Women & Love

Also by Mira Kirshenbaum

Too Good to Leave, Too Bad to Stay

Parent/Teen Breakthrough:
The Relationship Approach

Our Love Is Too Good to Feel So Bad:
The 10 Prescriptions to Heal Your Relationship

Women
&Love

Finding True Love While Staying True to Yourself:
The Eight Make-or-Break Experiences in Women's Lives

MIRA KIRSHENBAUM

Quill
An Imprint of HarperCollins*Publishers*

HarperCollins books may be purchased for educational, business, or sales promotional use. For information please write: Special Markets Department, HarperCollins Publishers Inc., 10 East 53rd Street, New York, NY 10022.

First Quill edition published 2000.

The Library of Congress has catalogued the hardcover edition as follows:
Kirshenbaum, Mira.
    Women & love / Mira Kirshenbaum.—1st ed.
        p. cm.
    1. Women—United States—Psychology.
    2. Love—United States.
    3. Man-woman relationships—United States.   I. Title.
II. Title: Women and love.
HQ1410.K57 1999   99-20576
305.42—dc21   CIP

ISBN 0-380-80222-8 (pbk.)

00 01 02 03 04 ❖ 10 9 8 7 6 5 4 3 2 1

To you, the women who've shared your stories with me. I thank you with all my heart for the help you've given to everyone who reads this book—and for your life-long fight to make sure that when it comes to love, you never settle for less than the real thing.

To my grandmother, Frieda, who was killed in the Holocaust before I was born. You've always lived in my imagination as a strong, heroic woman. Your loving spirit haunts these pages.

To my mother, Sonia, another heroic woman who inspired in me the desire to learn the truth about love.

And to my daughters, Rachel and Hannah. Whenever I think of the best in love for the best of women, I think of you.

THANKS

This book would not have been possible without the count-
less brave women who shared with me the truth about what
happened to them in the wonderful and scary and magical land
of love. More than any book I can think of, this is your book.
The truths here are your truths. The lives and stories laid bare
are yours. No matter how long I live, I will never be able to
thank you enough.

We can help each other only if we continue to reveal the
deepest, most meaningful truths about ourselves and our lives.
Our work—yours and mine—is on-going. Please e-mail me at
miraswomen@aol.com if you'd like to share your story with me
about what's happened to you in any of the eight make-or-
break experiences of love. Your story is important.

My phenomenal partner Dr. Charles Foster is my co-author
and researcher. Our partnership is 50/50, and every word of
this book is as much his as it is mine.

I can't thank the people at Avon Books enough for believing
in me and in this book. Jennifer Hershey, my wonderful editor,
understands what I'm trying to do and has worked brilliantly

to help me do it. Joan Schulhafer is a very wise woman and has put her whole heart into making sure that this book comes to the attention of everyone who needs it.

Howard Morhaim is not only my agent but my friend. He's seen me at my worst and given me his best, and for that I'm deeply grateful.

WE KNOW LOVE IS GOOD.
WHAT MAKES IT GOOD FOR YOU?

- It's not just how you feel about him. It's much more how he makes you feel about yourself.
- It's not about losing yourself in him. It's about becoming true to yourself with him.
- It's not about how great he is. It's about how great you can become alongside of him.
- It's not about how much you love him. It's about how he helps you love yourself.
- It's not just about his finding room in his heart for you. It's about his finding room in his life for your energy, drive, ambition, passions, and interests.
- It's not just about how good he is deep down. It's about how much you experience his goodness as you live your life together.
- It's not about how he makes you hungry to be with him. It's about how much he makes you feel at home when you are with him.
- It's not about the love you share. It's about your ability to fully, equally, deeply share your life together.
- It's about falling in like.

What good is a lifetime of love if it's not love like this?

CONTENTS

ONE

A Life Full of Love

For the first time in the history of the world a generation of women has come of age that has the power to say *No!* to crummy love.

It's because we care so much about love that we know nothing less than the best will do. We want love to feel like love, to be real and strong. We want intimacy to be rich and meaningful. We want the kind of love that goes hand in hand with our being honest and true to ourselves. We want to give love as much as we want to receive it. We understand that our love should be our emotional home.

It's time for us to demand the best in love. For the first time in history we don't need men to help us survive. We can put a roof over our own heads, put food on our own tables, pay our own way. We can even bring up kids on our own, if it comes to that. If we're going to have love in our lives, it ought to be great.

This book is dedicated to helping you find a way to:

- say *no* to bad love; to love that drains you, hurts you, robs you of your potential; to love that doesn't feel like love

- say *yes* to *real* love—love that delivers, love that's alive, love that fulfills your expectations, love that's honest and passionate and absolutely top quality
- get on the right path to have a life filled with love

I agree with you that love should change your life and make it great. With me it's personal.

    What's true for you is true for me. Love is the most important thing in my life. To a lot of people who think they know me, this is news. I come across as such a practical, commonsensical person. I hate bullshit, and I show it. Besides, women today are not supposed to be in love with love. I've taught my daughters to take care of themselves first and to seek love second. We're all concerned about the ways women sacrifice themselves in the search for love. I hate bad love.

    But every sacrifice I've made in my life has been for love. I've had many dreams, but a life of love has been my deepest desire. I like helping people, I like discovering new things, and to be honest I like having money and getting ahead, but I'd throw it all away to keep love alive.

Let's Throw Ourselves an Award Ceremony

There are so many twists and turns in the story of love in a woman's life, from sitting down to have coffee with an attractive stranger, to spending an intimate weekend in a beautiful cottage with the person you're falling in love with, to trying to bring the two of you back together after a terrible fight, to getting over a painful breakup, to enjoying a twentieth anniversary surrounded by the people who represent the life you've built together, to debugging the mystery of heartache. As you've gone through all the experiences of love in your life, I know you've searched for love that's real and true. That means *you're* the best.

It's time to honor and celebrate the most important people in the world: *you,* women who truly care about love. You're special because you stand for something. It's become clearer and clearer to me the more women I've talked to that *you are the Krazy Glue holding the world together.* That's because love is so important to you, because of all the love you have to give, *and because of all you've endured in the name of love.* Without you our world would be filled with anger, pain, and emptiness. Because of you, joy, meaningfulness, and connection are possible for everyone.

Looking for the real thing. The myth is that women who care about love are sappy. Let's explode that myth. You're a woman of substance. There's nothing sappy about you. You're a practical woman, a happy woman, a smart woman, a hip young woman, or an even more hip older woman. You're committed to being honest about what you need, and let the chips fall where they may. It's just that you need to feel good about the love in your life to feel good about your life as a whole.

Your story of love is the most joyous, painful, meaningful, confusing, and triumphant story of your life. But love isn't the *only* thing in your life. Being true to yourself is as important to you as being a loving person. In fact, you're a whole person with all kinds of plans and dreams. There are other things you care about a lot—like children, friends, family, and work. There are goals you're trying to carry out, whether they involve becoming President of the United States, president of your small business, or president of your PTA.

We're already taking part in one revolution—becoming freer and stronger than women have ever been in history. Women today are proud of that. Now let's have another revolution. Let's understand what it means for free, strong women to have a rich river of love running through their lives.

Why should you have to choose between the best in yourself and the best in love? I wrote this book so you won't have to. This book is your guide to getting the best out of love for the best in you—for your entire life.

How We Feel about Love in Our Lives Today

It would be nice if we could just relax when it comes to love. But love is under attack today. Your heart, and mine, are the battlefield. Sometimes the battle goes quiet, sometimes the battle rages, sometimes one side or the other wins. It's a battle between hope and despair.

Of course love has always been hard. A lifetime of love is still harder. And the conditions under which we all live today make love scary and difficult. Still, for most of us, most of the time, the hope of love triumphs. As it should. If you have hope, you're willing to keep giving love another chance. And hope *should* win. Love is your gift, your strength, your birthright. You're as made for love as Aretha Franklin's made for singing.

How do you feel about love in *your* life? That's important because when it comes to love, our attitudes matter a lot. Our attitudes grow out of what's happened to us. But then our attitudes also *change* what happens to us in the future, because so much of what we do grows out of what we expect will happen to us. You can't get the best if you expect the worst.

What Our Attitudes Add Up To

If you want to know how real women today feel about love, ultimately we feel many different things, *all at the same time.* Here's what different women have said when I asked them to sum up how they feel about love. Most women agree with most of these statements at one time or another. Our different attitudes toward love are like the layers in a multilayered cake:

- "You've got to be realistic. If you really want someone to love you, you've got to hide who you really are."
- "I'm passionate about this—without complete honesty love is no kind of love at all."

- "It's because of the way guys are—that's why love doesn't work."
- "Talk to me next year. Right now love has exhausted me. I've got love fatigue, and I'm afraid the whole thing is a waste of time and energy."
- "Love is like anything else. You have to be practical and come up with answers to the problems that come up in the course of your love life."
- "Love is as dangerous as walking alone down a back alley in a bad neighborhood after dark."
- "Love is the best thing in *my* life. You have to relax and enjoy it."
- "Call me a romantic, but I'm still yearning for real love."

And on and on the layers go, filling our lives with contradictions. We all share these contradictions, but we all express them differently.

It's a jungle out there. What do all our different attitudes add up to? If you add up all our contradictory feelings and thoughts and beliefs, and pack them into one tight ball, you'd get the following sentiment:

"Love sucks, and I want as much of it as possible."

I'm just reporting back the sum of what you've told me. I'm *not* saying "Love sucks, and I want as much of it as possible" is necessarily *your* attitude right now. It's just that if you add up all the different attitudes you've had toward love, and then combined them with all the different attitudes your friends have had, this is what you'd get.

Could there be a bigger contradiction? Here we are, right on the knife edge between hope and discouragement. Sometimes the "love sucks" side dominates—usually when things are going badly. More often the "I want as much of it as possible" side dominates—because most often we hope that things will go well. But overall the battle rages. And why not? There's truth in the contradiction.

Of course sometimes love sucks. Why else would we have so many problems with it and complain about it and feel so unsatisfied?

And at the same time, of course we want as much love as possible. Love is the best thing in life. For many of us love is the thing we do best.

Love is like deep-sea diving. It's wonderful, it's where the treasure is, but if you're not scared, you just don't know what you're getting into. (But if you don't get into it, you're missing out on something wonderful.) We have to understand that for many of us this contradiction lies at the heart of how we feel; why our feelings fluctuate; why we can stay so stuck and then suddenly take a leap into the unknown. I know you know what I'm talking about.

It doesn't matter where you are in your personal love story right now. Wherever you are—whether you've just graduated from The Baby-sitter's Club or you're a full-fledged member of The First Wives' Club—you're just chugging along, doo-di-doo-di-doo, doing the best you can to take care of yourself. Because, hey, it's a jungle out there. And when it comes to love—well, it's a love jungle. A girl can get hurt. A girl *has* gotten hurt.

And that girl is you. And me. And we've told each other too many stories about how we've gotten hurt. So we just chug along, doo-di-doo-di-doo, sometimes taking unbelievable risks, but inside we're scared. And what kind of idiots would we be if we weren't scared?

But in a way that fear is a good sign. We keep hanging in there anyway. So it must mean our hope of love is still fully alive. In spite of everything.

But What Is Love?

That hopeful part of us—what's it searching for? What is this thing called *love* we believe in so much?

As usual, you guys know all the answers. Here are the feelings that kept coming through over and over when I asked women what real love is. I think they're all good answers. You might be interested to see which ones strike the deepest chord in you.

THE TEN MOST POPULAR DEFINITIONS OF LOVE

1. *"Love is a capacity I have inside me."* Many of us believe love is a potential we have inside. Of course, it's something that exists between two people. But it's something that starts inside you and me as individuals. Here's how a woman put it, and I now know that she speaks for many of us:

> *Even if I'm not in a relationship, there's still love in my life. It's the love I have inside me. It's the love I know I can give. It's the love I can make someone feel for me. It's the capacity I have to feel love. A tree in winter that's lost its leaves is still full of life, the way I'm full of love. When the right moment comes, we'll come into bloom.*

2. *"Love must be excellent."* Second-rate love just doesn't make it. You're not saying that love has to be something that would send poets into rhapsodies. It's more down to earth than that. If you ask any great chef what excellence in food is, she'll say it's basically fresh, wholesome ingredients prepared in such a way that does justice to their essence. It doesn't have to be anything more than fresh bread or a hearty, healthy soup.

There's that same kind of excellence when it comes to love. Nothing tastes bad. Everything enhances the natural flavor and texture of who you are and the love between you and the person you love.

Here's an example: even though there's no special occasion, he simply tells you, speaking from his heart, that he really loves you. That's the love equivalent of one perfect ripe peach. And then, because he knows how tired you are, he rubs your feet.

Then, when you complain about a problem you're having in your life, he listens.

To most of us this is real love. To you perfectionists, excellence in love has nothing to do with turning up your nose at anything that's not perfect. It's just that love has got to be more than words. Love *is* as love *does*.

3. *"You can't separate real love from the real lives you make together."* Women who'd lived awhile were more likely to say this. Like this woman: "I've tried, believe me I've tried, but if I fall in love with someone and the ways we want to live don't jibe, our love just won't make it. It's like paper, stone, and scissors: paper beats stone because paper can wrap up the stone. Life beats love because life wraps up love. Love is enfolded in a life. But when the way you live makes your love flourish—that's the real thing."

4. *"Real love makes me feel safe."* Real love has that I-can-count-on-you quality—like a car you just know will start on the coldest day. Here's how one woman put it. "Look, you *know* when you're not safe in love. You're waiting for the next hurt. Maybe you'll be hurt by some devastating criticism. Maybe by something truly humiliating. Maybe just by some little act of selfishness. I'm not talking about how you step on each other's toes from time to time. And sure sometimes you get mad and have to fight to clear the air. But real love means knowing, absolutely knowing, that you're not waiting around for the next blow to fall. No matter how many goodies you get, if you don't feel safe, your love is crap. Fix it. Or find someone new. But don't call it love."

5. *"Love is a home for the truth."* As one woman said, "I don't know about anybody else, but for me love that cannot hold the truth is no love at all. You can't say you love each other when you have to watch everything you say. If it's like that, you're just living with the illusion of love. Now hopefully there's real love lurking somewhere behind the illusion. Hopefully your

love can learn to hold the truth. But what do you really have if you live a life where the *only* way you can manage to keep on saying I love you is to keep on telling lies?"

6. *"Real love is strong."* A lot of women agreed with what one young rock musician told me: "What's the point of love that wilts like a flower at the first breath of cold air? The kind of love I care about, the kind we should care about, is the kind that can pick itself up after it's gotten knocked down. Shit happens. People hurt each other. They lose each other in the crowd of life. They commit small acts of betrayal. Love that's truly excellent is strong enough to survive this. Let's get real. Love's got to survive the incredible stresses you go through having to earn a living."

7. *"Real love should feel good."* The simple idea that love should be a pleasure is a revelation to some people. But many women said that love means looking forward to the experience of pleasure in your love. I'm not talking about anything wild. Here are some pleasures women told me they got from love. "Snuggling into a warm bed on a cold night, holding your love, not talking, not wanting to fall asleep right away." "You suddenly find yourselves singing a song together." "Laughter." "Being with each other feels like when you've been away and you come home to a beautiful house."

8. *"True love brings out the best in you."* Here's what one woman said. "It's true that if there's this great love, you make sacrifices for each other. Sure. But if my love is the soil I plant myself in, then I want it to help me become my best self. Love isn't love if it cripples the best of who you are and amputates your dreams and sucks your blood in order to keep itself alive. If your love is real, you know you always have the possibility of being your best self and holding true to the things you care about."

9. *"Love means nothing without respect."* One woman spoke for many when she said, "You don't need to be told how won-

derful you are. You don't need for the person who loves you
to think that you're the most beautiful woman in the world.
So why does it matter so much that our partners notice when
we've gotten a new haircut? Because it's the true essence of
respect: to care enough about someone to feel you need to pay
attention to her. People who are nobodies are invisible. People
who aren't seen feel like nobodies. If you've had an exhausting
day and your partner realizes it and helps you out a little because he sees how exhausted you are, that's the kind of respect
that matters."

10. *Love is the kind of thing that when you've got it, you know
it."* One woman said, "You can have all the ideas in your head
you want, but real love is always going to surprise you. It
always seems to come out of nowhere. You're just going along
and then, *boom!*, it hits you. And you know it just as if you've
been hit by a safe falling out of a window. If it doesn't hit you
like that, it's not happened."

Wouldn't it be great to have this kind of love in our lives?
This is the kind of love we look for when our hope stays alive.
I have enormous respect for the understanding and values
women hold in the name of love.

For most of us, our last thoughts before we face the darkness of sleep—or even the darkness of death—are thoughts
about love and the people in our lives who are the main characters in our personal love stories. I know this is true for me.
Fine, then. Let's discover what we need—what *you* need—to
become the heroines of our love stories. The kind of heroines
who come through safely and find the love we're looking for.
The love we deserve. The kind of love that brings out the best
in us.

And to do that, we need to understand just what's really
going on in all the essential experiences of love in a woman's
life today.

Real Stories, Real Answers

Here you are, a smart, warmhearted woman with lots to give, and you want to feel there's real love in your life. But right now for many of us there's something missing when it comes to love. Maybe love itself is missing, whether you're in a relationship or not. Maybe you have love in your life, but you're just not getting everything you want from it.

And you look at yourself and you wonder what you're doing wrong, if anything. You know you're great, and that makes it feel as if a life full of love should come easily. And yet you're also aware that there must be things you do to make things hard for yourself. But what?

It's a mystery, isn't it? Why do so many of us have *Mad About You* daydreams but lead *Seinfeld* lives when it comes to love? For example:

- "It's so hard to strike a balance between love and everything else in life. Where do I draw the line? How do I know when it's worth making a sacrifice for love and when to emphasize other things in my life?"

- "I get so horny sometimes. Okay, but then I'll sleep with a guy and then something rises up inside me and it's like, oh, you slept with him, it must be love. But I don't even know the guy."
- "Anyone can make a mistake, but you're supposed to learn. Here I am falling for this guy I know is a bad choice, but he's exciting and my feelings for him are real too."
- "I've been here before in a relationship. Everything's fine for a couple of years. But then it's like there's this restless imp in me, like a bored kid who takes apart the toaster because she has nothing better to do. I want love to be exciting. But would I destroy love just because I'm bored?"
- "Sure, things don't work out sometimes, but if I'm not the one doing the dumping, I go nuts. If he rejects me, I just obsess about it like a maniac and I can't stop wondering what I did to screw things up."
- "I just started going with a guy, and the same old questions came up. Should I just tell him how I feel, but then we'll fight? Or do I just let stuff go and hope things will work out—except that inside I'm going nuts?"
- "I'm glad I got out of that relationship, but I've been on my own for a while now and I really want to be in love again. I'd really like to be hopeful about love again, but I got hurt and now I'm afraid."

Our love lives shouldn't be this way. For all the time you and I give to love, if love were our garden we should be living in paradise. But too many of us are in exile from the Eden that should be ours.

Putting our heads together. We know it shouldn't be this way. And we know that there are women out there who don't have anything more to offer than we do and yet for them the path of love seems to run much more smoothly. You've probably asked yourself at some point, what do these women know that I don't? Good question. They know things you don't know, you know things they don't. And when you put us all together, we know all the answers. What we've needed is to talk to each other. Even more than we've been doing.

It's Your Story

That's just what I did. In the survey I did for this book I talked to hundreds of women and asked them dozens of questions— all designed to uncover just where and how they'd gotten into trouble with love over the course of their lives and, more important, what they'd done to make love great. Then I tried to pull it all together in a form that could help all of us.

This is going to be a different book for different women. You might find that for you it's mainly a book of *real-life love stories*, because that's what it's filled with, and the true stories of women are eternally fascinating. Who doesn't love a love story?

Some of the women you'll meet have stories very different from yours. You might also meet a woman whose story is the mirror image of yours. But below the surface, we all share the same hurts and hopes.

You'll meet women whose lives were changed by love, and you'll meet women who, in their search for love, changed their own lives.

You'll meet women who found love, and you'll understand how.

You'll meet women who lost themselves in the search for love, and you'll gain insights into why.

You'll meet women who took too many risks when it came to love, and women who took too few.

You'll meet women who looked at the love they found and said, "I can do better," and you'll meet women who were made better by the love they found.

You'll meet women who were looking for anything but love and found love anyway, and you'll meet women who were looking for love and found themselves.

And you'll meet me too. Not that I matter so much. But in a book that owes its very existence to women laying bare their lives and their souls, it feels wrong for me to hold back. Besides, when someone talks to me about something I really care about, I need to know where they're coming from. You probably feel the same way.

But for you this might not be a book of stories at all. Instead, you might find that it's mainly a book of *understanding.* A kind of *Passages* for love. After all, if you want to understand your life, you have to understand the story of *love* in your life.

You know how we used to say, "First comes love, then comes marriage, then comes Mira with a baby carriage"? We were onto something. There *is* an underlying pattern to our love stories, yours and mine. We go from one experience to the next in a kind of cycle. This cycle of experiences is recurrent: you can go through it many times during the course of your life. And it's flexible: you don't have to go through it in exactly the same order as anyone else. And this pattern contains every make-or-break experience of love in our lives.

THE EIGHT MAKE-OR-BREAK EXPERIENCES OF LOVE

Here, in a nutshell, are the eight make-or-break experiences of love:

1. *Having your full share of love adventures.* This is where for the sake of trying something new you have adventures in the land of love. We need these adventures to learn about love. But they're scary. Will you have the courage to be open to love adventures? Will you get what you need from them? Will you avoid getting hurt?

2. *Finding someone to love without losing yourself.* Betty and Veronica would've called it dating. But in this experience you're playing for keeps. You're meeting people, getting involved with people, wondering how you feel—all for the sake of trying to find that one special person. But do you keep looking until you find the real thing or do you settle for good enough? Do you know what you're looking for? Do you know what you need?

3. *Feeling safe while falling in love.* This is when you feel not just in your heart but in your bones that *this* person is the *right* person. This is one of the peak moments in life. But just as when

you reach any peak, you're never more vulnerable than you are here, and you know it. Will you fall for fool's gold? Will you walk away from treasure because you're confused or afraid? Or will you wait for what's best for you and then grab it?

4. *Coming through a major breakup stronger and smarter.* We've all been dumped. We've all done some dumping. Sometimes it feels like a horrible tragedy. Sometimes it's good riddance to bad rubbish. But no matter how you feel, like it or not you're free again. Can you let go of the ways you've been hurt in the past, without forgetting to learn the lessons the past has to teach?

5. *Getting the best out of both love and sex.* Love is not sex. There are people you'll let into your bed that you won't let into your heart. There are people you let into your heart who don't work all that well in your bed. Maddeningly, wonderfully, sex chugs along in a path that's often parallel to the path of love. Will you be able to find a way to bring harmony between your love life and your sex life, or will they be at odds?

6. *Being truly yourself while you find a home for your love.* You've broken through into some form of commitment and now you find yourselves having to figure out a way to share a life together. This is the shakedown cruise of love. It's where you go from how you think you'll be together to seeing how you really are. Will your love survive your discovering what it's like to live with each other as you really are?

7. *Making sure your love survives the test of time.* What happens when love's placed in the hands of time? Time changes everything. You change. Your partner changes. Your lives change. Five, ten, twenty years after you start living together— what will it be like for the two of you to be together? Will time steamroller love? Or will love triumph?

8. *Finding the right balance between love and the rest of your life.* It's a lifelong challenge. We all find different solutions to

the question of what to do with love in our lives. It's a matter of finding just the right balance between love and everything else you care about. Will you discover new and exciting options that will make it possible for you to find the place for love in your life that feels right to you and works best for you?

What is it about these eight experiences that's "make or break"? It's your heart that can break. Not in the sense of those times when you've gotten hurt and cried—they're just the skinned knees of love. Your heart can break in the sense that you become *dis*-heartened, you lose heart.

These are make-or-break experiences because they either nurture your sense of hope or throw red meat to the hounds of discouragement. They either make you feel smart, capable, strong, even lucky, when it comes to love or they make you feel that love is just something better left to others because you don't have what it takes to get love right. They make you feel either that you can say *no* to crummy love and *yes* to real love, or they make you feel trapped.

I've got good news for you. Once you see where you lost your way, you can get back on track. Once you identify which make-or-break experience you've gotten stuck in, you'll know exactly what to do. Because you've always had everything you need to make love work in your life.

Another piece of good news is that you're not alone. Whatever path you're on, however far you've gone down your path, there are women who've been where you are now, and they have powerful advice.

You Deserve the Best

We're not setting an impossible standard for ourselves by wanting the best from love. We're real people who stumble through life, and sometimes it takes all we have to just get through the day. Some days I know I really don't do anything to show my husband I love him. Sometimes I put up with him treating me in a second-rate way. Sometimes I stumble through my day so badly that having made sure to wash my face at night is what I'm proudest of before I close my eyes. And so we all stumble along in our real lives.

Okay. So believing in real love doesn't mean we always *have* real love. But we'd rather aim for the best than think second best is okay. And speaking for myself I'd rather know I could do better than kid myself into thinking that mediocrity in love is something wonderful.

Coming together. As long as we learn for each other, we'll do fine. It's like orgasms. It used to be taken for granted that women didn't have any. Today it's understood that we're all entitled to orgasms, that having orgasms is normal, that having *multiple* orgasms is normal. Out of nowhere, suddenly there were all these orgasms. Your great-grandmother probably had her share. But you probably have a lot more. That's a fact of social history in our time. The transformation came about because we discovered that a lot of women were having multiple orgasms. Then we learned what these women did that made multiple orgasms possible for them.

Learn from the people who've already got what you want. That's been the basis of my work for over twenty-five years.

An orgasm is a matter of moments. Love is for your life. Here we are, women who care about love, who've devoted huge chunks of our lives and energies to love. We shouldn't beat ourselves up because it's hard to get it right. The real thing is always hard. Too often we fall short. But real love is worth striving for, because real love is what life is all about.

You deserve a life that's filled with real love. So let's do it. Let's share our secrets. Let's reveal our fears and deepest needs. Let's see why we get in trouble and what we can do to stay out of trouble. We know we need more love to be happy. So let's learn the secrets for how to feel smarter and stronger and safer *and more hopeful* when it comes to love in our lives.

THREE

Love Is Like an Itching in Your Heart

Make-or-Break Experience #1:
Having Your Full Share of Love Adventures

Climbing Mt. Everest. Scuba diving in the Great Barrier Reef. Adventures are a way of giving yourself the sense that you've really lived. They're a way of becoming strong. So we need adventures. But we also need to make sure that we don't get lost or destroyed in the process.

It's the same when it comes to love. Having love adventures is where we make experiments in the realm of love, and we all need our share. A fourteen-year-old has a love adventure almost every time she kisses a boy. A twenty-two-year-old has a love adventure the summer she spends in Europe and gets involved with three men she knows she'll never see again. A thirty-five-year-old in an iffy marriage has a love adventure when she sleeps with the first man who shows her some affection in years even though she knows their relationship will never go anywhere.

What makes this experience of love different from all the other experiences of love? You're not playing for keeps. You have no expectation that what you do with a person will lead to *forever*. This is the experience of having an experience *for the sake* of having an experience.

The girl's gotta have it. This is where a lot of us do stupid, crazy things in the name of love. But that's not why we get stuck here. *There's nothing wrong with trying things out.*

Here's the make-or-break part of this experience. If we get stuck here, it's because we do things that make us feel badly about ourselves. We get stuck because we fail to have enough love adventures. We get stuck because we don't learn from our love adventures.

But we need them. Get this: *61 percent of women over the age of thirty say they wish they'd fallen in love more; they wish they'd gotten involved with more guys; they wish they'd had more different experiences with love.*

From Fear to Freedom

Love adventures are good because it's through adventures that you get a sense of freedom and knowledge about yourself and life and love. Love adventures are like styling your hair: you need to experiment to find the hairstyle that's best for you. It's the same with love.

You've got to play with love to really know what it means to take love seriously.

Learning to fall. We understand intuitively when it comes to love what a neighbor of mine years ago learned when it comes to being an acrobat: You can only fly when you learn to fall.

This is not mysticism. It's sheer practicality. Already an accomplished gymnast, my neighbor had joined up with the Barnum and Bailey Circus to become an acrobat. They put her through their program. And for weeks this meant doing nothing but falling. At first falling from a standing position. Falling forward, sideways, backward. Then falling from a height. Then falling from a height while moving.

My neighbor told me she'd learned every fall a person could experience, and she'd learned what was necessary to survive that fall. Later when she was a daring young woman on the flying trapeze, she felt safe because she knew that she had everything she needed to protect herself when she fell.

That's what our love adventures can give us. Knowing how to fall. Knowing how to prevent falls. What better way to keep your hope alive?

What kind of fool I was. There's no way I could've handled falling in love with my husband if I hadn't had my share of love adventures before I met him. For a nineteen-year-old, I was fairly experienced in relationships. Even in junior high school I was looking for something more than the kid stuff around me. There's a picture of me in the ninth grade with long blond hair, tight skirt, and high heels. I actually look like an adventuress. In fact I was dating medical students while I was in high school. I started college when I was sixteen. And that's when my love adventures began in earnest.

My Orthodox Jewish mother would've jumped off the roof if she'd known what I was into. It's not that I was a slut. I wasn't. Not that there's anything wrong with that. Most women go through a year or so of a slut phase. But having love adventures isn't about sleeping around. It's about getting to know a lot of different people. It's about leaping before you look. It's not about who you let into your bed but who you let into your heart.

Years ago Helen Gurley Brown gave young women some advice: "Fall in love with the wrong man." *That's* a love adventure.

So during the three years of college before I met my husband, there were a lot of "wrong" men in my life, and a lot of "wrong" ways I had for handling them. For example, I remember one year when all at the same time I was involved with two of my professors, a graduate student, and a married man who said he was separated. I guess I'm literally in the position of having been involved with more men than I can now remember. Of course I do have the excuse that it was more than thirty-three years ago. Oh yeah, there was that bearded, Beatnik painter with ugly toenails with whom I lost my virginity.

You might think I'd been running around like a goof ball and a tease, but I remember clearly how sincere I was, how shy, how well intentioned. I just liked men. I was just looking for love. I was hungry for experience.

In the jungle of love. In the course of my love adventures I had the experience every young woman *should* have: I got to feel that everything was possible for me. Along the way a bunch of good and bad things happened. The worst was that I was once almost raped by a distinguished older man. He was a world-famous scholar whose apartment I went to because he invited me. I was seventeen, but I'd been wearing high heels for years and it was a principle of mine to go everywhere and do everything.

I still remember in my gut the feeling I had running half-dressed out of his apartment. I was scared to death, disgusted to the point of nausea, but more than any of those feelings I was proud that I'd taken care of myself. He had tried to humiliate me, but the way I shoved him into a chair so hard it fell over backward took care of that.

That's the whole problem and promise of love adventures right there. You want to avoid being horribly used and abused. But you also want to give yourself the opportunity to throw some asshole halfway across the room. Just so you know you can do it.

I remember feeling, okay, I've learned the lesson that you've always got to be prepared to take care of yourself, and that you always have to know what you're getting into before you get into it. I don't just mean learning that if you go to a guy's apartment he's going to expect to have sex. I mean learning that *whatever* situation you walk into people are going to have expectations and you'd better know what their expectations are and you'd better be prepared to take care of yourself. I've never forgotten that lesson. I remember it every time I walk into a meeting with anyone.

Having my fill of daddies. I learned a lot in my adventures. I learned that sexy-looking guys could be lazy lovers. I learned that there was a big difference between judging a guy by his résumé and by how it actually felt to be with him. Like a lot of women, particularly women like me who were fatherless, I'd come into womanhood wanting a powerful older man as a partner to feel safe. Well, I've had powerful older men as partners. That's what my love adventures were all about: teenager Mira using her blond good looks to get older men to fall for her and offer the promise of a relationship.

Without all those love adventures, it might have taken me a lifetime to learn what being with powerful older men did to my own sense of power. A very young woman in a relationship with a successful older man might be thought cute, she might be petted on the head for being smart, but she'll have a hard time being taken seriously. This isn't always true, of course, but it's generally true. How would I ever be an equal in any of these relationships?

And I also learned that I had some juice flowing in my veins that demanded that I always feel like an equal. I just hadn't understood that juice in my eagerness to fall in love with daddy.

Because I'd begun to understand that juice, I was able to fall in love with my husband, a boy one year younger than me and two years behind me in college. I was arrogant enough back then to believe that my love adventures had made me a connoisseur of men, and thank God, in my husband's case, I was able to foresee the kind of man he would become. But only because of my crazy love adventures was I able to have a chance of making a smart move when I felt it was time for me to play for keeps.

There's one more gift our love adventures give us. After you've sowed enough wild oats, you lose interest in sowing more wild oats. Been there, done that. We all come into wom-

anhood with a bit of wanderlust in our hearts when it comes
to love. If we don't indulge it, wanderlust just sits in our stomach, a bit of unfinished business that can haunt us forever.
You get the point. Love adventures are a Good Thing. Not
having had your share when you need it can mess you up.

Finding Safety in Adventure

It might seem like a paradox, but ultimately love adventures
are necessary for our safety. It's easy to get hurt in the land
of love. That can make us afraid. But, amazingly, the things
about love that make us afraid can be alleviated if we have our
full share of love adventures. Yes, you have to take care of
yourself. You have to make sure your love adventures don't go
on too long. But if you do all that, this is one of those times
where adventures can make things less scary.

Here's how. Let's run through the main fears we have
about love.

• Suppose you're afraid of being abandoned. Then your pattern when it comes to love adventures might be that you're
the one who always leaves. But that means cutting your love
adventures short. Or you might avoid them altogether. This is
the classic flight to commitment, even if it's with the wrong
person. The problem is that your fear of abandonment could
lead to fewer love adventures. *But you need those love adventures
to learn about the kind of guy who won't abandon you.* For example, maybe your love adventures will teach you that the kind
of guy who won't abandon you might not necessarily be the
highest quality guy. What good is avoiding abandonment if it
always gets you stuck with losers? But you've got to sort all
this out for yourself, and you need love adventures to do so.
• Suppose you're afraid of losing control. The problem here
is that you might arrange it so that you keep having love adventures where you won't really learn anything new. For example,

you might only get involved with younger men, the kind who look up to you, where you can play a kind of teacher role. But if you're always the teacher, when do you get to be the pupil? You need real love adventures to have real learning.

• Suppose you're afraid of being hurt. You might try to avoid having love adventures. That's understandable, but I can tell you how it plays out in real life. Women who avoid love adventures out of fear of getting hurt are the women who really get hurt. They don't know themselves, they don't know men, they don't know relationships.

• Suppose you're afraid of being trapped. Then you're more likely to get stuck flitting from one love adventure to another. Endlessly. But only the experience of flitting will teach you the true but empty payoff of focusing only on not being trapped.

• Suppose you're afraid of intimacy. Hey, we're all afraid of intimacy—it's the mosh pit where hearts get stepped on. You probably say you're afraid of intimacy because you've been having love adventures and you're afraid that means there's something wrong with you. There isn't. There's only a problem if your love adventures go on too long. There's only a problem if you fall in love with some perfectly great guy and walk away.

But when it comes to love adventures in general, the biggest mistake is not having them. Don't keep your heart in a box. As tender as it feels, it's tougher than you think. And it needs the experience. So do you. But watch out. You don't want to become a wanderer without a home.

Trapped in Adventure Land

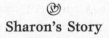

Sharon's Story

We all need to have our share of love adventures, but if they go on and on they can take on a life of their own. Instead of their being a series of events in your life, they become your life.

That's what happened to Sharon. I suppose you could blame it on the Sixties, except that in every era of human history when women have had any kind of freedom at all some have gone chasing after love adventures. Anna Karenina and Madame Bovary in the nineteenth century. Sharon and millions like her today.

If you want to visualize Sharon, think of any of the older women rockers, Stevie Nicks or Deborah Harry or Patti Smith. Without the music. A woman who's been around. Around and around and around. The way she put it to me was "I think I just had a wild need to live on an extreme edge. I wanted to really feel alive. I wanted complete freedom. I wanted love without strings. I wanted as much love as possible, but if I had to choose between love and freedom, I'd choose freedom."

Usually, though, the demands of life itself—the need to earn a living, the fear of what will happen if you don't settle down—force us to cut short our love adventures and zero in on someone to spend a life with. But Sharon had the misfortune in love of having a fortune in money from her grandfather. She didn't have enough money to buy yachts and helicopters. She had just enough money to buy the illusion that time didn't exist for her.

The minute she came of age she went to Hollywood. Not to be an actress but to be part of the scene. There was a cornucopia of older, handsome, married men there dazzled at the vision of a bright, attractive, dynamic young woman who passionately did *not* want to be an actress. That alone made her desirable.

Knowing all the right people. "I want to get to know you," was her line. One of the most powerful lines in the love adventure game. The first man she fell in love with was an agent. No one had ever wanted to get to know him. People just wanted things from him. But he had incredible energy and he knew the inner map of Hollywood, the people map, the who-knows-who-and-who's-done-what-to-whom map. Perfect. Their affair was all about enjoying each other's energy. They moved in a cloud of gossip.

He introduced Sharon around. It was 1969 and Sharon talked to everyone about the role Hollywood could play in changing America. They loved her ideas, all the older, married men. She thought she was influencing them. They listened to her and thought it was a great way to do market research: "So this is what the kids today want . . ." they thought. Sharon was someone to get to know because she somehow seemed Tuned In.

Then she met this producer who had made a movie that in some small way had changed America about ten years earlier, opening up people's minds to the need to solve our racial problems. She told him she wanted to get to know him, to really get to know him, and she fell in love with him and they had a ten-year on-again-off-again love affair. He broke her heart a dozen times, what with always going back to his wife and having sex with every actress who came within his orbit.

But Sharon was special to him—she knew that. It was precisely because there was some deep romantic current between them that their inability to do anything with their love was heartbreaking. The only thing worse than the pain of broken promises is the pain of the same promise being broken over and over. He kept promising he'd leave his wife for her. No other woman in his life was important enough to get that promise so many times. It's just that Sharon wasn't important enough for him to keep his promise.

Sharon got savvy enough about Hollywood so that some of the producers she knew recommended her as a kind of advisor/ mentor to promising screenwriters. She fell in love with every one she felt worthy of her help. Some of them simply used her. Some thought they were in love with her. Most didn't know what the hell to think. Sharon was unusual in that she didn't have that protective skin most women have that teaches them to hide the evidence of their loving feelings until they're sure the guy's receptive. If Sharon fell in love with you, you knew it. It's like she was daring you not to respond. How could you not get swept up in her radiant sense that you were wonderful, and that the two of you together were wonderful?

Waking up. Maybe it was so easy for Sharon to say "I love you" because love for her was still a game. Like a male rock star screwing every woman he lays his eyes on, and seeing how much of it he could get away with, and being amazed at how much he got away with, Sharon was the same way with love. She wanted a life filled with complicated love affairs and the risk of a broken heart. She was the Evel Knievel of love and had the scars to show it.

She burned out three friends because they couldn't stand her constant calls in which she pored over every shredded detail of her love adventures.

Sharon woke up when she hit forty. She was going through a dry spell. Her "I'll marry you one day" producer had told her he didn't think he'd ever marry her. He blamed it on his wife. A young screenwriter she'd felt very passionate about had dumped her to go back to New York and become a book editor. Then she met this guy more her age, a malpractice attorney, and he liked what he saw. So did Sharon. She wanted to fall in love with him and she knew the moves to make. But suddenly it all felt prescripted. Everything she did stank of déjà vu. After all those years of love adventures—when she wanted to feel the real thing it wasn't there for her.

But she made the moves and got a great guy. After so many years of love and no weddings, she had a wedding but wasn't sure about the love. Then . . . do you know that Roy Lichtenstein-type poster of a woman saying, "Ooops, I forgot to have children"? That's sort of what it was like for Sharon. After so many love adventures, when she finally got her nest she didn't have any eggs for it. What she said to me about having children was "When I was able, I wasn't ready; and when I was ready, I wasn't able."

I don't think any woman in the world has ever received more flowers than Sharon. I asked her to sum up her twenty years of love adventures. "It was great," she said. "I think it's given to few women to feel as alive as I did for as long as I did. That was the only problem. It just went on too long."

Hidden Love Adventures

Sharon doesn't serve as a warning against having adventures. She's a warning against *nothing but*. Love adventures are like high school: a vital part of growing up, but who'd want to spend twenty years in high school?

The danger Sharon represents usually appears in our lives in less dramatic forms. Sometimes what looks like a normal marriage from the outside is really someone's love adventure. Usually we get married because we've fallen in love and felt confirmed in our suspicion that this is the person we want to spend the rest of our life with. At least we think so. We hope so. But getting married doesn't mean it's not an adventure.

I would estimate that up to 10 percent of women who say "I do" see themselves as pre-divorced. Here's how one woman put it: "I don't know . . . I just always figured I'd be married a couple or three times. When Gary came along I said, wow, he'll get me out of this suburban hell I've been trapped in all my life. We'll go to the city. And then I can take things from there. I just felt that at some point I'd meet the right guy and I wanted to feel that I'd had the experience of already being married behind me."

The point is that a lifetime of love adventures can leave you high and dry, even when they come in the guise of a series of marriages. If you keep giving your heart away there is no guarantee you'll get anything back.

"I Just Don't Want to Get Hurt"

For every woman like Sharon who gets seriously hurt by having love adventures that go on for too long, there are dozens of women who pay a price for not having enough love adventures. We're so afraid of getting our hearts broken that we deprive ourselves of experiences that would make us feel free and would teach us valuable lessons about how love works and how we work in it. So we come to our committed, hopefully permanent relationships almost emotional virgins. But the price we've paid for safety is a deep kind of ignorance and the slowly dawning sense of feeling trapped.

Julie's Story

From Sharon to Julie is a trip from Hollywood to the Heartland. From a love life made of adventure to a love life devoid of adventure. Even if you need more adventures, I bet you're not as bad off as Julie was. I hope you haven't paid as big a price as she did.

Think of a girl growing up in the Midwest—southern Indiana—in one of your basic Fundamentalist Christian households. Poor, decent, hardworking people. But it was no Norman Rockwell family. Julie's mother and father hated each other and showed it. The family stayed together but her parents constantly advertised how emotionally far apart they were.

She didn't actually say this, but you can imagine Julie saying, "I've had all the love adventures I need after what I've seen in this stupid family." I grew up seeing the same kind of thing myself, so I can relate to Julie's feelings. For some of us, love is a safe harbor, and that's what Julie wanted.

Seeing the pain people can inflict on each other, Julie followed a very safe path, going to a bible college and marrying a man she met there who was a couple of years older. They shared the same beliefs, wanted the same things out of life, and there was something about him that made Julie think he'd never be mean to her the way her father had been mean to her mother.

So with no experience whatsoever of men and love—and

therefore no sense of how she worked or what she needed—
she married the kind of guy she thought she should love. And
so she convinced herself she did love him.

The years flew by, three children were born, and her youngest entered adolescence. Julie could feel in her bones the sense
of how her children were about to go off and taste life and
leave her.

Things hadn't been working out in her marriage, either.
Her husband turned out to be exactly as nice as he promised
to be. But as cold as an iron lamppost in winter. Distant, un-
communicative, deeply uninterested in Julie. Highly critical of
any desire she ever showed to spark up their lives, to bring
some *life* to their lives. As a small town banker, his main emotional relationship is with his image of his role in the community. It's taken her years but Julie's come to realize that he
sees her as an accessory, like a tie, and he's the kind of man
who always wears a tie clip.

They have sex a lot more often than you might think from
this description. Hubby's uptight, but he's horny. It's just not
particularly interactive sex. It's more like video game sex. He's
busy with all the buttons and levers but it has nothing to do
with making the buttons and levers feel any pleasure. Making
love with her husband is the sexual equivalent for Julie of
listening to someone in the next room talk to himself.

The good news is that over the last several years Julie got
a job at a Christian music recording company. Her job was to
coordinate recording dates with the artists. Being a warm,
pleasant woman Julie made friends with some of these musicians. She confided in them. They'd confide in her. She kept
telling herself, "I'm like a mother to them." But really she was
a woman, and they knew it and she knew it. With one of the
guys she got very friendly. She told him how unhappy she was
in her marriage, and he told her how unhappy he was in his.
Next thing you know, these God-fearing people were having a
wild love affair right out of Paris in the twenties.

The difference was that accompanying their pleasure in discovering each other were torments of guilt as bad as a bout of

food poisoning. She simply could not wrap her mind around what was happening. It was too good to be true, she thought, so it must be very wrong.

Any half-witted Parisian woman could've advised Julie on how to handle things better. Julie dealt with her belated love adventure by suddenly and with no explanation breaking things off completely with her new lover—the only man in her life who had ever made her happy. And then she told her husband all about it. She vaguely hoped that he'd see the desperate state he'd driven her to and then he'd change. Instead, he decided she was crazy.

Out of rage her husband made her stay, the better to punish her, and out of guilt Julie agreed to stay. She wasted four more years she could ill afford hoping things would heal and that the healing would transform the desert of their marriage into a bit of an oasis. But there was too much anger. Her husband's anger with her, her anger with him for being angry with her, his anger with her for being angry with him for being angry with her.

God bless her, Julie finally discovered there was enough fuel to keep this cycle of anger going forever. *Then* she got out. At least there was no question in her mind she was doing the right thing. It felt bad, washing up on the shores of middle age with only one love adventure, and that a tragic one. But her hunger for freedom was enormous. She decided to spend the next part of her life alone, and that decision made her feel happy. And safe.

"Be Good, but If You Can't Be Good, Be Careful"

Julie's story teaches us that sometimes there's nothing more dangerous than the attempt to hide from risk. Because she was afraid of having a broken heart, every experience of love in Julie's life was either a lie or was steeped in pain. Most of us are lucky to have more love adventures and to learn the valuable lessons that come with a heartbreak or two.

I've talked to women of all ages who felt they were able to agree with the following statement: "I've had my share of love adventures, maybe more than my share." And I asked them this: "You probably had plenty of ups and downs in the course of your love adventures, but that meant that you had difficulties and disappointments among everything else. What made it all worthwhile? What did you get from it that gives you some payoff now?"

Here's what they told me.

THE TOP TEN ADVANTAGES OF HAVING LOVE ADVENTURES

1. *It makes you feel ready to settle down.* I believe that most women enter adulthood knowing roughly how many love affairs they want to have. If you settle down before you reach your secret number, you always feel a little cheated. But if you have reached your secret number, when you do settle down you feel ready.

2. *You get to work the honky-tonk out of your system.* I don't know why, but both men and women seem to need to get a certain number of trashy relationships under their belts. Even a really smart guy needs to have his share of women with nothing in their heads and a lot on their chests. Women seem to need a couple of romantic flings with the Marlboro Man or the tattooed rock musician who's your parents' worst nightmare. How much better it is when these trashy relationships are kept separate from your committed relationships.

3. *You go past what you* think *you want in a relationship to discover what you really* do *want in a relationship.* You know how it is—you go shopping for a pair of shoes, you think you want one thing, you try on a bunch of different shoes, and you realize you want something else. There's nothing wrong with that. But you had to try on a bunch of shoes to get to that

place. It's the same with love. There are things you think you want to make you feel safe or happy or sexy. But you need to shop around to make sure. I would've bet everything I wanted an older, highly authoritative man. But after I tried on a few, well, I was very happy to fall in love with a boy my own age. And to be honest with you, now that he's grown up to become an older, highly authoritative man, it's not so wonderful and I sometimes find myself wishing I had back the not-so-sure-of-himself boy I married.

4.   *You learn how to judge which men can really give you what you want.* It's one thing to learn what you really want. You also have to learn who can give it to you. One woman who'd had more than her share of honky-tonk boyfriends realized that what she really wanted was a man she could respect. So she got involved with a guy who was a high-level corporate executive. An accomplished, easy-to-respect guy. You'd think. But she discovered that he felt his value as a human being fluctuated almost daily with the changes in the political winds at the office. She discovered you can't respect a man who gets his self-respect only from his job. She ended up involved with a veterinarian who was proud of what he was able to do and didn't need a job to prove it.

5.   *You develop the sense you can take care of yourself.* Remember the circus acrobat who learned to fall? That's what this is about.

6.   *You develop a picture of yourself as someone who's desired.* It's simple. If you make a commitment to the first person who comes along, there's always that doubt about whether anyone else would want you. This is important because if you don't feel you're desirable, your insecurity gives your partner way too much power. We all need to be able to say to our partners, "I don't need you for me to feel confident that I'm desirable."

7. *You learn to forgive yourself for the mistakes you've made.* If you get involved with one guy and he turns out to be a loser, you can get very self-critical about your bad judgment. If you get some love adventures under your belt, you might discover that you were able to choose solid guys. Or you might come away with the philosophical perspective that most guys have flaws once you get to know them well. These are just a couple of the ways experience with love teaches self-forgiveness.

8. *Because life is complicated, when you have the same kind of love adventure over and over and get the same result, you learn what it is that's the same that you need to avoid.* It's very hard to draw a single clear lesson from a single highly complex event. Let's say that for the first time in your life you drink too much, and then the next morning you wake up with a headache. Have you learned a lesson about the cost of drinking? Probably not, because you might figure that headache came from not having enough sleep, or having eaten the wrong thing, or maybe it came out of nowhere. But if you drink too much over and over and keep waking up with a hangover every single time, it becomes much easier to draw a simple lesson from this complex event. It's the same with love. If you have one love affair with a guy with a lot of problems because your love is tangled up with your hope that you can save him, but that guy shows neither improvement nor gratitude, well who knows why that happened? But if you keep getting bad results with fixer-uppers, well, there's your lesson. No fixer-uppers.

9. *You learn to understand what makes a relationship the real thing and not just a fling.* Imagine someone sends you a dollar in the mail every time some teenage girl somewhere in the world wonders if she "really loves" the boy she's seeing, and if he "really loves" her. You'd be another Bill Gates. But we all struggle with this question. And the reality is that there's no way to answer it unless you have a lot of experiences to compare it with. You want to be able to judge good wine? All

you have to do is drink a lot of different wines. It's the same with love.

10.   *You give yourself a sense of having lived.* We all feel we've missed out if we haven't traveled to certain special places. A Caribbean island, Paris, the American West, Venice, Hong Kong maybe. If you haven't been there, you feel as if there's something missing from your life. As a result you're filled with restlessness and dissatisfaction. Well, one of those special places is the land of love affairs. Imagine being able to eliminate restlessness and dissatisfaction from the most important relationship of your life because you went into it having had your fill of love adventures. What a gift to give the love story of your life.

What about you? Have you had enough adventures to give your love life what it needs? There's no magic number. What's important is whether you've gotten for yourself what you need to get from love adventures. That's what you can diagnose for yourself now. Answer the following ten questions, based on the Top Ten Advantages of Having Love Adventures:

1.   Do you feel ready to settle down?

YES_____ NO_____

2.   Have you had your share of bad boys, fixer-uppers, and guys you know are just no good for you?

YES_____ NO_____

3.   Have you had enough love affairs to achieve a deeper, more enlightened understanding of what you want in a relationship?

YES_____ NO_____

4.   Have you gotten deeply involved with enough different men to be able to judge which men can really give you what you want?

YES_____ NO_____

5.   Can you say with some degree of confidence that if you fall in love with someone you can still take care of yourself?

YES_____ NO_____

6. None of us thinks we're perfect, but do you have a sense
    of what it is about you that many men would find desirable?

    YES_____ NO_____

7. We've all made mistakes in the land of love. Do you have
    the experience and understanding to forgive yourself for
    yours?

    YES_____ NO_____

8. If you think about falling in love in the future, do you
    have a clear, confident sense of what you damned well
    better stay away from?

    YES_____ NO_____

9. Do you have enough experience to know the differences
    between being flattered by someone, being horny for
    someone, feeling taken care of by someone, and really
    being in love with someone?

    YES_____ NO_____

10. Can you say fairly confidently, when it comes to love
    experiences, "Maybe I haven't done it all, but I certainly
    feel I've lived"?

    YES_____ NO_____

If you have only one or two *no's*, it's a sign that you've had
your love adventures. And, even more, it's a sign that you have
pretty much everything you need to do just fine in the land of
love, whether you're an old married lady or a hot twenty-six-
year-old prowling the streets of the big city.

But I'm sorry to say that answering *no* to three or more
questions pushes you over the edge, based on the experiences
of many, many women. If you answered *no* three or more times
to the above ten questions, then you've got some unfinished
business in the land of love adventures.

Don't be scared. You don't have to run out and disrupt
your life. If you're in a committed relationship right now, you
certainly don't have to run out and have an affair. *Don't* run
out and have an affair. Don't even stroll slowly into an affair.
It'll probably cause too much damage, and it isn't necessary.

You can get what you need in other ways. Here's the prescription.

What to Do If You Need More Love Adventures

If you're young and unattached, there's really no prescription for you. Just do what comes naturally. Follow the spirit of this chapter. *Don't be afraid of having a number of romantic entanglements.* Remember, you can't throw your heart away. Your heart is the one thing you always keep no matter how many times you give it.

But whatever your age, and whatever your relationship status, every question you said *no* to represents a piece of unfinished business.

• If you said *no*, for example, to the question, *"Do you feel ready to settle down?"* then you have some wild oats in you. But if you don't feel ready to settle down, ask yourself what's missing, even if you're married. Maybe you need to give yourself a summer in Europe. Maybe you need new friends. Maybe you need an exciting hobby. Maybe you need a lifestyle makeover. I don't know what it is, but there's obviously an itching in your heart, as the Supremes sang, and you've got to find a way to scratch it. Before it really gets to you.

• Suppose you said *no* to the question, *"Have you had your share of bad boys, fixer-uppers, and guys you know are just no good for you?"* Well, congratulations for being very honest. Now think about what you're saying. You're saying that you still haven't satisfied your appetite for bad boys. This is a feeling some women have. You can't deny your feeling. But you've got to realize you can ruin your life by actually getting involved with a guy who's Trouble with a capital *T*. The best way to deal with this feeling is to accept that you have a Mother Theresa Complex—you want to help those who really need help. Fine, but Mother Theresa didn't get romantically involved with the people she helped. Help people who *truly* need it. Become a Big Sister. Work in a shelter for battered women. Read to the blind. If you're man-crazy, work in a shelter for homeless men. But save your heart for a guy who can and will give more than he gets.

• Did you say *no* to the question: *"Have you had enough love affairs to achieve a deeper, more enlightened understanding of what you want in a relationship?"* Okay, so you're saying you're still not sure what you want. Let's sort this out, fast. You're either in a relationship or you're not. If you're in one, the question is what do you want from this relationship that you're not getting? I've never met a woman who didn't have answers. Be honest with yourself. Then be honest with your partner.

If you're not in a relationship, the question facing you is really what do you want from your next relationship? That's all you have to do: think one relationship ahead. After all, you might not think of your "next" relationship as a permanent one. A lot of times we just want a guy because we're going through a period in our lives when we just want a guy. Our lives are in transition. Settling down isn't in the cards. But again, you've got to be honest with yourself. If the "next" relationship *is* one you want to be permanent, then that should be your focus when you think about what you want from a relationship—what you want from a man you're going to join your life and fortune to forever and ever.

• Did you say *no* to the question: *"Have you gotten deeply involved with enough different men to be able to judge which men can really give you what you want?"* If you said *no* to this question, my best advice to you is to get to know men *outside* of the world of love. Make friends with men. Talk to men at work. Have an acquaintanceship relationship with more men. Become the kind of woman men feel they can talk to because they're not afraid you'll tie a rope around them or criticize them or get all judgmental on them or start acting girlie.

• Did you say *no* to the question: *"Can you say with some degree of confidence that if you fall in love with someone you can still take care of yourself?"* Nothing is more important than our being able to take care of ourselves. I'm going to write a book about this one day—that's how big this issue is—but it boils down to this: Know what you need. Have money of your own and a way of getting money. And have support—friends and family who can advise you, help you, listen to you. *Every* woman can do better on at least one of these. Figure out where you need to do better.

• Did you say *no* to the question: *"None of us thinks we're perfect, but do you have a sense of what it is about you that men would find desirable?"* If you answered *no* to this, you need to take inventory. Ask the men in your life: "What is it about me *as I am* that makes you want me to be in your life?" If they give you a one- or two-word answer, ask for more. If a guy gives you an answer that feels false or empty, one that makes you feel hurt or dismissed, maybe you don't want that man in your life. You can also ask your friends. Most of all, ask yourself. Write down on a piece of paper "The Ten Things about Me That Would Make a Man Lucky to Get Me." Force yourself to write down ten things, even if they feel stupid or unimportant, even if you don't feel all that great about them. But you deserve to feel that you're desirable.

• Did you say *no* to the question: *"We've all made mistakes in the land of love. Do you have the experience and understanding to forgive yourself for yours?"* If you answered *no,* I'll bet anything that it's really just one big mistake that you feel badly about. One thing you can't forgive yourself for. Okay. Ask yourself who the wisest person you know is. It could be a friend you're no longer all that close to. A member of the clergy. Your grandmother. Whoever. Tell that person what you did and ask her or him what you can do to put it behind you. If he or she says, "It's nothing. You were just a kid. Let go of it," then for God's sake just let it go.

• Did you say *no* to the question: *"If you think about falling in love in the future, do you have a clear, confident sense of what it is you damned well better stay away from?"* If you don't, I'll tell you. No losers. No assholes. Stay away from guys who will make trouble for you either because they need help or because they'll make you miserable. A woman living alone with the ugliest cat is better off than a woman married to a loser, a nut case, or a bastard, even if he's famous or a millionaire.

• Did you say *no* to the question: *"Do you have enough experience to know the differences between being flattered by someone, being horny for someone, feeling taken care of by someone, and really being in love with someone?"* If you don't know the answer to this question, and you're not in a relationship right now, you just need more love adventures. If you are in a relationship, you have to ask yourself honestly, "What do I need to feel loved?" Take a piece of paper. At the top of it write down, "I'd really feel loved if . . ." Finish that sentence as many different ways as you can think of. Read back to yourself what you've written down. And circle what you think of as your *three* most important answers. That's it. Now you know.

• Did you say *no* to the question: *"Can you say fairly confidently, when it comes to love experiences, 'Maybe I haven't done it all, but I certainly feel I've lived?'"* If you answered *no*, actually most of us go through a crisis from time to time where we're suddenly hit by the sense that we haven't really lived. There's nothing wrong with being hit by this feeling. It's just a way for you to force yourself at key intervals in your life to think about what's missing, what new slices of life it's time for you to take on. We should all be thinking about this. It's a lifetime project.

Your Love Adventure Insurance

Suppose you're saying, "Yeah, I do need more love adventures." Maybe you need them because you've been afraid of getting hurt, and that's kept you from having your share. And you can get hurt. The good news is that most of these hurts are easily survivable, like the pains and sprains we get learning to ski. Since you can get hurt so badly *not* having love adventures, you can't worry too much about the hurts that come from having them.

But you do have to worry about real damage. That brings up a good question: What are the major mistakes women make when they have love adventures, and how do you protect yourself from these mistakes?

Having love adventures is like going to Las Vegas. If you want to avoid getting hurt, here's what to do.

1. *Walk in with your eyes open.* Know what you're getting into. Know what the odds are. Know what you're willing to lose. When it comes to love this means, for example, that a summer romance is usually just that—over by Labor Day. It means that falling in love with a struggling artist is unlikely to end with a commitment but is likely to take a lot from you. That's okay if you feel you have a lot to give and you don't need to end up with a commitment. As long as your eyes are open and you see what's real. There's one way in which love is just like the craps tables: If you think you're going to beat the odds, you'll get creamed.

2. *Have an exit strategy.* Always make sure you're able to get out. Know what the signs are that it's time to get out. Know how to get out. Have the resources you need to get out. Don't have children as a result of any love adventure. Have children with someone after you've had your adventures, after a particular adventure has ripened into true love and commitment and a period where you really find out whether the two of you can make a life together. And do hold on to your money. Never put yourself in a situation where you don't have the dough to walk away from a love affair.

3. *Learn how to play the game.* Know what it means for you to win. Have an idea of how to win. There's a reason why love adventures and falling in love are separate experiences. A love adventure is play. It can feel like you're playing for keeps, but it's a ride in the amusement park of love. It's seeing what

it's like to be with a certain kind of guy. It could be seeing
what it's like to be with a woman. It could be seeing what it's
like to get back with an old boyfriend now that you're feeling
more empowered than you were years ago. It could be any
kind of experiment. Most often, you win if three things happen.
You have the love adventure. You learn something new about
yourself. You avoid getting badly hurt.

4. *Don't play if you're desperate*. When it comes to love, desperate, lonely women who feel badly about themselves are like
people who gamble their rent money on the craps tables.
They're going to lose and they're going to get into trouble. This
means protecting your heart when your heart is vulnerable.
Just don't have love adventures when you're in a weakened
state, on the rebound from being dumped, going through a
period when you're feeling lonely and hungry for love. If you
are feeling vulnerable, here's what you need instead of love
adventures. Women friends. Men you become friends with.
And never get involved with someone who wasn't your
friend first.

These four things are all you need to be safe while you're
having adventures. Keep that gambling analogy in mind—all it
means is, no blind adventures. It's fine to dive off a cliff into
a pool 150 feet below—it's insane to dive into that pool before
you've swum around and checked out how deep it is. And if
you haven't proven yourself as a diver, practice on the baby
board first. If you'd tell your daughter not to do it, you
shouldn't do it.

You see, the danger with love adventures is the same danger
people run into with gambling: you get into trouble when
you're desperate for a thrill or desperate for money or desperate
for love.

But looking at the story of love in your life as a whole, the
biggest danger comes from not having your share of love
adventures.

Ain't Nothing Like the Real Thing

Make-or-Break Experience #2:
Finding Someone to Love without Losing Yourself

With love adventures you were looking to have an experience in the land of love. With *this* make-or-break experience you're looking for true love. The kind that will last. You may take your time. You may be ever so cautious. But by the end of this experience you're hoping you'll have found the whole enchilada.

Here are some moments from women's experiences of looking for someone to love:

• Three serious relationships haven't worked out. Now you find yourself complaining about how hard it is to meet good guys, guys who say, "I'll call," and then call. Guys who make you glad they called. But in spite of your disappointments, you keep doing things to meet someone. The worst depression of your life came when you gave up on meeting someone to love.
• Your marriage is on the rocks, and before you know it you start having whole new relationships with guys, flirting and talking about yourself in a way you haven't since way before you got married. You roam through AOL chat rooms looking

43

for people with interests similar to yours, but always find yourself heading off for private chats with men you take a fancy to.
• Even though you've gone out with a guy for months, and most
of the time he sleeps over at your place, you're still wondering how
you feel about him and aren't even sure how you'd feel if you knew
he loved you. Because deep down you're still looking.
• You go for long walks every day in the park near your
house now that you're single again, and in spite of your vow
to stay single you keep running into the same woman and
you've started to talk. It bothers you to find yourself hoping so
intensely that the two of you will connect.
• You're living with a guy and you've said "I love you" to
each other, but deep down you're wondering if you really do
love him and if he really is right for you. Let's face it. Sometimes we say, "I love you," just to see how we feel inside after
we've said it.

It was the best of times . . . This can be the best of times
and the worst of times. *Fifty-four percent of women agreed with
the statement, "I had the best time when I was dating, but I'd
never want to go through it again."*

*The worst part about it? Most women said it was the time
they wasted. The scariest part? Most said their biggest fear was
hooking up with the wrong person.*

*The best part? When the sun rises and you slowly discover
you've found the right person.*

The battle rages. The battle between hope and discouragement
is all-important here. There's the fun and anticipation of meeting
new people. And the dread at having to tell your life story yet one
more time to someone who's telling you his life story yet one more
time. There's the tremendous surge of hope that comes from thinking that maybe you've connected with somebody good looking
who's not a jerk and who seems to like you.

Most of the time we're fueled by hope. But here's the make-
or-break part of this experience. Should we get discouraged,
we're at terrible risk of losing out on love. We just stop going

out. We refuse to be fixed up. We reject overtures. What's easier than just not looking for love? No wonder this is a make-or-break experience. This is the launching pad. If the rocket won't launch, there's no journey to the stars.

Looking for the Real Thing

This experience is deeper than just dating. Maybe *dating* isn't even the right word. There's something old-fashioned about it. It feels too formal—you know, the guy calling the girl to ask her out and then picking her up in his car, dinner and a show, bringing her home, kissing her at the front door—all like a movie from the fifties. And it feels silly, like Archie and Betty meeting the gang at Pop Tate's Choclit Shoppe.

We may be going through the experience of looking for love even if we're married. A lot of married women aren't sleeping around and would say they're committed to their marriage, but they're still checking out guys as if to find an answer to the question, "Would I be happier with this person than I am with my husband?" A lot of women check out men's souls the way men check out women's bodies. We're looking for something we haven't completely found. If you haven't found love in your current relationship, then you're looking for love whether you know it or not.

You get stuck in this experience the same way you get stuck going shopping. If you don't know yourself, or if you feel rushed, or if you sell yourself short—any of these can result in not being happy with what you get.

You're looking for someone because you want to be loved. You want someone in your life who will truly, thoroughly, and deeply love you. You need to know he'd weep true, bitter tears if you died. You need to know he'd cut off his left arm for you, if that ever came up, but that he'd also take out the garbage without being asked, because that will come up and because sometimes it's things like that, little actions, not big words, that let you know you're really loved.

And how in the world do we manage to find someone like that? It helps if you know you can trust yourself.

You're Smarter Than You Think

We've all said things like these: "I can't believe I went out with a guy like that." "I can't believe the guys I went out with." "I can't believe the kinds of relationships I had." "I can't believe the things I did with guys."

What's up with this? We could just say women are idiots and go home. Problem solved. We're all a bunch of goof balls. Or are we? Maybe, just maybe, you were never *smarter* than when you were doing those stupid things you did during that period when you were looking for the real thing.

I don't think we're idiots. I've talked to women for many many years, and I've known some scared women, some inexperienced women, some women with nowhere to turn, but *very few idiots* when it comes to love.

We all need love to live. How could we be idiots about that? Our most basic instincts are tied up with knowing about love. It would be like calling squirrels idiots when it came to finding acorns because they spent so much time looking for them. But finding acorns is their job, and it's a tough job. In fact, they're brilliant at it. And we're brilliant at our job. Even if it throws us into contact with more than our share of nuts.

Here's a woman whose love history makes her look a lot stupider than she really is. She wasn't screwing up the process of looking for someone to love. She was doing it in a way that made sure she took care of some important business. For Dana, part of finding someone to love was finding herself.

☙

Dana's Story

While still in college Dana lived as a homeless woman for three months. Looking back she feels lucky that she survived. The stories she wrote about her experiences on the street—stories about fear, loneliness, hunger, boredom, but also about some wonderful bonds she made with some surprising women—forced a difficult choice on Dana. She couldn't shake from her mind the faces of women driven to the street by one form of abuse or another—drugs, violence, you name it. Dana decided to help these women.

Ten years later, Dana was running a shelter for homeless women, plus directing a pilot project for rehabilitating them by educating them in the humanities, arts, and sciences instead of just training them to be data-entry clerks.

Have I proved to you that Dana is not an idiot? I hope so because you might wonder when you learn a little about Dana's dating history.

Experimental men. Back in college there was the professor. Not the professor from Gilligan's Island—he at least was single (wasn't he?). No, this guy was a married professor with a wife too rich to divorce but who completely "didn't understand him." One day, he said, somehow, he and Dana would join their lives together. Just not now.

The worst part of the relationship wasn't his unavailability. It was his contempt for her. He was the poster boy for every woman who's ever said, "I could never like a guy who really liked me." Their relationship basically consisted of sex and criticism. Of his being turned on by her body and turned off by everything else about her.

And Dana ate it up with a spoon. The whole time she was fighting for other women's rights she was ignoring her own. But she felt flattered. She had lots of time to herself—the professor was the original Cling Free guy. She had lots of sex (which she admitted was not very good). And best of all, because he was so hot for her body and so mean to her the rest of the time, she felt 100 percent free to have as bad an attitude as she wanted. He didn't care if she acted like a bitch. The professor was a vacation from having to be nice!

Unfortunately he was also a vacation from having nice things happen. She told her friends, "This sucks," but she felt as if it could go on forever, and maybe it would have if he hadn't gone off to do research somewhere. She never got a single call or letter from him.

Bad boys. The next guy—I kid you not—went by the name of Scar. "So where's your scar?" Dana asked him after they made love the first time. "It's not about my *having* a scar," he said, leaving Dana to figure it out. You get the point. Scar was a street guy. One of her homeless women fixed Dana up with him. He claimed he was trying to rehabilitate himself from a life of dealing and doing drugs. When she met him he was working as a bartender. He claimed he was trying to save up the dough to start his own club.

The fact is he made her crazy. Practically every word out of his mouth was some tall tale or other. He rarely said anything definite. The things he said that were definite were rarely true. But he was incredibly handsome. A romantic figure. A babe magnet, and he had the babes to prove it. One thing he would give Dana the professor would never give: He would say he loved her. "You are the love of my life." When he said it he sounded like the most believable guy in the world. Then Dana would see him with other women.

These two are just a sample of Dana's relationships during this period. Most of the guys were classier than Scar. Most were nicer to her than the professor. But they were all impossible relationships. So was Dana an idiot?

And the point is . . . I asked her what the worst part of these relationships was. She said, "None of them knew me." I asked her what the best part was. She said, "None of them knew me." I asked her to explain. She did:

> *You know, there's a part of me that feels I want my husband to be the first man to see me really naked. I know that sounds incredibly old-fashioned for a slick chick like me who's stripped down for more than my share of guys. So I guess I'm talking about naked souls here.*
>
> *The first week or so I was on the streets living like a*

homeless woman—and remember that was a lie because I had money and family and everything—I realized that I really was homeless in the sense of completely not knowing who I was as a person, and if you don't know who you are, you don't know what you want. You need something real to happen to find out who you are.

I wanted to be somebody but I didn't know who I wanted to be. You know, like people who want to do something artistic but don't have a specific artistic activity in mind. That was practically the first thing I realized about guys: If you don't know who you are that's no problem for them. They'll tell you who you are. Two seconds with a guy and you can have a complete identity. But it probably has nothing to do with who you really are.

I hated every minute I was so completely invisible to these guys. But I loved being in control of being invisible. You asked me about "dating." I would never have called it that, but that's exactly what I was doing. Marking time until I figured out what I needed to figure out. I don't know, I guess some women need to figure out who they're comfortable with. I always knew that. I wanted to marry a guy like my dad. How boring. I just couldn't accept it. But I didn't know how to be comfortable with myself.

Needing to Know Yourself

Dana understood deep down that until she knew herself, intimacy would be impossible. *She didn't want to fall in love with a guy and then wake up ten years later to realize that who she really was didn't fit in that relationship.* Dana was faced with the challenge of finding a way to know herself. Her preventing intimacy from happening was her way of rising to this challenge. In a sense she was saying to these guys, "Stop. Wait a minute. I don't know enough about who I am yet. What's the point of revealing my 'true self' when I'm just a work in progress at this point?"

It's not as if Dana was cold-bloodedly devoting ten years of her life to going out with the wrong guys. She was almost as confused and annoyed with herself as her mother was, and you can imagine how her mother felt about Dana's relationships. But deep down Dana knew she was serious about looking for the real thing. And instinctively she understood that the more you know about yourself, the more the person you end up with will actually be the real thing. In the meantime, you dilly-dally with Scar and the professor.

You can't find a true love until you discover the true you.

⊗

Deb's Story

Dana managed to stay out of a serious relationship until she could figure out who she was. Deb was so desperate to marry she was denying who she was. Even to herself. And that was a big deal for her. Almost a sin. She was a member of the Episcopal clergy, and she'd worked hard to get where she was. Much of her spiritual work involved trying to come to terms with her true self. But her desperation led her into self-deception.

Why was Deb so desperate? Hey, you don't have to put any of us on the couch to get an explanation out of us for why we'd be hungry for love. Love hunger is the deepest, most powerful hunger there is. After you've got food in your belly and a warm, dry place to lay your head at night, you want someone in your life who cares about you. You want to feel you really matter to someone. Roommates can be great, but sometimes they only make you realize how much you want someone who'll really love you.

To sum up her postcollege dating history, the years passed, and guys didn't click with Deb or she didn't click with guys. Next thing she knew she was thirty-three and the arithmetic of love was scaring her witless. She couldn't see how she'd get to be a bride in less than two years even if she found the right guy immediately. Add a couple of more years before the first kid comes and suddenly she's thirty-seven. And that's assuming everything goes right.

Anyway, her arithmetic led to instant marriage panic. But she'd learned a lot about herself over the years. Like how, if truth be told, she was a woman who liked to be in charge. And she was afraid of not having any money. And she was a little bit of a snob—the thought of being with a guy who didn't know the right fork to use was horrifying to her.

But don't for a minute make the mistake of thinking that any of this means Deb was cold. She wanted to be held and loved and told she was wonderful and have her face kissed just like everyone else. And if she would ever find a guy who knew what fork to use and let her manage the money, she would be as warm and kind and affectionate as anyone.

He should have been perfect. Then she met Jeff, an Episcopal clergyman himself (so he was perfect, right?), and there was a collision between her love hunger and the truths she knew about herself. She felt that if she told him the truth about who she was, what she liked, and what she needed—"Hey, Jeff, guess what? I like sex, money, and being in control. How does that turn you on?"—well, her best guess was that she'd lose Jeff. And that would be a big loss, because Jeff seemed to love what he saw in her.

The need when we're looking for love is to find someone who will really love us. Deb was saying what millions say, "It's so important to me to be loved, so what if the person who's being loved isn't exactly me?"

You do what you gotta do. Deb did what we all do. Instead of deliberately, cold-bloodedly, manipulatively going into hiding, she softly, gently, mostly unconsciously deceived herself. For example, Jeff had a missionary bent to him. The idea of working out of an inner-city church appealed to him. Well, how in a million years could Deb say to him that she thought the idea sucked? Having a missionary streak made him the perfect guy for the woman she was supposed to be. Saying it

sucked would make Deb look awful. So she found herself getting forced into believing that wanting an upper-middle-class
lifestyle—which is how she'd been brought up—was merely a
bad habit, something she could slough off as easily as the desire
to eat bacon for breakfast.

So what would you see if you spied on those early dates between
Deb and Jeff, when they were getting to know each other? You'd
see a woman behaving the way we've behaved for hundreds of
years. You'd see Deb drawing Jeff out, listening to him with interest
and sympathy. You'd hear her say, "That's wonderful," when he
told her how he wanted to live with poor people.

Deb's deceiving herself wasn't just about ideology, either.
It was also about that in-your-skin feeling when you're with
someone. Jeff conveyed in a thousand little ways that he liked
being in control. For example, whenever they'd go out together,
instead of his planning their evening with her, he would just
say, "I'll pick you up at seven. Dress up." If she asked where
they were going he'd try to avoid telling her, like she was a
spoilsport for not wanting to go out on an Evening of Mystery.
And Deb heard herself say, "You make such great plans. It's
so nice not to have to think about it," as if she were the kind
of woman who was just waiting for a guy to come along and
be in control of things. And she didn't say to herself, "What a
big fat hypocrite I am." She thought, "Gee, it's about time I
learned not to always have to be in control."

Setting It Up Right

Deb thinks she's found the real thing. Dana knows she hasn't.
But Dana's closer to finding love than Deb is. Right now Deb's
going through the painful process of revealing who she is to
Jeff. They're doing it in couple's therapy. The ostensible reason
they went to look for help was that Deb was somehow mysteriously unhappy in the relationship. But the reason wasn't so
mysterious. It was that she was struggling to bring a new

woman into the relationship. The woman she really was. And that wasn't the woman Jeff knew.

How many of us do what Deb did when we go through the experience of looking for someone to love? Here are just a few examples of women who hid small but essential pieces of who they really were, not because they were shallow, conniving tempt-resses but simply because they were women hungry for love. They'd learned what most of us learn, that love is hard to find in this world. For them this meant compromising with their sense of who they really were. Not for sleaze, but to please:

- A woman makes her prospective partner feel that it's fine with her if he works thirty-six hours a day and is never around.
- A guy talks endlessly about the computer stuff he's inter-ested in and the woman hides how bored she is from him.
- A woman lets the guy she's dating think that having a fam-ily is as important to her as it is to him, when in fact she had a bad experience with her own family and would really prefer not to have kids.
- A woman acts as though she never watches television be-cause she's afraid it will turn the guy off if she reveals how much she likes all kinds of TV shows from *The Simpsons* to Elsa Klensch.

We don't say, "Oh, look at me, I'm hiding who I really am just to find someone to love." It's not like that at all. Instead it's all about not knowing who we really are (like Dana), or deceiving ourselves about who we really are (like Deb). It's about sincerely wanting to be the kind of person we know will work in this relationship. Sometimes it's just about waiting for the right time to let the other person know who we really are.

"But I Just Want to Find Somebody . . ."

However it happens, however benign the motivation, a mis-taken impression gets created. Two people are moving along two very different paths, and they're thinking they're on the same path.

Back when I was first involved with my husband we were both philosophy majors in college. We both liked literature. The first night we met I read my husband a part of a paper I'd written about *The Brothers Karamazov*. That might not make me seem wildly attractive to you, but it turned him on. From the very first night he thought he was getting involved with a woman who cared intensely about literature and philosophy.

I wasn't lying to him. I wasn't a phony. I thought I really cared about that stuff too. But I was an immigrant street kid from the Lower East Side of New York. My parents struggled to run a small lamp store. I was an infinitely more practical, problem-solving-type woman than he thought I was. Part of me was afraid he'd be disappointed if he knew how practical I was.

But it broke my heart when I saw how much he was falling in love with who he thought I was. This experience is about finding someone who'll truly love us. I saw he could truly love me. And get this: I *wanted* to be someone who lived for literature and philosophy. I didn't like the practical person I was afraid I truly was (and that I truly am). After all, I was only nineteen. How well do we know ourselves at that age?

Will the real me please stand up? Now think about what this did. I wanted us to be extremely close. But talking about literature and philosophy supposedly defined what it meant for us to be warm and close. I was paying for my innocent deception. How could I feel close when the things we were talking about were things I didn't really care that much about?

I started being annoyed at him for how little he really knew me. But how could he know me if I wasn't showing myself? How could he like me if he'd be disappointed in what I had to offer if I did show myself? So for me as for so many of us, this guy was in a relationship with a me that wasn't the real me. And then I'd be annoyed at him because I didn't feel we were as close as I wanted us to be.

How many of us go through our lives annoyed at our partners for not knowing us very well when we're the ones who've kept part of ourselves under wraps? And then we wonder why intimacy doesn't feel like intimacy.

Love Hunger

We're all hungry for love. Maybe you're too cool to admit to being hungry for love. But come on. I've rarely met anyone, the toughest guy, the toughest woman, who wasn't really eager to find someone who loved him or her. Have you? I've never met anyone who wasn't willing to make sacrifices if that would make it possible for the person she loved to love her back. If you measure love hunger by a person's willingness to sacrifice, then you see how much most women, at least at some point in their lives, are driven by love hunger. Let's face it: it's freer, easier, tidier to live by yourself. Why would any of us ever want to go through the work of combining our lives with someone else's if we weren't filled with love hunger?

Midnight cravings. I can't remember a time when I wasn't filled with love hunger. And that's a truth about love hunger that's not commonly recognized. Most of us have felt it, and most of us still feel it even after we've found someone—we wish there were more love in our relationships. (Which is why you can be going through this make-or-break experience even if you're in a relationship.) And it's not just words you're looking for, but real feelings. When you want a pizza, it's not enough to know that Domino's exists—the guy's got to actually show up with the pizza.

"How did you manage that?" we wonder when we see women seeming to just sail through this experience of love. I wondered the same thing.

Here's the secret they told me: you need to be a good shopper. That's what this experience is. You're shopping for a lifetime lover. If you're controlled by love hunger, you'll screw up. Love hunger makes you scared, when what you need is guts.

Love hunger makes you stupid, when what you need is to be smart. And love hunger makes you lose touch with yourself, when what you need is self-knowledge.

Shopping for Love

Love and guts. Being a good shopper requires *guts.* You've got to be willing to walk out without buying anything. And that's hard if you're shopping on a Friday afternoon for a Friday-night cocktail party with clients from work. It's hard if you feel deprived and you just need that one dress to bring home to feel satisfied inside. It's hard if you're eaten up by the feeling that your friends have good stuff and you don't. It's hard if you've fallen into a habit of always bringing something home with you, no matter what.

Women have gotten hurt because we've been more afraid than men are to walk away from a relationship. We blame men for their fear of commitment. But we hurt ourselves by dreading the thought of walking away.

Maybe it's our biological clock that's responsible for that. But this is how love has been disempowering. Like when I first met my husband and I didn't apply to the graduate schools I wanted to apply to, because they were very far away and that would have meant our not being together. I got hurt because I was afraid to ask him to move with me across the country.

But we don't have to stop believing in love. Let me give you the advice I've given my own daughters: Believe in love, but be willing to walk away when it doesn't look like you're going to get the real thing.

Love and smarts. As you know, being a good shopper takes smarts. You've got to know what you need, what works for you, who you are. At the very least you have to be able to avoid making horrible mistakes.

For example, jeans are a fashion icon. Tight jeans on a woman with a fat ass are a fashion disaster. You've got to be

smart enough to know your own ass. Isn't that the greatest
clothes-shopping motto: Just stop and think for a moment. Do
you really want this? Do you need this? Will this be good for
you? Can you afford it? Will you quickly grow sick of it?

Again, it's the same when it comes to looking for someone
to love. Maybe a guy turns you on. But even though he makes
your panties wet it doesn't mean he'll be great to live with for
the rest of your life. The guy who turns you on today could
be a big drip tomorrow and a pain in the neck later on. So
shopping takes guts and smarts. And so does looking for someone who'll really love you, the real you. Let's take this analogy further.

Love and self-knowledge. Suppose you're going shopping
with two of your friends for a dress you're going to wear to a
party that's a big deal for you. A lot of people you know will
be at the party, plus a lot of people you want to impress. Well,
there are plenty of bargains in the store. Plenty of dresses that
are the latest style. Plenty of dresses that make a statement.
Plenty of dresses that look good on the rack. You look and
look and look.

You're looking for that dress that's going to make both of
your friends say, "That's *you*. And it makes you look wonderful." You're looking for something that picks up what's special
about who you are, some flavor you have that everyone who
knows you recognizes, a spicy quality, perhaps, or a quirky
sweetness. And when you find the dress that's truly you, it
makes your search worthwhile. Then instead of having a dress
that wears you, instead of having a dress that looks like it has
nothing to do with you, you have a dress that—check out the
language—*becomes* you.

Guts. Smarts. Self-knowledge. Women who find the real
thing have all three.

When you'd kill for a date. You've got to watch out for
dating mania. This is when you fork over thousands of dollars
to dating services that promise treasure troves of gorgeous guys

but deliver only musty scrapbooks of fading losers. This is when you read books like *The Rules*—there are actually dozens of books like this. They're all about getting the guy. As if winning at love were like ensuring that no matter what else happens you don't leave Bloomingdale's without that Big Brown shopping bag. And you and I both know who those books are aimed at: you and me in our desperate hours when we talk to our friends about wanting to get married and about our biological clocks ticking and about feeling lonely and about wanting to find someone to love us.

When Winning Makes Us Losers

It's during those years when we're looking for someone to love that dating becomes focused on *winning*. You hook up with a guy who satisfies enough items on your checklist without violating any of your major no-no's, and that's it, bang!—you're willing to do whatever is necessary to *get* the guy. You don't care how. All you want is to cruise down that highway from Dating Forest through Love Valley and on to Marriage City.

And *that*—when we focus on winning—is when we start setting ourselves up for a love life without intimacy. Focusing on winning in love means you're always so busy trying to get him to want you that you forget to ask yourself if you want him, or if he'll want the real you.

Letting it all hang out. That's not the only force operating during this experience. When we're young we can be incredibly idealistic about honesty in love. We feel we have all the time in the world and there are a million guys out there—so let it all hang out and let the chips fall where they may. We also get smarter as we get older. We learn what happens when you hide your real needs: You can't feel intimate with someone who doesn't know you, who can't know you because you've been in hiding. And so if you want love to feel like love, you've got to be yourself.

That brave young woman and savvy older woman is always a part of all of us regardless of our chronological age. But the scared woman who's afraid she won't find someone who will really love her, that woman is a part of all of us too. We understand her. We know how she feels.

Welcome to the Real Love Club

I asked women what they'd say to this scared woman so hungry for love. Their answers were consistent. Based on what they told me, here are The Top Ten *Real* Rules that have proven their value to women who care about love and have managed to find someone who can give them real love.

Don't you think it's time we stopped engaging in stupid patterns while we date and then act surprised when the relationship that comes out of that dating isn't filled with the real thing? So let this be our new motto: Date for Real Love. If that's your motto, these are The *Real* Rules.

THE TOP TEN *REAL* RULES

Real Rule #1: *Make smart go/no-go choices after the second or third date.*

Real Rule #2: *The sooner the guy gets to know who you really are and what it's like to connect with you, the better.*

Real Rule #3: *Give yourself options.*

Real Rule #4: *Know that you're setting the patterns from the very beginning, so make sure that the patterns that get set are the patterns you want to live with.*

Real Rule #5: *Intimacy requires self-knowledge.*

Real Rule #6: *The right person for you is the person who feels right to you.*

Real Rule #7: *Go for the steak, not the sizzle. All the smartest women think of dating as the search for substance.*

Real Rule #8: *Because you're worth it . . . So don't settle for anything less than someone who's good for you and your future.*

Real Rule #9: *The important thing isn't how you feel about him but how he makes you feel.*

Real Rule #10: *Don't connect with someone over where you are now—connect with him over where the two of you want to end up.*

Let's take these one at a time.

Real Rule #1:

MAKE SMART GO/NO-GO CHOICES AFTER THE SECOND OR THIRD DATE.

It's about not wasting time. And it's about not overlooking a treasure. Here's how to decide whether or not to go on a second or third date with a guy, based on my asking women what they wish they'd paid more attention to, both on the plus side and on the minus side.

On the plus side, I don't have to tell you what you already know. Obviously a handsome, smart, charming, funny, sensitive guy with a good heart and a good job is what you're looking for. But what about good qualities that are often overlooked? You can be reasonably confident a guy's worth checking out further if the following things are true about him:

**THE TOP FIVE THINGS TO LOOK FOR IN A GUY
YOU MIGHT NOT THINK OF LOOKING FOR**

1. *He delivers on his promises.* A guy who underpromises and always comes through is worth a thousand guys who break their promises.

2. *He's easily open.* He shares good things, bad things, everything. He tells you things about himself without your having to probe.

3. *He's a solid guy compared to guys in his reference group, and compared to guys in your reference group.* A "reference group" is a bunch of people it's appropriate to compare someone to. It's a no-go sign if the guy you're dating just doesn't stack up to his reference group. That's the technical definition of a loser.

4. *He's there for you when you need him.* A guy who's just a little bit more attentive and responsible when he knows that something's important to you—that's a trustworthy guy.

5. *He's fun to be with.* Fun is the glue of love. You have an idea of what's fun for you, and if he's fun to be with in that same way, then you've got something *really* solid to fall back on.

On the minus side, here are the guys you should run from. Let me be clear. It doesn't matter how cool he is. It doesn't matter how much you have in common. It doesn't matter how excellent his excuses are for why he is the way he is. But if he falls into any of the following categories, then ultimately he'll make you miserable.

THE TOP TEN KINDS OF GUYS YOU SHOULD RUN FROM

1. *He's obnoxious.* Say a guy's a boring whiner, but so what because he has a prestigious job? The thing is, though, that the way someone actually makes you feel is a hundred times more important than facts about him you don't experience.

2. *He's a hider.* There are always these facts that you find out too late. You feel you never know what's real, solid, and true. And nothing ever is with him.

3. *He's an empty promiser.* He keeps saying he's going to do things that for 101 different reasons he ends up not doing. Your anger and disappointment with this guy will become huge if you stay with him.

4. *He's a gross exaggerator.* A guy who exaggerates all the time will ultimately seem like a very small man.

5. *He's a blamer.* If you begin to get the idea that whatever goes wrong is always someone else's fault, run. Fast. Ultimately this guy has no conception of what it means to take responsibility. Plus, sooner or later he'll start blaming you.

6. *He's a manipulator.* If you ask a question, he makes you feel somehow in the wrong for asking. If you mention that if he's going to be late, he should call, he makes you feel there's something wrong with you for needing that. He manipulates things so you always feel in the wrong.

7. *He's someone who has a radically different vision of how to live than you do.* No matter how great a guy is, if the way he wants to live is seriously different from the way you want to live, your relationship will end up being a tug-of-war.

8. *He's got too many problems.* A guy who has a recent track record of screwing up is a guy you've got to stay away from. Let your heart go out to whomever you want, but don't give it to a guy with problems.

9. *He's just fishy.* Trust yourself. An amazing 77 percent of women who've been screwed by a guy say they felt there was something wrong but they just didn't want to listen to their feelings.

10. *He's a liar.* If a guy lies to you about something big, then you've got to assume you're dealing with a guy who han-

dles difficulty by lying. A guy you're just starting to date who tells a big lie is a guy you should run from.

Then there's the one who got away. I asked women about times when they gave a guy the kiss-off and later regretted it. So what are the things women *regret* dumping a guy for?

THE TOP FIVE THINGS YOU MIGHT THINK ARE PROBLEMS BUT AREN'T

1. *He's not your type.* You might find out he's more your type than you think. It depends on what you mean by your type. Too often it's really about superficials of appearance and lifestyle. Be open-minded.

2. *He's not as successful as you'd hoped.* If his dreams are real-istic and he's got what it takes to achieve those dreams and he's going about it in a sensible way, then give him a chance.

3. *He seems too shy.* Give a shy guy a chance to feel comfort-able with you, and see what happens. He might change once he feels safe.

4. *His previous relationships have been disasters.* You've got to find out why things didn't work out. Because he beat the crap out of his previous wives? Then run. Because he made poor judgments about the kind of women to get involved with? Well, if you're different from those women, then why shouldn't it work out with you?

5. *You're just too different.* The only differences you have to watch out for are the differences that cut at the root of how you want to live your life. Some differences are a source of distance and irritation, but some differences are a wonderful opportunity for the two of you to get what you want as individuals.

Real Rule #1 was all about the quick-and-dirty guidelines. Okay, you've kept the potential winners and weeded out the guys it's better not to bother with. Now how do you proceed?

Real Rule #2:

THE SOONER THE GUY GETS TO KNOW WHO YOU REALLY ARE AND WHAT IT'S LIKE TO CONNECT WITH YOU, THE BETTER.

The solution is easier than you might think. Did you ever take a tour through a historical house where they put up a rope barrier in front of some rooms, so that you could look in but you couldn't walk in? That's what you do with a guy when you take him on a tour of your House of Intimacy.

Maybe it's just your third or fourth date. Open a door and show him what intimacy with you would be like. You don't have to actually let him go into that room. You're just telling him what you want from intimacy without making him experience it.

For example, maybe intimacy for you involves literally walking around naked. To be true to yourself, *tell* him about your wanting to feel comfortable enough with a guy at some point to be able to walk around naked. At least this way he knows that the thermostat might be at sixty-two now but if you're going to get close it's going to go up to seventy-five. You don't have to actually walk around naked. Maybe you wouldn't feel comfortable doing that anyway at this point. Maybe he would misinterpret it. But by telling him about it now, you're protecting your future intimacy. He's been warned. And that's your protection. Your honesty protects you.

To take another example. Maybe you feel that when two people are really close, they can fight with each other without it making them scared that the relationship is going to collapse. Being true to yourself doesn't necessarily involve launching the guy into some fight that will scare the hell out of him. But open the door and show him the room. Let him know what your vision of an intimate relationship is. Tell him that it involves two people being comfortable enough with each other to fight.

You can give him time to set the pace for when he moves into that room. Maybe he's someone who grew up in a family where fighting was a rare, scary occurrence. He'd like to feel free enough to fight—so he does share your vision of intimacy. He's just not ready to jump into it right now. But he needs to know what to expect.

A lot of intimacy is spoiled because we spend our time running away from bad surprises. And because we spend too much time dealing with the way one of you is disappointed at how disappointed the other is in what he's discovered. None of this is necessary, if full, early disclosure of everything *you'd* want to know going into a relationship is the basis for what you tell your partner. If you'd want to know it about him, tell it to him about you.

Real Rule #3:

GIVE YOURSELF OPTIONS.

If only we were as smart in love, you and I, as we are in shopping. If we go to buy a watch or a pair of shoes, we'd have a fit if we walked into the store and there were only two or three items to choose from. We don't really know all that well exactly what we want. We don't know what will look good on us. We don't know what will fit. We don't know what will coordinate with the other things we have.

But when there's a large selection, we sort of enter into a dialogue between our own needs and feelings and all the watches and shoes on sale. They educate us about what's possible. Most of all, a large selection teaches us not to settle. The more items to choose from, the more possibility there is of finding something just right.

What does this have to do with finding someone to love? Maybe nothing. We all know cases of someone who moves to a new city and the first guy she meets is perfect. But, hey, sometimes people win the lottery too. If you talk to women who've been down this road, maybe a couple of times, you hear a very specific regret over and over, and a very specific word of advice.

Here's how one woman put it:

ॐ

Gail's Story

"I can't believe I did this *twice*. My first husband—well, I was in the chorus in college and he was in it too. There were twenty guys in the chorus and he's the one who asked me out. What are there, three billion guys in the world? There were maybe five guys in the chorus I would've even considered going out with, and I married one of them. With a whole bunch of reservations. Okay.

"Then I'm divorced and I move to New York with this really good job in publishing. I'm thinking, wow, New York men. It's like walking into Tiffany's with a million bucks in your pocket. Okay. Six months later I've got three girlfriends in the city plus a couple of women I'm friendly with at work, and they each have one brilliant idea for someone I should go out with, and they set me up. Five setups.

"So in my head I'm thinking I've got millions of guys to choose from, because I'm in New York. In reality I've got five. I'm back to where I was in college where there were five guys I'd date. There's a world full of men and I choose my second husband from one of these five guys. I mean we were attracted to each other, but I never began to ask myself what I needed and wanted. I should've put in personal ads and taken classes and gotten involved in this singles organization my church has. I don't know, but I think I could've had a hundred guys to check out who were checking me out. So after two divorces my advice is give yourself some options."

A lot of women said what Gail said. Basically, "You've got to give yourself a lot more men to choose from. That's really how to win at dating."

Here's the rest of Gail's story. It's pretty simple. She took her own advice. She went on a campaign to meet one hundred eligible men. "I might die trying," she said, "but at least I'll die happy." She put in personal ads, she joined clubs, the works. She soon realized that in the past she'd been a total sucker for the first guy who was nice to her. The problem is that her first two husbands were nice guys who ultimately had little to give. "I'm going to wait for a nice guy who's got something on the ball."

Gail waited. She found him. It took a year. That felt like a long time. But her first two failed marriages took eleven years. You do the math.

Real Rule #4:

KNOW THAT YOU'RE SETTING THE PATTERNS FROM THE VERY BEGINNING, SO MAKE SURE THAT THE PATTERNS THAT GET SET ARE THE PATTERNS YOU WANT TO LIVE WITH.

Everything you do at the beginning of a relationship sets a pattern. Even if you do something once—even *that* can set a pattern. If a guy's always late when he picks you up and you never say anything about it, you've set up a pattern or rule about not commenting on his being late. You know you've set up a rule if when you finally do say something after he's late seventeen different times he acts like the injured victim and says, "How come you never said anything before?" It's the old "Speak now or forever hold your peace" idea.

A home for your love. Here's the thing. Going along with patterns you don't like absolutely destroys the possibility of intimacy—you won't feel at home in the relationship. It's just that if you talk about the rules between you and make an issue of your patterns while you're just going out together and things are still sort of casual, you might be afraid it will make you seem like such a pain in the neck that there won't be a relationship for you to be intimate in. What guy's going to want to go out with a woman who talks about "our patterns" on the second date? Fine.

But for millions that just means getting stuck in a relationship where you hate the patterns or have to fight to change the patterns, and that's even worse. So you've got to find a way to talk about it sooner rather than later.

Here's another example. Let's say that on your second date the guy criticizes you three times. Little things. You were talking about movies and you said you liked, among other things, *Gone With the Wind,* and he said it was a stupid movie. Not just that he didn't like it but that you were stupid for liking it. Then when you went to the restaurant he commented on the way you talked to the waiter, somehow implying that it wasn't classy of you to talk in a friendly way to the waitstaff. Then when you told him about a conversation you had with your boss where you asked for help, he said that was a big mistake and you should never let your boss know you need help.

Okay. Three strikes and you're out. But what's more tempting than saying nothing? What's easier? He was a nice guy about his criticisms. He dropped them after he said them. What a micro-managing bitch you're going to look like if you tell him what he really did and how you feel about it.

So don't be a bitch. But don't let a bad pattern get set. Say something or break up. The things you go along with today will haunt you for the rest of your life.

Real Rule #5:

INTIMACY REQUIRES SELF-KNOWLEDGE.

I'm going to tell you a shocking truth. I think, God help me, that most women most of the time know themselves pretty well. It's not always easy to admit the truth. And we need to give ourselves time to grow up. But by the time we're truly grownup women, we know enough about ourselves to make intimacy work. But you have to be sure. If you don't know yourself, intimacy won't work.

The reason this rule is necessary is that there are certain circumstances that place self-knowledge in short supply. Being too young is one of these circumstances. The reason it was stupid for me to get married at nineteen was that no matter how open and honest I was, I was revealing to my future husband a work in progress. A first draft, a first *page*, of a book that would undergo enormous changes. We love each other, we're good people, but the reason we were able to survive coming together as teens was *sheer luck*. As our simultaneous rough drafts started jelling, it just worked out that when one of us zigged, the other was zigging in the same direction.

Another circumstance that can deprive us of self-knowledge is coming out of a highly emotionally charged experience. Maybe your business just failed. Maybe you just got a huge, head-turning promotion. If something's happened to throw everything up in the air, you need to let the dust settle.

Real Rule #6:

THE RIGHT PERSON FOR YOU IS THE PERSON WHO FEELS RIGHT TO YOU.

You're talking to your friend about this new man in your life and she picks up on the way you're slightly less than sky high about him. You've complained a little about how he's boring sometimes and he could have more money and you've been with guys who were better in bed. And your friend says, "Are you sure you're not just settling?" And you tell your friend about how he's the best guy you've met in the last three years. Fine. But is he good enough?

How good is good enough?—that's the question here. If you've ever gone shopping for a couch, you know what I'm talking about, much less gone shopping for a guy. There can be a huge difference between good and good enough. Sometimes, of course, it's easy. The guy's great, no questions asked. Or it's instantly obvious that he's not for you. But most of the time it goes like this: You're very quickly hit with the sense that there's something really good going on here with this guy, but at the same time there are things you have questions about. It's a mixed picture. But that's why we date. *Dating is the process of confirming or disconfirming your hunch that there's something wonderful about this other person that outweighs any possible defects.*

So how do you know when you're settling and when you've found someone really good? This is where we make the mistake of evaluating the other person in the abstract. It's where we make the mistake of saying, "Hey, if the guy's good enough, it's true love." But remember that dating is like shopping. And in shopping it's a big mistake to evaluate your purchase simply based on your idea that it's the latest style or that it's a bargain.

You know you've found someone good when you're honest with yourself about what you need and who you are. And you'll know you're not settling when you see how open and honest you can be in this relationship. Because only then can you know what kind of a fit you and the guy are going to be together.

Women who are successful at finding real love are like great clothes shoppers. They look past the surface. Their eyes seize on what others have overlooked. They go for fit, not flash. They go for quality, not drama.

Real Rule #7:

GO FOR THE STEAK, NOT THE SIZZLE.
ALL THE SMARTEST WOMEN THINK OF DATING AS THE SEARCH FOR SUBSTANCE.

What would you think of a guy who looked for a wife based on the size of her tits? I once had a radio interviewer, when I was promoting one of my books, tell me on air that all he needed to know about a woman was how big her tits were.

You and I think that a guy like that is just stupid. Gross, of course. But mostly stupid.

And yet I know brilliant women who fall for a man because he has puppy-dog eyes. I know certifiably smart cookies who just gotta have a guy with ripply stomach muscles and nice buns. These are the very same women who'd be creeped out by a guy who judged them by their breast size. *You* would never go out with a guy just because he has cute puppy-dog eyes or nice buns. But there are all kinds of things that come across as sizzle, and we have all kinds of ways of ignoring substance.

Here's a list that will make the contrast clearer:

* *Sizzle* means choosing a guy because he has a romantic job. *Substance* means choosing a guy because he has a good job.
* *Sizzle* means choosing a guy because he spends a lot of money. *Substance* means choosing a guy because he knows how to hold on to his money.
* *Sizzle* means choosing a guy because he wears smart clothes. *Substance* means choosing a guy because he's smart.
* *Sizzle* means choosing a guy because he has a nice car. *Substance* means choosing a guy because he has a nice family.
* *Sizzle* means choosing a guy because he made one incredibly romantic gesture. *Substance* means choosing a guy because he makes your little everyday moments feel romantic.
* *Sizzle* means choosing a guy because he has a lot going for him in the present. *Substance* means choosing a guy because you're confident he'll have a lot going for him in the future.
* *Sizzle* means choosing a guy because he impresses your friends. *Substance* means choosing a guy because he impresses you.

Choosing substance over sizzle means choosing the person you want to be. The kind of woman who always needs advice from her friends? That's where looking for sizzle will land you. Or the kind of woman whose friends turn to her for advice? That's who you'll be if you look for substance.

Real Rule #8:

**BECAUSE YOU'RE WORTH IT . . .
SO DON'T SETTLE FOR ANYTHING LESS THAN SOMEONE WHO'S
GOOD FOR YOU AND YOUR FUTURE.**

This is one of the most dramatic statistics I've ever seen. It emerged in the research we did for this book. For every woman who feels she screwed up during this experience of love by being too picky, *ten women* feel they've screwed up by hooking up with a guy who *they knew* offered them less than they deserved.

Now think about what this means. It's possible you'd wither on the vine because you're too picky. That does happen. But it's *ten times more likely* that you'll waste your time and break your heart and miss out on having kids maybe and subject yourself to a messy divorce and stress yourself out completely by *not waiting for a guy who had more to offer*. Then before you throw your heart away you need to remind yourself of your true worth.

TV and magazines are filled both with images of exceptionally beautiful women and also of unusually accomplished women. After you see a picture of a swimsuit model and then read an article about a scuba diving professor of marine biology, it's easy to think that these are the kinds of women appropriate for the really good guys. After all we know that these are the kinds of women the best guys aspire to. Every guy you ever went out with has had ten-minute bathroom dates with Playmates of the Month. Then we look at ourselves and feel we have to lower our sights.

But you'd be amazed. You deserve someone great, because you're worth it, and you can get someone great too. You just have to remember that being too picky is a tiny little danger compared to the huge danger that comes from throwing yourself away on a guy who's not worthy of you and who'll make you miserable. How do you know you're being too picky? If all your friends say there's no way you can do better than this guy, and if being with this guy feels really good to you, *then* you're being too picky if you think you can find someone better.

Real Rule #9:

THE IMPORTANT THING ISN'T HOW YOU FEEL ABOUT HIM BUT HOW HE MAKES YOU FEEL.

This may be the most important rule of all. And it's one of the easiest, because you just have to check inside yourself to know.

It's nice if you feel the guy's great. It's much more important that he makes you feel great.

It's nice if you love the guy. It's much more important that he makes you feel loved.

It's nice if you believe the two of you can be happy together. It's much more important that you actually feel happy with him now.

The point is that your guts are the judge. I know a woman who stayed with a man for eleven years because she kept telling herself that she should be happy with him. And there was nothing bad about him. He seemed like a guy she should be happy with. But he was never able to make her feel happy. Finding someone to love is not about some idea in your head. It's about how you actually feel, day to day, skin to skin, eyeball to eyeball. If it doesn't feel good to be close, it'll never get close to feeling or being good.

Real Rule #10:

DON'T CONNECT WITH SOMEONE OVER WHERE YOU ARE RIGHT NOW—CONNECT WITH HIM OVER WHERE THE TWO OF YOU WANT TO END UP.

This rule is in honor of all the women who've sobbed out the question, "Why do I keep getting involved with losers?" I'll make it simple. Where you are is not who you are, and the younger you are the more this is true. We're all in transit, particularly in our twenties and even in our thirties.

Think about a very common type of woman in her twenties. She's not making much money. She's vaguely moving from one career that wasn't right for her to some possible new career that may or may not be right for her. The future is all question marks. Meanwhile she's leading a low-rent life. A lot of good guys are going to look right past her. The cities and small towns of America are filled with young women like this. And so of course they connect with guys who are sharing the same aimless, low-rent life they've got. And what the hell—you want to be able to complain to each other, plus that's what's available.

But so many of these connections wouldn't take place if you and I asked ourselves, "This guy . . . he fits where I am now. But is this where I want to be? Where do I want to be? What's my best guess? What's my dream? And would this guy fit in there? And if this guy doesn't fit in with where I want to be, why would I hook up with him now?

Diagnosing What You Need

If you just want a guy in your life to pay the bills, open jars, and father your children, just say so. But save yourself time and trouble and stop reading. You've got to recognize that by settling for just a guy, you're setting yourself up for a life without intimacy. And then you lose the right to complain that you and your partner have a lousy relationship.

But if you want love that feels like love, then why not see what you're doing (if you're dating right now) or what you were doing (back when you were dating) to prevent yourself from getting the real intimacy you want. That's what we're going to diagnose now: the degree to which the barriers to intimacy for you lie in this make-or-break experience of love.

So answer the following three diagnostic questions *yes* or *no*:

1. Do you hate being alone?

2. Do you hate conflict and confrontation?

3. Are there things you hate about yourself you think about a lot?

Just consider what it means if you've said *yes* to all three questions. You're going to be so eager to get a guy, so reluctant to struggle with him, so determined not to show the real you, that the gap between the relationship you're creating and the relationship that would fit you is enormous.

We all have things about us that put us at risk of answering *yes*. Suppose there's something about your body that makes you self-conscious, for example, and you've answered *yes* to the question "Do you hate being alone?" If you're going to want to get a guy no matter what, you'll be tempted to hide your body. And *that* means a lifetime of sex in the dark. Millions of women hide in the dark because of something they don't want their partner to see. And I'm not just talking about what's on the surface.

How many of the three diagnostic questions did you answer *yes* to? I'll tell you something. A good solid definite *yes* answer to any one of them means that during this experience of love you are at serious risk of setting things up for yourself so that intimacy will be hard for you later on.

This diagnosis is good news because you've finally put your finger on what's prevented you from filling your life with the love you deserve.

Prescriptions

What do you do? You're either looking for someone to love or you're going through one of the other seven experiences. Let's deal with each case:

If you're dating. Think ahead. What is it about you, the real you, that a guy is going to have to know and accept for you to feel that the two of you are truly close? These are the kinds of things your best friend would know about you. Write them down: *"The seven truest things about me."* I'm talking true confessions here. I don't want to put words in your mouth, but based on what women have told me, I'm talking about things like:

- "I don't really like kids."
- "I like to spend a lot of time making love."
- "I get bored easily."
- "I want to have a lot of money."
- "I don't know how, but I want to change my life soon."
- "I'm actually kind of a wild woman."
- "I can't wait to stop working and stay home."

These are all things women have told me they just didn't feel ready to let guys know. But because they couldn't say them when they were dating, intimacy was more difficult once the relationship got going.

Now here's what you do with your seven truest things about you. *You tell them to the guys you're dating.* You don't have to blurt them out on a first date. You don't have to get through them all at once. But before you get physically naked a *second* time, he's got to know most of these true things. Because here's how guys work. If you keep getting naked and don't reveal who you really are, if you reveal it later, it's going to be as if you've completely changed all the rules on him. Then he'll get mad and dump you.

It's not love if the guy runs screaming from the room when he sees you naked. It's love when he sees you naked and then still takes you in his arms and shows you that he wants you even with all your imperfections. And I'm talking about your naked soul. If you feel he wants you after he's seen you naked, you know his wanting you is real. Then you're safe. Then you don't have to spend the rest of your life worrying that the lights will come on.

If you've found someone. I don't know if the two of you started off on the right foot, but it's never too late to start off on the *real* foot. "Let's get to know each other all over again" is a good idea for people in any relationship. But it's the perfect prescription for someone who answered *yes* to any of the three diagnostic questions. I'm not talking about working on your relationship here. I'm talking about the foundations of intimacy.

Just say to your guy, "I'd like us to get to know each other really well. I'd like our relationship to reach a new level of honesty. And I don't mean by 'honesty' that we tell each other things we don't like about each other. That's not what I want. That's just putting out negativity. When I talk about more honesty, I mean I tell you things about myself, even if they have nothing to do with you. All I want is for us to feel closer. So can we trade secrets? I'll tell you one thing about myself and you'll tell me one thing about yourself. What kind of thing? You know, the kinds of things we should have told each other way back when we were dating but never did."

Create more love for the rest of your lives by regularly, every week or month, trading secret revelations. Not criticisms. Just truths about yourselves. The kinds of things you'd tell your best friends. You don't have to do anything beyond sharing them with each other and then talking about them for a while. Think of how intimate you've gotten when you've shown each other physical details about your body when you've gotten naked. You don't have to fix anything. But you have to make sure you experience more emotional nakedness with each other, and more acceptance. And therefore more real love.

FIVE

Taking a Chance on Love

Make-or-Break Experience #3:
Feeling Safe While Falling in Love

It's the paradise of love, the orgasm of romance. It's what we all dream of when we're not in a relationship, and what we all wish we could get back to when we are in a relationship. I'm talking about *falling in love*.

This is the experience of realizing that someone has captured your thoughts and feelings, that this person makes you feel wonderful, that this person *is* wonderful, that you'd be willing to make changes in your life for him. It's the reason you look for that special person. It's the way you know you've found that special person. It's what we always want to last forever.

This is the experience of being as madly, passionately in love with someone as you're capable of being. We're excited because suddenly there's the promise of a whole new future, filled with delight, where so many of our deepest needs will finally be met. So why is it that *74 percent of women say falling in love is a wonderful, scary, disturbing experience*? The *wonderful* part is not news. The news is how scary and disturbing so many of us find this experience.

78

Fear of Falling

Well, why wouldn't we be scared? When you're just checking each other out, you haven't jumped off the cliff yet. But when you've fallen in love, *you're falling*. Obviously when you actually feel in love you're full of hope. But even here the battle between hope and despair lies in wait.

Here's the make-or-break part of this experience. What if you fall in love and the whole thing collapses? What if you decide you can't trust yourself? What if as a result of past hurts you prevent yourself from falling in love—so that you trip over despair before you get to hope? We want to fall in love, but we wish it came with fewer crashes. We're never more vulnerable to discouragement than when hope has floated us high in the air.

We must learn everything we need to keep hope alive, so our hearts will always be open to the possibility of falling in love. You say you're already in a relationship? Then you want to be open to the possibility of falling in love with the person you're already in a relationship with.

Zing went the strings of my heart. It can happen five minutes after you meet someone. Love at first sight is real. Sure, sometimes you later realize that you were experiencing a moment of emotional vulnerability and fell for the guy just because he was nice to you. Sometimes the guy's just gorgeous and you confuse love with lust. We've all had to sort these things out. But a lot of times smart, sane, grown-up women fall fast and stay that way. Thirty percent of marriages that last more than ten years started when two people fell in love at first sight.

Or falling in love can take months to happen. First the guy was an acquaintance, then a friend, then a guy you found yourself spending time with . . . and then something happened. Maybe it was when he helped you move, maybe it was the aftermath of that horrible week when your dog was so sick, but that's when you realized, after so much time, that you'd suddenly and completely fallen for him.

It can sometimes take years to *realize* that it's happened. You dated this guy in college and it was perfect. Maybe too perfect, and you wanted a little adventure. So you drifted apart, you thought you fell in love with some other guy, married him. But it was a shaky marriage, and all the problems there at the very beginning that you'd hoped would go away—well, the problems are what stayed, and the marriage died. Then you run into that guy you knew so long ago from college. And you see how deeply connected you are to him. Oh my God, you realize, *that* was the love of my life.

This is the big one. The truth about falling in love is even better than the romantic poetry that gets spouted. The myth is that falling in love is for the purpose of giving birth to a relationship. Once the relationship is born, the time of being in love with each other fades. The embers may continue to glow. Sparks occasionally fly up into the night air. But magic time is over. That's the myth.

The truth is something I wouldn't have believed myself until I talked to so many women who'd been through it. *Once the relationship is launched the two of you can fall in love with each other again.* Falling in love can happen over and over within the same relationship. We're not like Adam and Eve. We don't get expelled from paradise, never to return.

What Falling in Love Is Really Like

It's time to open a window into what this experience of falling in love is like for women today. And that's important. Most of us go through this experience and know only what we feel like inside. A lot of the time we're confused. Then we see other people going through it and all too often what it looks like they're feeling and experiencing is very different from what we know we're feeling and experiencing. And that too often makes us feel like oddballs. Which is fine if you are an oddball. But maybe the weird things you think you're going through when you're falling in love are totally normal. And you deserve to see that.

What are the keynotes of magic time? I asked women of all ages about this: "What special moments do you remember from that period when you were falling in love? How did you know that this was the person for you? *How did you know that this was the real thing?*" I know these are questions that haunt all of us. The heart can be a labyrinth in which the pure note of love is hard to detect. That's why so many of us need a little help from our friends if we're going to figure out whether we're really in love or not.

Let's do it, let's fall in love. Let me begin with myself. I've done it. I've fallen in love. And it was with the last kind of guy in the world I would've thought would have done it for me. I'd always gone out with older guys. Like when I was fifteen my boyfriend was a twenty-four-year-old medical student, and when I was seventeen my boyfriend was a twenty-nine-year-old college instructor. It wasn't about the bragging rights—I rarely talked about my boyfriends. I just desperately wanted someone, a substantial guy, who could take care of me.

So imagine my surprise when I met this guy who was a year younger than me and two years behind me in college, and *that's* when lightning struck. I think what happens is this (and think about the last time you fell in love and whether this was going on for you): things are happening in your life that bring certain needs to a head. Needs that resonate down into your deepest self. Maybe you were going out with egotistical guys and you needed to experience someone who'd pay attention to you, who'd have room in his head and his heart to see you. Maybe you were looking around at your particular world and feeling unsafe, and you needed a guy you knew would be able to take care of you. Maybe you'd gotten involved with one too many nuts and you just needed a guy who was sane.

Sometimes when you get involved with the kind of guy you'd always been attracted to you're surprised that it wasn't as magical as you'd thought it would be. That's because finding a guy like that wasn't really tied up with your deepest needs. Now you can see why we so often fall in love with a guy who's not our type. Because we go out with guys who are our type and then these unmet needs start building up and building up and building up and this guy like my husband comes out of left field and knocks you for a loop. Because there's something about him that goes right to those unmet needs.

"How Did You Know It Was the Real Thing?"

When it happens you're suddenly in magic land. What is that like? I can still remember what it was like for me. The three-day weekend late in August when we stayed in bed the whole time. No, it wasn't a seventy-two-hour sexathon, although we certainly committed our share of sex acts.

The truly special part of those three days was the way we spent the whole time totally absorbed in each other. Telling each other stories about our pasts and our dreams for the future. Singing songs we remembered from camp that we were amazed to discover we both knew (it had never occurred to me that someone else would know all the words to John Jacob Jingle Heimer Schmidt). Telling each other about the things we liked and disliked and being thrilled to realize that we liked and disliked many of the same things. Motown and Jack Kerouac and Alfred Hitchcock were among the many things we liked—and that was another neat thing: discovering that we were the kind of people who just liked a lot of things. I'd known too many guys who turned themselves on by talking about the things they didn't like.

Anyone who's ever been in love has stories about days, even weeks, even months when you were nuts about each other. Literally. You acted like nuts. You were completely absorbed and obsessed. I remember once during that period I got into an elevator in a building and burst into tears. Out of nowhere. And yet if I said, "because I was in love," I know you'd understand.

It's the real thing, baby. Let's make sure we get clear what falling in love *isn't*. It's not infatuation. Infatuation is one-sided. It's your obsession. You can't get the guy out of your mind. Your head is filled with dreams of being with him, of doing things with him, of his doing things to you. You're trans-fixed and absorbed by his wonderfulness.

It's happened to all of us. Now here's why it's not the same as falling in love. Because it hasn't been put to the test of actually being with the other person. It's not based on a relationship, on time you spend together. I'll just tell you what women have told me: "Even though you're gaga about someone—and your gaganess can feel like the realest, deepest, truest feeling you've ever had—it's no guide to what it would be like to be with that person. If your feelings aren't confirmed by mutual attraction, mutual interests, and the sense that the more time you spend together, the more time you want to spend together, *on both of your parts,* you're not falling in love. You're just infatuated. And infatuation, when it's not reciprocated, is the mas-turbation of love."

This is what it's like. When we talk to each other and look back and separate reality from self-deception, here's where women say, "This is what was going on when I knew I was really in love."

Which of these fifteen scenes from falling in love have you experienced?

Scene #1:

ACTING LIKE KIDS AGAIN.

A thirty-five-year-old loan officer remembers: "I can't believe the things we did when we were falling in love. We were suddenly like these crazy kids again. It was so strange—there was that one night when I stayed over at his place and that's when we knew we were in love. The next day we just didn't go to work. Instead we went to the zoo. It was even worse than that. We acted like complete children at the zoo. We'd have these conversations with all the animals, and then on the way home we each pretended we were our favorite animal—I was the zebra and he was the gorilla. We talked and acted like we were this zebra and gorilla in love making a new life for themselves. It seems so silly now but it seemed so right then."

Scene #2:

EXPERIENCING THE SWEET JOY OF TOTAL ACCEPTANCE.

A thirty-one-year-old graduate student, a woman with what used to be called *a past*—years of honky-tonk living, getting drunk, having sex with strangers, occasionally getting paid for it. Then the seven miracle years when she turned her life around, just because one day she'd walked past a pretty-looking community college that made her feel she'd be safe and clean in there. And what an amazement to discover that she was really, really smart. But that first year in graduate school she hadn't talked to a single guy because she understood that when people get to know each other they talk about their pasts. It was amazing how it happened with Marty, but first they just talked about their coursework, then they could tell they liked each other, then he told her things about himself growing up and she felt very understanding and accepting as he told her these things. Somehow that made him melt, and piece by piece she felt she could tell him about her past. Everything she said was okay with Marty. It was almost hard for her to tell the difference between the sense of total acceptance and the experience of falling in love. Maybe there is no difference.

Scene #3:

EXPERIENCING A SURGE OF ENERGY.

A thirty-eight-year-old lawyer remembers: "Nothing could have prepared me for it. I don't think I'd realized what a low energy state I'd fallen into. I just thought it was normal, going into your thirties and what with work and the stress of a divorce you're just exhausted all the time. But when I started falling in love with Sammy I felt this surge of energy every day all day. I don't think I'd ever felt energy like that ever before. Instead of coming home from work and wanting to collapse I just wanted to get together with Sammy and do something. It could be, let's say, Tuesday and we'd get together at seven and make love and then go out to eat and then sit around talking and I just don't remember feeling tired getting up the next day to go to work."

Scene #4:

WHEN YOU GET TOGETHER AFTER BEING APART, IT'S AS IF THE SUN HAS COME OUT AFTER MANY LONG GRAY DAYS.

A thirty-seven-year-old teacher never thought she'd fall in love again after her husband died. It had been the real thing with him. But after five years of living as a single woman Ellen met Tim. She went very slowly, of course, because she didn't want to be hurt, and because she couldn't quite believe what was happening. But eventually she reached the point where she was wondering if she was in love with Tim. Could this be the real thing again?

They both worked, and they were both busy. So they couldn't get together as often as they would've liked. But when they finally did hook up, say on a Friday night, Ellen noticed that as much as she'd been looking forward to seeing Tim, when he stood at her door and walked into her living room she felt all happy and sunny and warm inside. It was like taking a bite of your favorite dessert, where you know it's going to be good but when you actually feel it in your mouth it's always so much better than you remember.

And this is how Ellen knew she'd fallen in love with her second husband.

Scene #5:

CONNECTING WITHOUT WORDS.

A twenty-three-year-old student remembers: "We sat on the grass and there was this period—it felt like hours—when all we did was stare into each other's eyes. Then we'd stop staring and kiss for a long time with our eyes closed. But then the kiss would end and we'd look into each other's eyes again. We had no need to say anything. It's like every desire was satisfied, every thought was communicated, without words, just by looking at each other."

Scene #6:

PHONE CONVERSATIONS WHERE YOU DIDN'T WANT TO STOP TALKING TO EACH OTHER.

A thirty-seven-year-old office manager remembers: "Jeez, the phone calls. Oh my God. Like, I'd get home from work and, you know, be busy with this and that, and then he'd call me or I'd call him—he was the first guy I felt comfortable calling—and we'd just start talking and the next thing I'd know it would be three, four, five hours later. We would talk until three in the morning. Without feeling tired at all. We'd be tired the next day getting up for work. But then that night we'd stay up late talking on the phone again. I have no idea what we talked about. But I'd give anything to have that kind of energy again."

Scene #7:

MISSING EACH OTHER ENORMOUSLY.

A forty-two-year-old high school teacher remembers: "I'll never forget this poem I read once. This was it, the whole poem:

> *my days are full*
> *but sometimes only of your absence*

I remember feeling like that when we were falling in love; it was incredibly intense, like when you get the flu. We were in different colleges, so we could only get together on weekends. I'd spend all week, every minute of every day, with this heavy sack of sand in my gut weighing me down; it was this sense of missing Jake. I don't think that feeling ever went away, of needing him like when you're dying of thirst, but there'd be periods when it would just take over and—I don't know, I thought I'd go crazy sometimes."

Scene #8:

"WE COULDN'T DO ENOUGH FOR EACH OTHER."

A thirty-six-year-old photographer remembers: "I guess I'm one of those awful women who just hates to cook. And I'm usually pretty bad at it—which is probably why I hate it.

"Then I met Dick and when we were falling in love he'd come over to my place in the evening and all I wanted to do was feed him. I mean I'd make muffins. I'd roast a chicken. He mentioned he liked mushrooms so I bought them and cooked them—I'd never known what to do with a mushroom before. It's a good thing he didn't say he liked fresh venison because I swear to God I'd have bought a gun, shot a deer, and cooked it for him.

"It was amazing, that wanting to do stuff for someone. And

he was doing stuff for me—he saw I had this lousy stereo but he knew I liked music and he showed up one night with this whole new stereo system for me, and he said it was for him so he wouldn't have to listen to music on my stereo. But it was for me."

Scene #9:

THE WHOLE WORLD SEEMS BEAUTIFUL.

A forty-eight-year-old nurse remembers: "My parents fell in love back during World War II when my father was a serviceman stationed in London. And there'd be an air raid and they'd have to go into a shelter. Mostly people were scared and tired and pissed off, but my mother tells me that when she and my father heard the sirens and the bombs in the distance they'd go down into the shelter and huddle together happy.

"It was like, when you're madly in love even an air raid can feel beautiful. I always felt that story was overly romantic but when I was falling in love it really was like that. Everything in the world was beautiful. I'd get on the bus going to work and talk to old people and the old people seemed younger or wiser or friendlier. It was like my happiness was so powerful that it was literally transforming the world around me and making it better."

Scene #10:

EXPERIENCING A NEW LEVEL OF OPENNESS.

A twenty-nine-year-old journalist remembers: "I'd always thought guys were this other species. Even if you got involved and had sex and had feelings for each other you'd keep the guy at arm's length. I just thought there were things you didn't show guys about yourself.

"It was completely different with Joe. I don't know if this is why I fell in love with him or if it happened after I fell in love, but the things we let each other see about ourselves were just amazing, and no matter what we said it was okay. Until Joe I'd always felt I had to hide this passionate, emotional, wild part of myself. In the past every time I showed this side they'd treat me like a nut. But I just thought of it as my energy. Joe thought it was wonderful. I could get angry, I could get upset, I could say crazy things and Joe just accepted it all. He wasn't just tolerating me either. He really liked what I had to hide from everyone else."

Scene #11:

YOU CAN'T STOP THINKING ABOUT EACH OTHER.

A twenty-five-year-old receptionist remembers: "I think I'm falling in love with him right now, so you caught me at a good time. I think I'm in love because . . . here's what I find myself doing all day every day. My guy's a cop. Mostly he's just out on patrol. And I find myself imagining every single minute practically where he is and what he's doing. It's like I live his life, feel his life, inside me in my heart the way he's probably experiencing it. I mean, I don't know what's going on but I'll be thinking I bet he's having lunch and he'll call me and it'll turn out he's just had lunch."

Scene #12:

CREATING YOUR OWN PRIVATE WORLD.

A thirty-eight-year-old stay-at-home mom remembers: "Maybe you'll think this is corny, but it was almost like we were creating this special club where we were the only two members. But there were all these secrets we shared. I'm not going to tell you the names we came up with but we came up with whole names for every single little part of our genitals and every other part of our private anatomy. We'd start making love and it would be like this whole cast of characters would parade into the room. And because Katie and Matt were on the *Today Show* the first morning we woke up together, every morning we'd call each other Katie and Matt.

"Then one night after we made love, right when we were starting to fall in love, we turned on the radio and there was Whitney Houston singing "I Will Always Love You." He started singing to me along with her. And it became like the national anthem of our love. There were all kinds of special things like that. Like we could be anywhere and he'd say, 'Do you feel like a having a sub?' and I'd know that he was wanting to make love right then and there. And we'd talk about what we wanted on our subs and even though it didn't make sense we'd know that we were talking about doing different things with each other in bed by describing our sub sandwiches."

Scene #13:

HAVING DREAMS FOR YOUR FUTURE TOGETHER.

A thirty-three-year-old psychotherapist-in-training remembers: "You know, we weren't yet at the stage where you talk about marriage—that was scary to both of us. But there we were, falling in love, what the hell, we'd already fallen, and we were talking about how we wanted to own an orchard with apple trees and cherry trees. And we'd have three kids and sheep and . . . the point is that we were planning for this future together and we weren't even ready to move in together but talking about our farm felt like love."

Scene #14:

THE MORE YOU KNOW HIM THE MORE YOU LOVE HIM.

A twenty-two-year-old day-care worker told me: "It never happened to me before. I'm so totally picky. Every guy I've ever gotten involved with it was because they looked so hot but then I'd get to know them and I'd find all these things wrong. I was afraid it was me, like I'd have to go into counseling to find out why I hate men. But then I met Johnny, and okay, he was hot too—I mean, I could never get involved with a guy who didn't have great hair and a great stomach—but we'd talk and everything and I'd see him with his friends and then I saw him with his parents and the more I got to know him, the more I liked him. I mean, just the way he was with his little sister, I thought I didn't even know how great this guy was."

Scene #15:

EXPERIENCING A RENEWAL OF TRUST.

A fifty-five-year-old doctor remembers: "I'm afraid this is going to sound weird because I don't think you're supposed to feel the way I feel. I've been married for twenty-nine years. One Saturday I got a call from my daughter. Things were shaky in her marriage. They'd drifted apart. They didn't have much of a relationship. She wanted to know if there was hope. I don't know, I said.

"But here's my experience in my own marriage. It was that same Saturday my husband and I had had a big fight in the morning because he'd interrupted me a few times and that just brought up for me ways I felt he didn't respect me. So after twenty-nine years you have the same fight over and over.

"But later that day I was telling him why I'd gotten so upset and talking about my hopes and disappointments for myself. He started talking about his own life. After all these years

together you can do that—talk about your life. And I was just
filled with this sense of comfort and safety and trust. That
there was no one else in the world I felt understood me the
way he did. And that sense of specialness and trust—I felt in
love with him, like when I *fell* in love with him so long ago.
It was the same feeling.

"You know, he was the first man I ever had an orgasm
with, the only man actually. I had that same sense of being
able to surrender myself to him. You can fall in love again and
again I think with the same person. You can have the same
feelings you had when you were falling in love with that person. That's what I told my daughter, and she started crying."

Making Sure It's Real

Is falling in love a promise of wonderful things to come, a
glimpse of the beginning of a beautiful truth? Or is falling in
love a snare, a delusion, an opportunity for self-deception, a
playground for the hungriest and most immature parts of
ourselves?

Falling in love, that most wonderful of times, on the verge
of all our dreams coming true, is also that most dangerous of
times when we're suddenly faced with the possibility of falling
into our worst nightmares. And we know it. That's why some
of the craziest things we do as women happen around the time
when we're falling in love.

You want to be able to trust your feelings. That's what
makes you hopeful. But sometimes we confuse the intensity of
our feelings with the helpfulness of our feelings. If you keep
going nuts over nothing, or over worse than nothing, at some
point you'll stop being able to trust yourself and you'll fall over
the cliff into despair. The solution isn't blind self-trust. The
solution is being smarter about what you do as a result of what
you feel.

Real love has nothing to do with choosing blindly. It has everything to do with what you get after you've chosen.

⚘

Dawn's Story

Six months ago Dawn, a twenty-nine-year-old interior decorator, was feeling free as a bird. She'd finally gotten over the collapse of the third major relationship in her life up to that point. She felt okay about everything in herself and her life except her history of relationships.

How do you sum it up in four words? "Too many cool losers" was the phrase Dawn used.

Looking for keepers. Dawn understood all too well that the very things that gave her the hots about these guys were what ultimately broke them up. They all had this wild, cool quality that made them incredibly attractive, but then she'd want to introduce them to her sister or her parents. And the minute she even thought of doing it the sheer impossibility of building a life with these guys became all too clear.

So six months ago Dawn decided that if she ever got involved with anyone again it would have to be someone she felt would be a keeper. That was her dream: finding a man she could imagine being the father of her children, the kind of man who could put his kids through college.

Then she met Ross. Though still in his twenties he owned his own car dealership. Ross was smart, educated, and cultured. Dawn met Ross as a client of hers, and there's nothing like decorating a guy's apartment when it comes to learning whether he's a jerk or boob or an okay guy. Not only did Ross know art and design, but they had similar tastes. Best of all, he was a keeper in the sense that he was a guy living a grown-up's life.

"I wish it felt more naughty." Just before she fell in love with Ross, Dawn remembers thinking it would be too obvious

if she fell for him. Somehow because he looked so good on paper it would feel a little mechanical, she thought. These were disturbing echoes of her previous relationships. With those guys their inappropriateness somehow made her love seem more genuine. Because Ross was so perfect, it would feel less like falling in love and more like following orders. Where was the wonderful, wild leap?

It bothered Dawn that she was thinking like this. "Am I saying I'm not supposed to fall in love with a guy unless he's no good for me? I've got to be one sick puppy if I can't fall in love with the kind of guy I really should be falling in love with."

Then they went for that ski weekend they'd talked endlessly about taking. At one point late in the afternoon they were doing this cross-country thing and they stopped in a clearing surrounded by tall pine trees and kissed. While they were kissing a snowshoe rabbit hopped past and then stopped for a long time staring at them. It was when she saw the rabbit looking at them holding each other in the snow that Dawn thought she fell in love with Ross.

"I'm glad it was just the two of us," she said.

"Me too," he said.

There was something unresponsive about the way he said, "Me too," that sent this ever so slight chill into her. By Sunday night Dawn had the courage to ask Ross if he'd ever been in love.

"I used to think so, but I'm not sure anymore," he said, as if he were saying love was just something he wasn't connected to.

Two weeks later Dawn was telling her sister she was in love. Mostly it was because Ross was suddenly the new reference point for everything in her life. Everything she thought or felt—she wondered how Ross would feel or think about it. Her evenings were dominated by Ross's call, how long it lasted, what it felt like, what they talked about. Often he didn't call, and it felt like a disaster. But it's not that they talked about anything so special when he did call. Lots of times she felt he just didn't want her around.

We all need to feel safe. "I didn't know what was real," Dawn said to me. "You think this is it, I'm in love. But so many of the signs weren't there, too. I feel we're the same. But what does it mean if your 'soulmate' seems to want to keep you at arm's length? Maybe he's not my soulmate. Maybe he's a guy I have a lot of things in common with on the surface but our hearts have nothing in common. I don't know, but love to me is a time when you feel like the guy is making this leap toward you—I certainly felt that toward those loser guys I'd gotten involved with—but in terms of love Ross is just sitting there. Maybe he's just lazy.

"It's just not fair. It felt so much more like the real thing with those guys I'm glad to be rid of. I always said I could do better. Now I'm doing much better, maybe the best I'll ever do. And it's like I can't imagine falling asleep in the middle of having sex but I could imagine falling asleep in the middle of falling in love with Ross.

"So I'm scared. I know I deserve better. And what's scarier than that: you're totally in love with Mr. Right and it's not good enough."

"Don't crowd me." After a while in this falling in love period Ross showed something that made him seem a lot more like the guys Dawn had gone out with in the past. That business of seeming not to want her around—that started to come through in other ways. Dawn had understood that she shouldn't crowd Ross but now she was getting the sense that it just wasn't cool to want to go anywhere with this relationship. Being in love with each other was fine as long as the relationship wasn't going anywhere.

The sick part was that when Ross was holding her at a distance, Dawn couldn't help wanting him even more.

They were still in the period of falling in love (as long as they didn't get too close) when they started having fights. And that was tremendously confusing. One Wednesday night she'd gone over to his place and he'd been unusually tender and loving toward her. He told her things he valued about her like her intelligence, which he'd never mentioned before.

An hour later she was screaming "Fuck you" as she stormed out of his apartment, slamming the door behind her as hard as she could.

It had started when she asked, "Do you think we should talk about taking our relationship to another level?" She'd been prepared for his not wanting to take the relationship to another level, like moving in together. She wasn't prepared, however, for his not even wanting to talk about it.

"Are you the one for me?" They were now stuck in a kind of no man's land. It's a place where you feel madly in love, so that you're having the full experience of falling in love with someone, and yet things feel bad. You feel this guy's your soulmate, and yet you wonder if he's any kind of mate at all.

Many women report that falling in love is surrounded by questions and doubts and difficulties. Dawn's story is more like what happens for women today than the stuff you see in the movies. And that's good news for you. Aren't you tired of feeling lousy because your real life doesn't measure up to what you think you're entitled to? It's like everyone else is having a good time except for you. Thinking of Dawn's story as being more near the norm helps you relax a little. It's not supposed to be a fairy tale. And you don't have to get down on yourself because it isn't.

And in fact things worked out for Dawn. One night she called Ross crying. She said to him, "I think I have to dump you before you dump me."

He came over. He took her face in his hands and said, "Can't you see that we're the same here? We're just two people afraid of getting hurt. Someone always wants to go more slowly. The other person always panics. So I'm the one with us who's wanting to go more slowly. It doesn't mean I don't want you."

Dawn asked a great question. "What are you scared of *with*

me? How can I make you feel less scared?" They talked—the logjam was broken.

⊛

Linda's Story

Can we trust our hearts? That's a question we all must ask if we reflect on ways our hearts have led us astray.

This is the question Linda was asking as she experienced the miracle of falling in love. It was a special miracle because she hadn't counted on it happening to a divorced woman with two kids, which is what she was.

But what can you do when you find you're falling in love with the exact same kind of guy as your first husband? Linda was working as the secretary to the chairman of the department of computer science at a major university. Geek central. The hub of nerd city. Her first husband had been one of these computer guys. A nice guy really. And he seemed to enjoy falling in love with her so much, like it was a totally new experience. His enjoyment of it really enhanced the experience for Linda.

But ultimately he was completely absorbed in his own work, and he was incredibly impatient with the slightest stupidity. Linda remembers telling him what she thought he knew, that she was no genius, computer or otherwise. He said he loved her the way she was. But if she said anything less than brilliant, he'd cut her to pieces. Then on top of that, he'd keep falling into these depressions. But not when they were falling in love.

Déjà vu all over again. Now here she is with Philip, and there are a lot of similarities between the two men and between her two relationships with these two men. Things are just heating up with Philip, so Linda doesn't know if she's going to follow the same downhill path once she reaches the crest of the hill, but the uphill path is very similar. She knows she's no intellectual match for Philip. He takes the same incredible delight in falling in love, like a teenager in a man's body. He'll bring balloons home for her, and teddy bears. He'll write these silly romantic notes, where he pretends he's this lovelorn teddy bear, and he wants her to be his teddy bear. And when they make love, he always wants to know what he can do to make things better for her. He's just so eager to please.

But inside Linda's afraid the core of this is some expectation Philip has that Linda's going to keep making everything wonderful for him the way things are wonderful now.

Whoa, there, big boy. Linda is afraid it's all going too fast. Philip talks about their moving in together. Philip's brought up the *M* word. Linda knows Philip's sincere, but she also knows how hungry he is for love. She's afraid that the speed at which things are moving is less a sign of love than the way a salesman rushes you along to close the deal he's afraid you're going to back out on.

Linda's scared that the teddy bear thing and the balloons and all the rest of the cute, lovey-dovey stuff can't last, that there really won't be much to their relationship when it's gone (the way it was with her first husband), and that when the rocket fizzles she'll have blown it with her friends too.

Part of her confusion is the way all her friends tell her Philip is the one. When she tells them how wonderful he is, they say they're jealous. Philip's going to be rich one day, and they'd like balloons and teddy bears from their guys. It's sad when they go out of your love life. It's even sadder, though, when they leave nothing behind. Meanwhile Linda feels she's being rushed by her friends just as much as Philip's rushing her.

The whole thing pisses her off. Falling in love is supposed to be great. Philip *is* great. The way things are between them right now is great. Great, great, great. So where does all the fear and suspicion come from? And should she trust it? It's a decision we've all had to make.

I'll tell you what Linda decided. She said *no* to Philip. She decided to trust the queasy part of her feelings. Did she make the *right* decision? You never know. She's seeing other guys now. But it feels right to her. Most of all, she's glad she didn't drift.

Preventing Mistakes

What a funny thing falling in love is. So incredibly wonderful. I think the best memories for most of us out of our whole lives are from special, magical moments when we were first in love.

And yet what a scary, confusing thing falling in love is. That's the part that's not talked about much, except when we talk to our friends on the phone. Maybe that's part of the problem: We feel badly when we talk to our friends because our real lives have more shades of gray than the falling-in-love stories we see in the movies or read about in books. I can't tell you how many women have questioned whether they were really in love because the experience they were going through was full of shadows, compared to the pure light they imagined falling in love was for other people.

There's a real danger in all of this that has the power to hurt the possibility of real love and true intimacy later on. The danger's very simple really. You're falling in love. But things aren't perfect either. And you want them to be perfect. So you try to do whatever is necessary to hold on to the perfection of this time when you're supposed to be most in love.

Maybe that's the ultimate danger of falling in love. It's so wonderful that you don't want to shake things up by introducing a note of reality. And maybe that's ultimately why we're so scared of falling in love, because we know it's a wild ride governed by its own set of rules. The good part is that it launches the rocket ship of commitment. The scary part is that once the rocket ship is launched, it's hard to choose to get off.

"Oh No! I'm Falling in Love! Not That!"

The good news is that as turbulent as this experience is, there are only two dangers. When you start falling in love there's the danger that you'll say *yes* to the relationship when you should be saying *no*. And there's the danger that you'll say *no* to the relationship when you should be saying *yes.*

It's falling victim to these dangers that puts us at risk of having our hope turn to despair. They're huge dangers but there are only two of them. And they can be dealt with. And that's great because if I could wave a magic wand and eliminate the fear of falling in love, I'd do it. What's worse than being afraid of something wonderful?

Sometimes our fears protect us and sometimes they get in our way. That's why we need to learn to see what's real. Sometimes our fears prevent us from seeing what's real. But sometimes they help us discover what's real.

So here's what we'll do. Based on the lessons that have cost so many women so much wasted time and so many wasted tears, I'll present the two dangers women face when they're falling in love. Then I'll show you how to diagnose whether you're facing that danger now. Then I'll show you, if you are facing it, what you can do to take yourself out of danger.

Falling-in-Love Danger #1:

"I'M SO IN LOVE, THIS MUST BE RIGHT." BUT IN FACT IT'S WRONG.

This is a rookie mistake, except that women of all ages make it. It's so easy to make. When you fall in love, you're saying, "I'm so head over heels, I'm experiencing so many of the scenes of falling in love, I can confidently say this is a great relationship and we're going to have a great future." The danger of course is that you're wrong. Excited, but wrong. Your feelings are real. But they're based on someone who's not worthy of your feelings. *You are in danger if your feelings prevent you from seeing what's real.*

Infatuation is an example of this. You're nuts about a guy, but you're not in the kind of relationship with him where you're two people developing loving feelings for each other.

You're nuts about a guy who doesn't know how you feel. Or doesn't care. Or doesn't feel about you the way you feel about him. Talk about loving something that doesn't love you back!

Look, feel whatever you want to feel. But know that the strength, power, and passion of your feelings have *absolutely nothing* to do with whether there's anything good for you here. Because your feelings are not based on reality, they can become supercharged. After all, you haven't confronted anything real.

The danger is that you'll get into a one-sided relationship that will hurt you. The make-or-break part of this is that if you keep getting into relationships that are wrong for you, you'll get soured on the idea of love itself.

Hester's Story

Hester was the girl we all knew in college who was too busy studying to go out on dates. Premed. But she was still a woman. Halfway through her senior year in college it suddenly hit her—her loneliness, her hunger for love, her need to be told she was wonderful and beautiful, her sense that she was only a few months away from totally missing out on what every other woman gets to experience—a college romance.

Suddenly this handsome guy whom she's known for four years starts paying attention to her. Tom's moody and sometimes critical. And he's got a lot of weird paranoid-type ideas about how big corporations are all out to hurt everybody. But at first he's sweet and romantic, so much so that Hester finds herself having sex with him within the first week, which is *way* earlier than the timetable she'd set for herself if she'd ever meet someone.

Then they start moving on separate paths. Tom starts acting more moody and critical. He finds a million things wrong with her. He doesn't stop with her either. He starts telling her how her parents and brother have hurt her. He keeps telling her how disappointed he is in her. But from her point of view, they'd just started falling in love. Since she'd decided he was wonderful, what he was saying must be true. Since he seemed to be pulling away from her, she felt desperate to win him back by changing herself.

You can just smell a disaster waiting to happen. And what will happen to Hester's hope of love if she keeps saying *yes* to situations like this?

Can I trust my feelings? Hester is an example of someone who had feelings that say, "This is something wonderful for you," when in fact she's having these feelings about someone who's very bad for her. Hester had never been loved as a woman. For her high school didn't count, not that much went on for her there anyway. Suddenly, a full-grown woman, already accepted at a medical school, she's facing this guy who threatens to leave her, who threatens to deny her the love he's just started stimulating in her.

Those are the big fears for women facing falling in love danger #1: *fear of rejection* and *fear of not finding love.* You're so afraid of rejection that you run the risk of saying *yes* to a love you should be saying *no* to. And you're so afraid of not finding love again that you run the risk of saying *yes* to a love you should be saying *no* to.

But how do you know if this applies to you? You're safe as long as you're still able to look the other person and the relationship straight in the face, without being blinded by passion or panic, and ask, "Is this good for me?" And know you'll give yourself an accurate, honest answer.

Only when you take care of the gold *in you* will you find the gold of real love.

Making Sure It's Safe

Here's how to tell if you're able to do this. How many of the following five statements can you say and mean if you're falling in love (or could you have said when you were falling in love)?

1. "I have a good chance of getting anyone I want."

2. "I've been in love before, I'll be in love again."

3. "Any guy would be crazy not to want me."

4. "I have to check out a guy pretty carefully before I'll let myself fall in love with him."

5. "I've been carried away by how I feel about someone in the past, so now I've learned to go more slowly."

If *four or more* of these statements apply to you, then you're probably not in danger of falling for someone who'd obviously be bad for you. Life can be full of surprises, but you have what you need so that your feelings will not prevent you from seeing what's real.

When it's not safe. But if only *three or fewer* of these statements apply to you, then you'd better watch out. You may fall victim to your love hunger. You may be so afraid of rejection or of not finding someone that you run the risk of saying *yes* to a love you should be saying *no* to.

You're like the person who goes clothes shopping at the mall before she's had a good meal, gets there discovering she's ravenous, and immediately heads for the food court. Well, as you know, it's one step from the food court to diet jail. It's not a place filled with food that will love you back. Hungry women are in danger. Well, if three or fewer of these statements apply to you, you are one hungry woman when it comes to love.

Don't go any further with this relationship. Not yet. If you're thinking of moving in together, don't. If you're talking about getting married, wait awhile. If you're thinking of changing your plans, don't. Tell the guy, "I owe it to myself, I owe it to *us*, to get perspective on all this." Use the words women have used for ages: "This is moving too quickly for me." If the guy's good news, he might be disappointed but he'll accept this. If the guy's bad news, he'll try to get you to see that there's something wrong with you for wanting to slow things down.

Then give yourself a month to see if this guy is really as great as he seems. It's like the old dieting trick of passing a bakery, being tempted to go in and snag a goody, but then saying you'll go back and get that goody if you still want it a half an hour later. The point is that you've got to slow down the emotional momentum within you and the practical momentum between you and the guy so you can see things in the clear light of day.

But what do you look for in the clear light of day when you feel you're falling in love with someone? Here's what women tell me:

THE TOP TEN BEST QUESTIONS TO ASK YOURSELF ABOUT A GUY IF YOU'RE AT RISK OF SAYING *YES* WHEN YOU SHOULD SAY *NO*

1. *Is he pretty much okay the way he is?* Never, never, never get involved with someone who won't make you happy unless he changes. He's gotta make you happy as he is, without changing.

2. *Does he make good choices?* If there are too many bad choices on his resume, there's too much risk of bad choices in the future.

3. *Is he kind?* A ton of sorrow doesn't buy back an ounce of mean. And if he's not kind when you're falling in love, he'll be one mean bastard once he's got you. No excuses acceptable.

4. *Does he always have to be right?* When some disagreement comes up—whether it's over politics, about who said what to whom at some party, or the "right" number of kids to have—does it bug the hell out of him if you don't come around to his side?

5. *Can he learn?* Watch out for a guy who's always got his way of doing things and won't do things differently. You can train a dog; you should be able to train your guy. (Although, *you're* at fault if you want to train him to be an essentially different person.)

6. *Do you feel good about showing him off?* There are people whose opinion really matters to you: if you showed up with your boyfriend and said this is my guy and they sat around talking to him—do you predict you'd be feeling you had to make apologies for him?

7. *Does he do normal things?* I mean normal for someone of his education and occupation and background. Use your judgment, but a guy with weird stuff going on now will be bad news for you later. No excuses.

8. *Is he open to other people?* Guys who don't have friends, who don't want you to have friends, who shut other people out of your life—guys like this are bad news. His wanting you only for himself is not romantic. It's sick.

9. *Is he stupid?* Stupid guys will mess you up. Common sense, the ability to figure things out, the possibility of having good ideas—this helps assure that your heart has made a good choice.

10. *Do his actions match his words?* A guy who doesn't promise much but delivers what he promises is worth a hundred guys who promise you the moon but can barely deliver a moon pie. Catching a guy lying or hiding stuff from you fits in here too.

There you have it, the answer to the age-old question: "How do I know if I should love this guy?" If you're so blinded by your hunger for love that you can't see clearly enough to

answer these questions, take enough time to clear up your
blindness. Trust me: The feelings humming within your breast
will not be strong enough to keep a love alive if your honest
answer to one of these questions is a thumbs down.

Falling-in-Love Danger #2:

"I GOT HURT BEFORE, SO I'LL PROBABLY GET HURT AGAIN IF I FALL IN LOVE."

Now let's see how to avoid the mistake of saying *no* when you
should be saying *yes*. The make-or-break part of this is that if
you keep rejecting good guys, you'll run out of time, out of
hope, and out of guys.

Here's where we talk about fear of intimacy that runs almost like an epidemic through the lives of young women today,
although of course women of all ages are affected by it.

You were in love before. You got hurt. You're in love again.
You're afraid you'll get hurt again. The keynote of fear of intimacy
is that falling in love feels like bad news: When your heart sends
you that letter that you're falling in love, it feels like you've gotten
a letter from the IRS telling you they're auditing you. But it can
be hard to diagnose whether you're really one of those women
who is so panicked by being carried away by love that you *mistakenly* think you're in danger. That's what we want to avoid here:
running away from something good (just the way with love danger
#1 we wanted to avoid embracing something bad).

How do you know if this applies to you? Good question,
because most women do fear of intimacy a little differently. Ask
yourself if any of the top ten most common fear-of-intimacy scenarios here apply to you.

THE TOP TEN MOST COMMON FEAR-OF-INTIMACY SCENARIOS

Scenario #1. The minute you fell in love you wanted to leave.
If you were living together before you fell in love, you might've
moved right out of the apartment. *Does this apply to you?*

Scenario #2. The stronger your feelings for someone, the more you need to slow things down. You insist on slowing things down even if you and the guy are just getting to know each other and you start liking what you see. *Does this apply to you?*

Scenario #3. You fall in love, then you find yourself picking a fight, then you wonder where your anger came from. One woman who was falling in love suddenly broke up because the guy "wouldn't help her paint her bathroom," even though she'd never asked him to help. *Does this apply to you?*

Scenario #4. Here you deal with your fear by pushing for a level of commitment the guy couldn't possibly agree to, and then of course he runs away. He gets blamed for your panic. *Does this apply to you?*

Scenario #5. Because falling in love feels like you're losing control, you do something big to regain control. You issue an ultimatum, for example. If he can't live up to it, you've "proven" your falling in love was a mistake. *Does this apply to you?*

Scenario #6. This is where you overanalyze the relationship. Every potential flaw and defect gets magnified. *Does this apply to you?*

Scenario #7. This is where, out of fear, women subject the relationship to an extreme test. If the guy can put up with your doing bad things to him, you think, "Wow, I'm sure safe with this guy." *Does this apply to you?*

Scenario #8. You go into your hair-trigger mode. You set your alarm system to respond to the slightest thing. If he makes one little mistake, you're out of there. *Does this apply to you?*

Scenario #9. Afraid of your falling in love, you suddenly show some hard-to-take part of your personality—your anger, for example—and shove it in the face of your relationship. This is just like scenario #7, except that instead of doing a terrible deed you show some terrible part of yourself. *Does this apply to you?*

Scenario #10. You're with a guy and things seem to be okay. Suddenly he does something that reminds you of a guy you were involved with before who hurt you. That's it. You dump him. *Does this apply to you?*

  Diagnosis. If one or more of these scenarios applied to you, then you are at risk from falling-in-love danger #2: you fall into the category of women who are so panicked by being carried away by love that you mistakenly assume you're in danger. You could get hurt and not even know it: by running away from a perfectly wonderful relationship.
  I can understand why you'd be in this situation. Think about all the fears that come into play in these scenarios.

  "Can I see what's real?" You're afraid you can't trust your perceptions. Just the way delicious food makes your mouth water with the promise that it really will be delicious, falling in love is your heart watering at the prospect of something wonderful. But if you've fallen in love in the past because you thought something wonderful was in front of you and you were wrong, then how can you trust the promptings of your heart?

  Will I get stuck? And you're afraid of getting stuck. When people fall in love they have this goofy way of doing things that changes their lives. Eloping. Moving in together. Turning down that great job in a different city. Spending a good chunk of money on a 50 percent share of a couch. And then your arrangements trap you, and you find yourself doing what you don't feel ready to do.
  These fears are where the Top Ten Most Common Fear-of-Intimacy Scenarios come from. But no one's really afraid of intimacy, any more than people are afraid of happiness. People

are afraid of bad things happening to them in their search for intimacy.

Prescription. There's no point in my telling you that you shouldn't be afraid. But you don't need to run and shut the door on something wonderful. What you do need to do is take care of yourself. Isn't that what you're really looking for? A way to open your heart without getting hurt.

Here's what to do that works; I'll explain what it means in a moment:

Let your heart set the pace. Don't say or do anything to let the arrangements you make get ahead of your comfort level.

When they're diagnosed with this problem, women say, "I'm afraid of things moving too quickly." So here's how to make sure they don't, based on suggestions from women who've been down the road you're going down.

• *Think of your relationship as a maybe thing, and talk about it that way.* It's true anyway, plus you need it to be this way if your heart is going to feel it's in the lead. Do what other couples do: say things like, "We'll go skiing next month, if we're still together." "If we keep on seeing each other, and if we still feel the same way about each other, do you think maybe we could talk about the possibility of moving in together at some point down the road?" "Maybe we could spend a week together at the beach this summer, if we're still together." It's amazing how using words like *maybe* and *if* can give you that feeling that you don't have to run.

• *Find out what information you need and get it.* When we freak out, our feelings might be all over the place, but the reason is usually very specific. If you accept yourself as someone with fears, and if you can identify what specifically you're afraid of, then you can figure out what you'd need to know to stop being afraid. For example, you got hurt because you were married to a charming but lazy bum, and now your new guy talks about liking to go on vacation. Another bum! Or is he? Find out. Get to know him. Talk to his friends. See how he's operated in the past. *Then* you'll get the specific answers you're looking for.

• *Don't change anything in your life—don't give up your apartment, don't switch jobs, don't pass up that great opportunity somewhere else—until you feel sure.* This again is one of those situations where you're making sure your heart is in the lead. It's probably not so much falling in love as feeling trapped by love that's scaring you. But it's changing something in your life that will make you feel trapped. Be aware of this too: making plans for the future is a way of changing your life, and future plans can make you feel just as trapped as present changes. So don't run from the relationship, just run from anything that will make you feel trapped in it.

From Falling in Love to Making a Commitment

Since millions of women have asked this question for thousands of years, it's just possible you're asking the question: "Yes, I'm falling in love, but should I go forward—should I marry this guy?"

There are three things you have to check out. *You need to say* yes *to all three of them to get a* go *for commitment.* Here they are. Keep score.

1. You need to know that you're having real experiences of falling in love. Let me list all fifteen scenes from falling in love for you again:

You act like kids again.

You experience the sweet joy of total acceptance.

You feel a surge of energy.

When you get together after being apart, it's as if the sun has come out after many long gray days.

You find that you can connect without words.

You have phone calls when you don't want to stop talking to each other.

You miss each other enormously.

You keep finding that you can't do enough for each other.

The whole world seems beautiful.

You experience a new level of openness.

You can't stop thinking about each other.

You create your own little private world.

You create dreams for your future together.

The more you know each other, the more you love each other.

You experience a genuine renewal of trust.

You know whether you're having these experiences. If you haven't been having even one of these experiences, then you're kidding yourself if you call what you're going through falling in love. But if you have been having two or more of these experiences, and you have a feeling that there's more to come, then you've scored one *yes.*

2.   You need to know the guy's okay. We've dealt with that under falling-in-love danger #1. You went through a checklist there. If your guy flunked the test, you can't make the commit-

ment. But if he passed, then you've scored another *yes*. Two out of three so far.

3. You need to know you'll be happy with this guy. Well, some people feel that's such a mysterious and subjective area that no one can say anything about it. I understand that position: it says you make your best guess and take your chances. But, again, women who've been through what you're going through teach me that we can be much more definite.

Just ask yourself what your top three priorities are when it comes to spending the next years of your life with someone, when you think about actually living with that person day after day. I know—there are millions of things we want and hundreds of priorities. The *fact* is that when your big three are taken care of, everything else falls into place.

So let's say that the thing holding you back is that there's not as much sex as you'd like, it's not as orgasmic as you'd like, and it's not as emotionally fulfilling as you'd like. Okay. That's a disappointment. But what you have to ask yourself is this: *Is A-level sex one of my top three priorities?*

Are you saying that A-level sex is why you're here in the first place?

You get my point. *You can feel confident you'll be happy with this other person you're falling in love with if you're confident he'll do an okay job of satisfying your top three priorities.* That's what *priority* means.

> The people who make us happy are the people who come close to making our big dreams come true.

So write down your top three priorities, no matter who you'd be with. Then ask yourself if your guy gets a decent grade on your top three priorities. If so, you've scored your third *yes*. Three to victory. You can feel confident about moving from falling in love to making a commitment.

A Lifetime Bonus

Let me pay off on a promise I made you. Do you remember that I said that falling in love is not something that has to last for a moment? It's true. If you're in a good relationship, you can feel like you're falling in love over and over again as the years go by. Impossible, you say?

Au contraire. It's simpler than you'd think. Women do it all the time. The key is this: Don't sit around waiting for those falling-in-love feelings to sprout magically all by themselves, out of nowhere. Instead, focus on real moments from your life together when you and your partner were falling in love. Things you did together that captured the experience of falling in love. Snapshots from your falling-in-love scrapbook.

Now here's why you should get ready for magic.

More magic moments. All these moments are repeatable. To repeat them, you just have to do them again. Let me repeat that. You can repeat the moments that make up the experience of falling in love. If you did them once, you can do them again. Sometimes you'll find that you and your partner are having these moments without your even realizing it.

It's true that we can never get back that period in our lives when everything was new. But you can recapture the moments that made that period feel new. And then you'll feel you're falling in love all over again.

I Will Survive

Make-or-Break Experience #4:
Coming through a Major Breakup Stronger and Smarter

Yes, you *will* survive. You will survive and *thrive*. There are eight kinds of breakups—as you'll see—and most of these are by *your* choice. But even in those cases where you've been royally dumped and it feels like your heart's been broken and you're sure your life's been screwed up—even in those cases, eventually you'll be back on course doing better than ever.

Let's never ever forget this, you and I. Sure it's painful going through a breakup. Sure your life is disrupted. But it's not pancreatic cancer—it won't kill you. We need to remember this because women who are desperately afraid of going through a breakup are disempowered in their relationships, and therefore don't get their needs met, and therefore are sowing the seeds for a bad relationship, which will lead to a breakup anyway.

That's the make-or-break part of this experience. If you're committed to the idea that you'll never settle for less than the best, then you're willing to go through a breakup because you know what it will do to you to spend your life stuck in a second-rate relationship. But if you're controlled by your fear of going through a breakup, you'll never be able to fight for a relationship that's nothing less than the best. And settling for the second-rate destroys your hope of getting the first-rate.

Breakups are a huge, *natural* part of a woman's love life. What we think is the norm—you date, you marry at 27, and settle down forever—is really the exception. In fact it's usually a myth. Here's a story that illustrates how many ways the modern American woman experiences major breakups in her life.

☙

Carmen's Story

She's just turned forty and Carmen's current boyfriend reports being surprised by how playful she is, particularly when they're intimate. She's so playful that he sometimes finds himself wishing she were just a little more serious. This would sound very strange to people who know Carmen at work on Wall Street where she's a well-known market strategist for one of the hottest financial houses around.

Act One. If you don't know what you're looking for, believe me you'll never find it. Bob was Carmen's high school and college sweetheart. They first slept together when Carmen was a junior in high school, and sex was just great. Eight years of going steady, with no doubt that they'd get married. Puppy love seeming to ripen into love between two adults.

Within a year of college graduation they got married. Six months after that it hit Carmen that the whole thing was a gigantic, terrible mistake. The reality of living with him showed her something she didn't like. She can't say why or how. It was just a feeling. She loved Bob, but she fell out of love with him and knew she couldn't stay married to him.

And yet she hung around for seven more years. Breaking up is hard to do, particularly when you're the one who has to do it, particularly when your parents tell you, hey, what can you expect, marriage ain't no picnic. Carmen is more than willing to make tough calls when it comes to the financial markets. But it took her seven years of sleepless nights to accept that it was over with Bob and finally break up with him.

Act Two. Dating. Looking for someone to love. Making up for love adventures she missed out on. Going through a lot of breakups with men she didn't care about. The casual verbiage of easy break-ups: "I don't think we should see each other anymore," "I don't see us going anywhere," "I really see you as more of a friend," "I'm not ready to be in a relationship now."

Act Three. A new man in her life, and Carmen fell madly in love with him. Within months the relationship evolved into one of those situations where they each had their own place but she was mostly staying over at his place. Call it semi–living together. They made a lot of trips to San Francisco where they shared a romantic dream of settling down together one day. They'd spend some of their time on these trips checking out neighborhoods and houses.

Then when Carmen was thirty-one she found out that this guy was kind of doubly cheating on her by sleeping with another woman and taking that woman to *their city*. Before Carmen could get out three words of her anger, he burst into tears and said, "Carmen, it's all over between you and me. I'm so sorry." Imagine that: you catch your lover cheating and he dumps you. Once she got over being stunned, Carmen realized her heart was broken.

Act Four. Back on the dating scene. Not right away of course, because the last breakup had really hurt. But sooner rather than later, because it's getting ridiculous—a woman in her thirties, attractive, successful, warm . . . it sounds like a bad personal ad. It's different this time, though, for Carmen.

The second visit to the fun house just isn't so much fun. It wasn't so much that Carmen hated the guys. She hated the games, and most of all she hated herself with the guys. She felt

she had to hide how powerful she was and at the same time
hide even more carefully how deeply romantic she was. Plus
she's really scared now. Love's a place where you can get hurt!
But you gotta keep on keepin' on.

Act Five. Carmen meets Joey. Imagine John Travolta from
Saturday Night Fever, if he'd aged fifteen years and gone to
trade school. And been visibly intelligent and owned a growing
little electrical contracting business, with well-placed uncles
and cousins who could get him jobs. That's Joey. What the hell
is Carmen doing with a guy like that, you might wonder. But
he's "a real man," as Carmen put it, and he's sweet and kind
and most of all she feels "a real connection" between them.
They have the same background. Plus, for the first time in her
life, she's with a guy who can fix all the little things that break
in the house.

She gets married again. It's good at first. But gradually over
the course of a couple of years she realizes she doesn't want
to be married to Joey anymore. It's not like her first marriage,
where she instantly realized she'd made a terrible mistake. This
is weird in its own way, because there's nothing she can point
to as a mistake. She just doesn't want it.

But how do you end something like this? Like two porcu-
pines making love: very, very carefully. It almost doesn't look
like an ending. She announces she wants a separation, and he
moves out but only months later. After a year of separation
she can compare what it's like living with him and not living
with him, and Carmen decides she wants a permanent
separation.

Act Six. Real life really is like a soap opera. There's a happy
ending somewhere in Carmen's story just waiting to burst out.
Maybe the happy ending lies in the man that she's dating now
that she's forty. I know him. He's a good, solid guy, Carmen's
equal socially, financially. Okay, so he works too hard. Who
doesn't? He likes Carmen. He wants them to get serious. He
wants to have children. This could be it.

But Joey is still in the picture, in and out, hanging around like a yeast infection you can't quite get rid of. Except Carmen doesn't quite want to get rid of him. So the new guy calls and sometimes Joey answers. Obviously this is yet another kind of breakup, the non-breakup breakup. What else do you do, though, when you only want to break up with someone 90 percent and not 100 percent? This arrangement would be perfect, if it didn't have the risk of destroying the bright new future Carmen might have with the new guy.

I could've chosen almost anyone's story; it would've told the same tale Carmen's told. How breaking up is never the same experience twice. How the experience of breaking up is filled with echoes that just get louder. How we need to feel that this is a part of our lives that doesn't scare us.

A New Look at Breaking Up

The only thing sadder than the loss of love is the loss of the hope of love. And yet I find myself feeling incredibly upbeat as I sit here because I know a secret. It's a secret you could only know, I think, if you'd talked to as many women as I have who've gone through a major breakup. It's a secret you could only know if you got past the tears and heard the stories of what happened after the tears.

The secret is that *when a relationship ends that's usually the right thing.* You're usually better off. Maybe not in the first few days or weeks. Maybe at first the pain feels incredible. Maybe you have to go through a lot of fear and anger. But the secret is that there's a sense in which the death of that relationship was meant to be. The *fact* that you have to move on— and *where you go* when you move on—are a natural and surprisingly healthy part of the story of your life, part of who you are as a woman.

Looking back, here are the things women say most often:

- "I'm better off now than I was then."
- "I just wish I hadn't stayed stuck for so long."
- "I wish I'd gotten out sooner."
- "I like myself better now."
- "It's about learning lessons that you need to learn."
- "I wish someone had helped me see how much . . . it's not just knowing the pain will end, but that you'll come into your own as a person."

A wonderful future awaits you. The understanding here is vital for everyone, whether you've just dumped him or, frankly, whatever experience of love you're going through. But you know who needs the stories and insights in this chapter the most? The women who think they need it least—women who at the moment are looking for someone to love. Or who are falling in love. That's when all the old wounds get re-opened.

Old angers cause you to get inappropriately angry and possibly spoil a good thing. Old fears can easily lead you to run away from something wonderful. They can even lead you to run into the arms of someone dreadful.

These are the dangers. You need to understand this make-or-break experience to avoid these dangers. But perhaps the biggest danger of all is getting so mired in negativity that you shut down to the lesson that almost every woman who's gone through what you're going through has learned:

Things can be better in the future you *actually* face than in the future you *thought* you were facing before your relationship came crashing down around you.

So—after we've cried and after we've been comforted—what do we need? No matter what you do, it's a fact that things will probably be better than they were. That will probably happen. Millions and millions of women do just fine after going through a breakup.

Okay, so how do we make sense of what's happened to us? There are ten fixed stages we go through when we break up with someone, just like the stages we're supposed to go through if we discover someone we care about is going to die. These fixed stages are experienced differently from one woman to another. And you might spend one minute in a particular stage, while your friend spends years in the same stage. But when a relationship ends, here are the stages we all go through.

THE TEN STAGES OF GOING THROUGH A MAJOR BREAKUP

Stage 1. Seeing that something's wrong. When it comes to breakups, I've stopped believing that disasters come out of the blue. Most of us feel the same way. When one of our friends tells us that the breakup came completely out of the blue we're somewhat suspicious. "There must've been a sign, a clue," we always say.

Usually there is. Like you fight all the time. Like you hate each other. Like you have nothing to say to each other. Like one of you acts like a huge jerk. Like sex ain't no good no more. You know the drill. The kind of stuff that makes you at some point corner your partner and say, "Honey, we have to talk."

Stage 2. Working on your relationship. It's like going to the doctor. We all go to the doctor. But when someone goes to the doctor a lot, it's a sign that they're dealing with big problems. That's what Stage 2 is—when the need to work on the relationship is so huge it almost starts to feel like a part-time job.

Stage 3. Realizing that it's serious. This is when you know you're in trouble. You try to fix your problems but nothing works. And you know that nothing works. That's critical. Stage 3 is the *realization* that your problems are bigger than you are.

A lot of women discover they're in Stage 3 through talking to friends. You know, you talk to your best friend about your husband and she says, "Well, did you try . . ." and you realize you've tried everything. After your friend realizes that you've tried everything, her very next piece of advice will land you in Stage 4.

Stage 4. Trying to live with it. When you can't change something, you try to accept it. Even women who have vowed to leave if they catch their husband cheating—when they do catch their husband cheating they consider the possibility of accepting it. And that means living with it. Okay, so maybe you only try to live with it for five minutes before you kick the bastard out on his ear. Maybe you kick him out and then regret it and then try to think of a way you could live with it.

Among women who talked to me about going through a major breakup, *here's the one comment I heard more than any other:*

"Now that it's all over, I don't know why I stayed so long. I just kept hoping. I wish I hadn't spent so much time trying to find a way to live with things the way they were." Now that would make things incredibly clear to us all, except that a lot of other women talk about how glad they were that they tried to live with it.

And that's what throws the door open to confusion.

Stage 5. Living with indecision. Men—can't live with them, can't live without them. And that's where you get to when it slowly starts to dawn on you that living with the problems in your relationship isn't going to make them go away. Now what? Now you live with indecision. This stage is a sinkhole. Years, decades, entire lifetimes have been swallowed up with people trying to figure out whether they should stay or leave. My own mother spent thirty years stuck in indecision with my stepfather. This stage is the only truly tragic stage in the process. Women can be happy on their own. Women can be happy committing to their relationship. But to spend time in limbo neither in nor out, neither here nor there, torn by the stress of trying to figure out what's best for you—that's enough to make you crazy.

Don't make the mistake of thinking that you stand still

during this stage. While they're trying to figure out whether their relationship is too good to leave or too bad to stay in, women do things like have a child, buy a house, go back to school, move across the country—all in the desperate hope that one of these actions will bring clarity. But clarity never seems to come. Not when all you do is sit around waiting for it to knock at your door.

Stage 6. Living with disbelief. Now don't make a mistake about something. That sudden new turning where it's absolutely clear that the relationship is over doesn't always mean that you actually separate at the same moment. You might continue to sleep together, to live together, to stay married. You might go to a lawyer, or you might cancel your appointment with a lawyer.

The point is that this stage is marked by disbelief. Let me make the sequence clear again. Indecision. Decision. Disbelief. You now know it's over, but you just can't believe it.

One reason it can be hard to believe—and this always amazes even the most experienced women—is that after you've made your decision and you know it's right, you find you're sleeping together again. Or, having had that final fight, you find you're nicer to each other, more relaxed with each other than you've been in years. You could scream, it's so confusing.

In this stage your friends start coming at you from all different sides, and this just aggravates your sense of disbelief. One friend yells at you for hanging around with him after you've made such a big announcement that it's all over. Another friend yells at you because she's convinced you're making a mistake ending things.

But you *have* broken up. That's already happened, no matter how hard it is to fully believe it.

Stage 7. A quick ending. It always happens like this. No matter how stuck you've felt you've been or how long you've been stuck, the end always happens very quickly. For example, the two of you had been fighting for a long time and you'd both been threatening to leave, but then there was that Sunday morning where it seemed like you were fighting as usual but next thing you know he says, "That's it, I'm out of here."

Or the two of you had been talking and talking and talking about your problems, and the possibility of divorce had come up a number of times and been rejected. Suddenly one of you says, "Maybe we really should get a divorce." And the other says, "Okay, let's do it." And you know for sure that you've turned a corner. Next day you go to see your lawyers.

It can even happen in a quiet moment when you're all by yourself. You'd been going over and over the same confusing facts and feelings of your life, without gaining any clarity. Suddenly, while driving down the highway or sitting in the bath, *boom!,* you know for sure it's over.

Stage 8. Discovering yourself and life again. But your disbelief ends quickly. The world is new again. You're new to yourself. Maybe you're living alone for the first time in years. And the shock of how weird it is to be alone has turned into a kind of amazed joy at how much satisfaction you get from living alone. This is what you dreaded, above all, and you find out it's fantastic. You feel freer, safer, more at home in your life than you've felt in years. Many women who are alone after their first marriage ends realize they'd never been independent adult women. And so part of the discovery during this stage involves getting to know who you are as a grown-up.

Every woman going through this stage discovers the following things:

- There's something she can do that she never thought she could do—for example, pay taxes, travel alone, masturbate, buy a house, fix the toilet.
- There's something she likes that she never thought she liked—for example, spending Saturday night alone in bed reading a book, watching soap operas, having a dog, working out.
- There's something she hates that she never realized she

hated—for example, watching stupid shows on television, eating meat, staying up late, going to parties, working out.

The point is that having broken up you realize that your previous relationship created a world for you, and that world created a self for you, and now you're living in a new world and that enables you to meet a new self, one that's much closer to the person you really are. Saying good-bye to a husband or lover and therefore saying hello to oneself as if for the first time is an almost universal experience for women in this stage.

And the very best part of all the discoveries you make in this stage is how desirable you are. There's something about a sick and dying relationship that makes a woman feel like a piece of crap. It could simply be because your partner kept putting you down, or humiliating you, or ignoring you. Making you feel like a stupid nothing. It could also be more complicated. Maybe he was a nice guy and you're the one who wanted out, but you felt incredibly guilty about wanting to leave and helpless for not leaving. Now that you're on your own, the guilt and helplessness are gone. And you feel great about yourself.

Let me say this as strongly as I can. Every woman who's gotten out of a relationship, no matter how badly she was dumped, *is less than a year away from a whole new sense of how terrific she is.*

Stage 9. Feeling vulnerable. "I'm feeling very vulnerable now." No one comes out of a breakup without the sense of having been hurt. Not only that, but the ways you were hurt felt completely unfair and completely surprising.

Thank God we have that protective instinct that enables us to see how we've been hurt and remember it so there's a chance we won't be hurt the same way again. The problem is that that protective instinct is crude and sometimes overemotional. If your car crashed if you were driving down a certain stretch of road, you become afraid of crashing every time you drive down that stretch of road, even though the road itself had nothing to do with your crash.

The same thing happens with love. The last time a man said he loved you, he went on to hurt you very badly. That's why you broke up. Now there's a new man in your life and you've had fun dating, but suddenly this new guy says he loves you. And suddenly you feel very scared. Suddenly in the middle of your happy trip you turned a corner and there in front of you is that stretch of road where you crashed last time. One more example of the endless echoes in the land of love.

There's no way to avoid these surges of vulnerable feelings. There's something you can do, though, to make things better for yourself. Zero in like a laser on exactly how you got hurt the first time. You didn't get hurt because a man said he loved you. You didn't get hurt because a man wanted to have sex with you. You probably didn't get hurt because a man wanted to "move too quickly."

In fact there are only two reasons why you got hurt. You got hurt because you didn't see who that guy really was. Or you got hurt because you didn't see who you were, how you really felt, what you really needed. Seeing clearly. Going slowly enough to make sure you see clearly. These are the secrets of safe driving. They're the secrets of navigating the hairpin turns of love. If you see clearly, you won't get hurt. No matter how many confusing echoes you hear.

Stage 10. Having a new life. The experience of discovering new things can last your whole life, and it should. But whatever happens with your process of discovery, at some point you realize you've found a new life. Maybe you're in a new relationship. Maybe you've settled into a pattern of dating. Maybe you've gotten comfortable being on your own. But it hits you that you're in a new place now. Yes, you went through a major breakup. There was pain and loss and fear. But you've moved on now and have reached a new equilibrium.

And there's something you need to know about Stage 10. *There is always something about it that's better than what you had before.* If there's one amazing lesson I take away from

women who've gone through this experience, it's that you do
get over the pain and move on to something better.

The only risk you run is getting so stuck as a result of
breaking up that you cut yourself off from the good things in
life that are in store for you. But it was probably meant to be
that the relationship would end. By being stuck you're blocking
a natural process.

Love lives forever only if it's right for you.

THE SEVEN BASIC KINDS OF BREAKUPS

Let's see, there are forty ways to leave your lover, a thousand
and one tales of the Arabian nights, and eight million stories
in the naked city. And there are seven basic stories of breaking
up. These experiences are important for you and me because
they locate just what we have to focus on to save ourselves
from getting stuck. Stuck how? Not in the old relationship.
You've broken up. It's over. The being stuck you and I have
to worry about as a result of these experiences is how they
carry over into the rest of your life.

- *Not* being stuck means being free to move on, having
  learned whatever lessons you need to learn, and having a
  clearer sense of what you need now.
- *Being* stuck means that the experience of breaking up pre-
  vents you from learning what you need to learn in one way
  or another.

But how? And what do you do about it? That's what we'll
figure out next.

So here's what we're going to do. I'm going to tell you seven
stories of what it was like for someone to go through a major
breakup. For each one I'll tell you about the core emotional
issues. That's where you'll find the key that points to how you
can get stuck and what you need to do to get unstuck as you
face the rest of your life.

As you read each story, think about the breakup you're going through. Or think about the last breakup you went through. Ask yourself, "Is this basically my story? Is this basically what it was really like for me?" It should be immediately obvious when you read it that *this* is your story. If you can't identify which story is yours by the time you've read all of them, ask yourself which one feels closest to what it's like for you. Then follow the diagnosis and prescription accompanying that story.

Breakup Experience #1:

YOU REALIZE YOU NEVER WANTED TO BE THERE FROM THE BEGINNING.

☙

Ann's Story

"Did you ever buy a pair of shoes and they don't feel right but you talk yourself into the idea that it'll somehow be okay and you'll eventually feel about them the way you'd hoped you would? That's what happened to me with my marriage. Maybe I confused hope with love, maybe I was just desperate to get married. Maybe it was my baby hunger talking.

"But it was never right, even from the beginning. He didn't feel right physically, to start there. He was a handsome guy, actually, but he had really big teeth and when we kissed I was afraid he was going to eat me. It was like kissing a piano. But that's not the main thing. We didn't click . . . you know, as people. You know how wives complain about being golf widows and things like that? He'd be gone because of work or he'd be out on his boat or something and I'd be *happy*. Every time he came home I'd be thinking, 'Oh shit, he's back.'

"And even though sex was good at first, it's the strangest thing because at some point I lost all desire to have sex with him. This is the hard part. It was tough to get pregnant. Finally after years I was able to conceive and I had a kid. That's when I saw that I'd never really loved him.

"I felt terrible about it. But I felt so guilty that I'd created a lie that I just couldn't leave."

That was several years ago. The only regret Ann has now is that it took her so long to leave. The big surprise for Ann is how much fun she's having now. She feels no pressure the way she did before she first got married to find someone, anyone, and settle down. Now Ann's life is just one big love adventure, meeting guys, getting to know them, not taking anything more seriously than she wants to. Now for the first time she feels she can let things ripen at their own pace. She feels free to be herself.

The emotional hallmarks of this experience. It's striking how often women going through Breakup Experience #1 feel their sense of love and being married collapses like a house of cards. It was there one day. Then something happened. Then it's gone.

And so of course you immediately feel incredibly trapped. You know you don't belong, and you just want to be somewhere else, anywhere else. Lemme outta here!

But on some level nothing had happened. Women who've had these feelings often have trouble making a case for how horrible their partner is. You're not leaving because your partner's terrible—you're leaving because you thought this was right for you, you thought you wanted to be here, and you were wrong. So along with wanting to get the hell out of there as fast as possible, you feel terribly guilty for having trapped him in a relationship that never ever should've existed. When you realize that the marriage was a lie, you're realizing that you've wasted years of your partner's life as well as your own.

Diagnosis and prescription. If this feels like your story, you might not really have a problem. Some women in your situation are able to focus in and say that *this* marriage to *this* person was a mistake, and these women are ready, willing, and able to move on and find love somewhere else. But some women get stuck. Here's what you should watch out for, because it's how women who've gone through a similar experience have gotten into trouble.

• *Where you might get stuck:* Paralysis. Women who wake up to the realization that on some level they've never been married and never wanted to be in this marriage often have incredible difficulty leaving. The marriage isn't horrible. Their partner isn't horrible. And just think about what happens when they tell their partner that they don't want to be married anymore:

He says, "Why not?"

She says, "I don't know. I just don't want to be married anymore."

He says, "Well, that's not a good reason. If that's all you've got, don't you owe it to me [or the kids, or the time we've spent together, or what we've built together] to stay and work on the relationship?"

And she usually says, "I guess you're right."

Prescription. If you're suffering from paralysis, you're trapped by guilt, hope, and inertia, but ultimately you will leave. And if you listen to the women who've gone down the same path as you, you'll hear them say, "The longer you wait, the worse it is. The sooner you get out, the better for everyone." So you have to deal directly with your guilt, hope, and inertia.

•*Guilt.* Okay, you've done something bad. You've kept your partner in a marriage you now realize never existed. If you need to talk to a clergy person to find a way to do penance, that might be good. But what you have to understand is that keeping your partner in this nonmarriage isn't fair and just adds to what you have to feel guilty for. Unless you can make a commitment to stay forever, leave now. That's the best way to have the least guilt in the long run.

•*Hope.* Different women in your situation hope for different things at different times. Maybe you're just hoping for your partner to turn so incredibly wonderful that it banishes all thought of leaving. Maybe you're hoping for him to do something so terrible that it becomes easier for you to leave. I know you need hope, but most of us are hungry for the hope that we'll know what's

right for us to do. *That hope's come true for you.* All that's left is
for you to act on it. Any other hope is unrealistic.

•*Inertia.* It takes a controlled explosion to launch a rocket,
and it takes a controlled explosion to launch a breakup, any
breakup. But you're in one of those situations where there's little
likelihood of such an explosion. Your partner wants you to stay.
You can't really think of a reason not to stay beyond your feeling
that you don't want to be there anymore. So where is the energy
going to come from to counteract the tremendous dead weight of
a house to sell, kids to deal with, friends to tell, lawyers to see,
parents to disappoint. Just finding another place to live?

Here's what you do to counteract this inertia. Decide today
that you're going to leave. Actually, you've already decided—
you're just acknowledging your decision. Wait a week. A week
from today check in with yourself to make sure you still feel
the same way. If you do, tell as many people as possible that
you're leaving. By making it a public act, you're gaining momentum from the sense of shame you'll feel if you don't act.

•*Where you might get stuck:* "I'm just not one of those 'love'
people." A lot of women feel that it's monstrous to walk away
from love and marriage. Here's how one woman put it:

> *My husband was a good, decent guy. Cute, too. Most women would
> be glad to have a husband like him. Then here I am saying it's
> nothing to me. A therapist asked—I guess to test how I felt—if I'd
> prefer living alone to living with Mike. I said yes. Well, just think
> about that. I can't love a perfectly good guy I started out thinking
> I loved. I want to be alone. I must not be one of those 'love' people.
> Maybe I wasn't meant to feel love or live it.*

I don't know. Maybe that was true for her. But it usually
isn't true. Just because it was never a marriage doesn't mean
you were never meant for love.

Prescription. Your prescription is to find out once and for
all if you really are one of those "love" people. Here's how.

You have to ask a question about the family you grew up in and your adult siblings today.

Unless you have clear, powerful evidence that your parents were off the charts, compared to most of the parents of most of your friends, then you should probably conclude you got everything you needed from them.

And unless you have clear, powerful evidence that your siblings cannot function in the land of love, compared to other people their age, then you should probably conclude that your siblings are normal screwed-up people like the rest of us.

Okay, so now we have the right frame of reference: real people, not ideal people. Based on this, can you make an overwhelming case, compared to other parents you know about, that your parents were incapable of love? And can you make an overwhelming case that your siblings are better off living without love? If you can answer yes to both questions, then maybe you're one of those rare people who just doesn't do well in relationships.

But you've got to go with the odds, and let me spell out what the odds are. At least 95 percent of people who break up because they suddenly realize they've never been in love from the beginning are in that situation because they simply hooked up with the wrong person for the wrong reason.

Bottom line: love is natural for all of us. In spite of the things that have happened, assume that love is natural for you unless there's powerful evidence to the contrary from your entire family's history.

Breakup Experience #2:

**A GOOD GUY KEEPS GOING DOWNHILL
UNTIL YOU JUST CAN'T TAKE IT ANYMORE.**

Linda's Story

"When we first met, he was already different from any guy I'd ever known. But I thought that was good. Yeah, he'd had these

weird parents who never sent him to school and he was so
incredibly romantic, writing me a poem every day, kissing my
hand—and this was a guy from Denver! But he owned his
own business—a restaurant—and I thought he was a sweet,
warmhearted guy with his feet on the ground.

"Now things were okay for a while, but then he just started
getting weirder and weirder. It began when his restaurant failed.
He blamed it on the bank being in collusion with his competitors.
It sounded kind of paranoid to me, but what did I know?

"Next thing I know his hair is getting longer and he's wearing a beard and overalls and he's getting fat and he's got these
weird ideas about how people are robbing him and he's going
to expose this and he's going to expose that. It's not just that
he was going nowhere fast, but he was dragging me down,
because when I should've been working I was worried about
him, or having to take care of him. Finally I just couldn't take
it anymore. I'd done everything I could. But I had to get out
of there. It broke my heart, but it also felt like I was saving
my life.

"It was the best thing I ever did. It felt like a tragedy at
the time. I remember going to my therapist and crying out of
guilt. And of course there was all the pain of basically wasting
my twenties on this guy. But look at it from another angle. I
was very very immature when I got married. A kid like me
would've had to have been very lucky to make a good choice
anyway. At least being with David forced me to grow up and
take my life seriously. I realized I'd have to succeed at work
to have any kind of security, and I think I'm much more successful now than I would've been otherwise. Of course I'm
dating again and I've started getting serious about this new
guy. He's not the kind of guy I would've looked at twice when
I was a kid. So I think it's all been for the best."

The emotional hallmarks of this experience. Most of all you
feel guilt. That's partly because you feel you should be able to
help him but you couldn't. And that's partly because you want
to leave but feel it's wrong. You also feel terribly angry, because

by changing the way he has he seems to have broken a deal he made with you. You also feel enormous self-doubt. What was up with you? How come you didn't know things would turn out like this—shouldn't you have foreseen it all? Shouldn't you have been able to handle it better? Shouldn't you have gotten out sooner?

Diagnosis and prescription. If this feels like your story, here's what you should watch out for as you move into the future, because it's how women who've gone through a similar experience have gotten into trouble.

• *Where you might get stuck:* The flight to safety. You've just gone through an experience of having the rug pulled out from under you. So now what you want more than anything is safety. That means finding an extremely solid guy or staying away from guys altogether.

Like anyone who's been disappointed, you think you'll be okay if you lower your expectations. The more you're worried about being okay, the more you'll lower your expectations. Not low in the sense of accepting anybody (that's the next diagnosis, love hunger) but low in the sense that "don't hurt me" is your only priority. Women who get stuck like this will sometimes get involved with weak, boring guys, underachievers who'll be dependent on them. Like someone who buys a goldfish after their dog's been run over.

Prescription. We all want safety, and we all deserve it. But understand what happened to you. You got badly disappointed. Something that should've turned out great turned out badly. But it doesn't mean that things that look great will always turn out badly.

Don't give up your high expectations.

Either you had a bit of bad luck and there's nothing you have to do differently, or if you think back you'll see there was some telltale sign of a serious problem. That's all you have to watch out for. As long as there's no sign of trouble, why not feel safe about going ahead with a new relationship?

• *Where you might get stuck:* "Help, I'm trapped in this relationship and I can't get out." The way the story should go is that once you realize that your partner has terrible, unsolvable problems that are dragging you down, you make a decision. Understand the course of your partner's disease or problem. If you feel you want to hang in there for the whole deal, then make that decision. But if you know that you simply can't or won't hang in there, get out now. It's painful, but it's over, and now you can begin again. But a *real* disease occurs when you get stuck in not being able to leave.

The hallmarks of this disease are things you think or say. For example:

• "He was so terrific, I know he can be terrific again."
• "He had so much promise—it would be a shame to give up on him."
• "I've invested so much time in our relationship—why give up now?"
• "He keeps begging me 'don't leave—I'll change.' "
• "I'm afraid he'll collapse completely without me."
• "He keeps making progress. I know he can solve his problems."
• "He says he just needs that one thing [a job, a lucky break in his career, for his rich uncle to die] and everything will be okay again. What if I walk out and a week later everything's better for him?"

I've left one thing out. This diagnosis applies to you if you've said or thought things like the above *and* if you recognize that you basically have a dead relationship.

Here's how to see if you have a dead relationship. If you've said things like the above and any *two* of the following statements apply to you, then you can safely conclude that you have a dead relationship:

- "We just don't want to make love anymore."
- "We're not interested in talking about anything except our problems."
- "I don't have any feelings for him anymore."
- "I don't have any hope for him anymore."
- "I don't respect him anymore."
- "We don't care about sharing any activities any longer."
- "I have nothing more to give him; I don't want to give to him either."

Dead is dead. And you can't let an addiction to hope chain you to the rotting corpse of a dead relationship.

Prescription. Most of us say we want to be in a relationship, but based on my research *women who got out of bad relationships generally did very well and were glad they'd left. Even if they stayed single.*

Here's what this means for you. Obviously you're scared of leaving. You're scared of being alone. But if the relationship's dead, things will probably be better for you on the other side even with all the hassles of going through a divorce and starting over on your own.

You have to be careful about something. You probably have friends who've been divorced and they've probably done a lot of complaining. Their complaints may have scared you. But the fact is that complaining is something that we women do when we talk to each other. We complain about our boyfriends and husbands, but we still love them. And we complain about our divorces, even though we're usually better off. The point is, don't confuse complaining with making a recommendation.

So do this. Wander down to your bookstore and check out some of the books on the shelf marked *Divorce.* You'll find books about what it's like to break up and start over. Unless it's one of those rabidly antidivorce books, I think you'll generally find these are hopeful, positive guides.

Acknowledge that the relationship is dead. Know you'll be

better off on your own. What more do you need to know that you can and should get out of this dead relationship?

Breakup Experience #3:

OUT OF THE CLEAR BLUE SKY YOU'RE DUMPED AND YOU JUST CAN'T FIND OUT WHY.

⊗

Vivian's Story

"Eddie and I had been sort of living together for I guess three years. I say sort of because my ex-roommate still kept a room for me at my old apartment, so maybe from Eddie's point of view I never *really* moved in with him. Okay, but the thing is that we were really great together. Where should I begin? I'd been bopping around New York for a couple of years after graduation and I was working as an assistant to this big editor at a publishing company. Eddie was one of her writers. He was one of those 'promising novelist types,' but he's actually doing well these days.

"He asks me out and we really click. I mean I kind of give him a hard time because I'm afraid that maybe he's using me to get in with his editor or find out stuff. But Eddie went to another publisher pretty soon after we met and it didn't change anything with us. Maybe from his point of view I was just playing hard to get. Aren't you supposed to do that?

"So there's this long period when, I'm telling you, everything's great. Sex is great. We talk all the time. We do all these really special things together, I don't know, like one weekend we wrote a whole play together and I wrote all the male parts and he wrote all the female parts and it was really good. We went to the pound to get a dog. And we both fell in love with the same dog there, and she wasn't a puppy either.

"Eddie's about six years older than me, and I guess he's had his share of relationships. I'm saying that because I thought

it meant something when he told me he loved me and that I
was the best woman he'd ever been with and that he felt happier with me than he'd ever felt before. It just seemed perfect.
Not *too* perfect, but perfect the way it's supposed to be perfect.

"So what happened? One day Eddie starts moping around
and getting all hard to connect with. I don't say anything. I'm
thinking maybe it's his work, or something. Then I start asking
him what's wrong, and he says nothing's wrong. That goes on
for I guess three weeks. Then one Sunday morning we're fin-
ished reading the paper and it's strewn around all over the
place and Eddie actually uses those words, 'Listen, we've got
to talk.'

"Then from that cliché he goes to, 'It's not you, it's me.'
The idea is that he doesn't want to be with me anymore but
he doesn't know why. He just wants me to move out. We'll
always be friends, and he'll always love me, blah blah blah.
But I'm fired. It's over. And there's no reason. Just vague stuff
like it's not working out.

"So of course I'm in shock. But I'm not so much in shock
that I can't ask him every question I can think of. Is it something I did? No. Is there some way he wants me to change?
No. Is there another woman? No. Is he thinking he's gay? No.
Is it because of that time I got mad at him when he was so
late and I said what's the point, you'll never be a Russell
Banks? No, because he knew I didn't mean it. Is it because my
breasts are too small or my ass is too big? No, he likes my body.

"I could go on and on. Everything was perfect, wonderful,
I'm the greatest woman in the world, we have the best relationship in the world, but he's just not happy and he wants us to
break up.

"It just made me crazy. We had the kind of relationship
people try to break into, not break out of. Was I missing something? Was I blind? Was I stupid? What killed me was that I
kept having this feeling that there was this totally obvious reason behind what Eddie was saying and that everyone could see
it but me. You know, it hurt like hell to lose Eddie. There will

never be another Eddie in my life. But the real pain came from being so completely in the dark."

The emotional hallmarks of this experience. There are three things we all need. (1) To feel good about ourselves. (2) To feel we have some kind of control over our lives. (3) To feel we can make sense of what's going on around us. Think of these three as the three legs to the stool of emotional strength. With this experience all three legs are knocked out from under you so it's very likely that you'll feel you're going to crash.

You have the blow to your self-esteem that comes from being rejected. You feel helpless because you don't understand what's going on. And you feel driven crazy by your inability to find out what's going on.

No wonder women respond with extreme emotions to this form of breakup. Basically your emotions are in an uproar.

Diagnosis and prescription. If this feels like your story, here's what you should watch out for as you move into the future, because it's how women who've gone through a similar experience have gotten into trouble.

• *Where you might get stuck:* Can't-let-go-itis. Let's put ourselves inside the mind of a woman who's suffering from can't-let-go-itis. Her partner's just dumped her, but she doesn't know why. Because she can't find a reason, she thinks there's no good reason. The whole thing seems to her like a tragic mistake.

This is where you hear those words that are the hallmarks of can't-let-go-itis. *Made for each other. Meant to be.* "I just know we're made for each other." "I just know our love was meant to be."

If a woman is saying this, why would she let go?

Because there doesn't seem to be any reason, she concludes that her partner just doesn't know his own mind. Often women suffering from can't-let-go-itis say, "If there was a reason for us to break up, you'd tell me the reason." And then the person suffering from can't-let-go-itis does everything you can imagine, and a lot of things you can't imagine, to hang on to the relationship.

There are many ways to cling. One of the most common is to try to guilt your partner into staying. One of the most common forms this takes is saying, "You'll cripple our kids psychologically if you leave." Or you say, "I won't be able to survive without you." You might even threaten suicide. All because the breakup makes no sense to you.

Prescription. You're entitled to ask for two things if they're still possible, if your partner hasn't completely broken things off:

One, more time. You're entitled to ask for a period of time like a month or three months in which the two of you will just go on as if nothing had happened. At least this way, even if your partner still doesn't know why he wants to end things, you'll know for sure that he does want to end things.

Two, outside help. You're entitled to know that it's not some easily fixable problem that's causing this breakup. Maybe, for example, sex is good but it's just not great. You're entitled to know that it's not some dumb sexual problem that you could easily fix with the help of a good therapist.

Another kind of help might be individual therapy for your partner. Maybe he's going through some kind of weird, premature midlife crisis. Maybe he's scared about something going on inside him that he feels he can't talk to you about. All this can be resolved surprisingly quickly with a good therapist, and if the two of you have been together for any length of time, you're entitled to this attempt.

But if time doesn't make a difference and some therapy doesn't make a difference and your partner still has this desire to leave for no discernable reason, there's only one smart thing for you to do. You can destroy yourself fighting this and you can use yourself up trying to make sense of it. Or you can accept it and let it go. Think of yourself as one of those tornado survivors. You'll never know why your house was singled out, and you'll never be able to change what's happened. All you can do is say, "Sometimes things happen that don't make any sense." And move on.

Most women come through something like this and years later realize that their partner was doing them a favor. The point is that when the time is right for you, you will understand why this happened. At the very least you will understand why it was for the best.

• *Where you might get stuck:* "I won't stop until I find the answer." What you do here is stalk with words, rather than with actions. You're looking for answers, not reconciliation. You might be hoping for reconciliation, but you're putting all your energy into getting answers.

The most common form this takes is bugging your partner constantly, "Why? Why? Why?" Everything he says, every off-hand remark, every event in his day becomes a chance for you to unleash a torrent of questions.

This mild-sounding disease can actually be very deadly. I've seen women drive their friends away because they were so crazed by their search for understanding why they were dumped. I've seen women ruin every new relationship because they push the new guy to talk about the woman's old relationship. As if the new guy can give her insight into the old guy.

Most women eventually let go of their need to understand why. But in the meantime they waste time and make themselves miserable.

Prescription. First, ask yourself what your partner's most obvious reason might be to break up with you. What big, fat, simple, obvious reason is staring you in the face? I've seen so many cases where women were mystified even though the answer was right under their noses. If it had been a snake, it would've bit them.

For example, one couple had gone along for years fighting a lot when they were together but never really having much time together because of their work. Suddenly the guy says that he doesn't want to be married anymore but he doesn't know why. The woman wasn't stupid. She asked him, "Is it because of all our fighting and our not seeing each other much?" Bang. She hit it with her first shot. But he said no!

Who knows why? Maybe he said to himself that he'd stayed so long with all the fighting and not seeing each other that it couldn't be the reason. Maybe he thought that if he gave their old problem as the reason, she'd give him a huge argument.

The point is that if there's something that's obvious to you for why he would want out, *believe it* even if he denies it.

If this doesn't work, listen to what your partner says carefully. I've had couples sit in front of me talking about his not knowing why he wants to leave. She keeps saying why won't you tell me. He keeps saying I don't know. But I've been sitting there and I've heard him tell her very clearly why he wants out. He's just said it but neither of them can hear it.

How could this be? It's usually because the truth is too simple, too stupid, or too weird. For example, he says he doesn't know but then as a kind of throwaway he says, "Maybe I just need to live alone." Maybe he's telling the truth. Maybe that's exactly why he would walk out on a wonderful relationship with a wonderful woman like you—because he's never really lived alone and that's what he wants now.

Okay, suppose you've looked at the obvious reason and that doesn't make sense to you. Suppose you've sifted through what your partner has said and you really can't find anything there. Here's a mistake you must avoid. Don't, I repeat *don't*, push him for answers to your questions so passionately and persistently that he gets to the point where he's willing to say anything just to get you off his back.

Think about what you really need to know. Ask your partner something like this, "Look, I know you don't know why you want to end this relationship. But even if it's not a reason why you want out, can you give me any feedback for something you think I should do differently in my next relationship?" Maybe there's enough good feeling between the two of you for your partner to be willing to answer this question. And if he won't answer it, ask your friends. Listen to them.

Breakup Experience #4:

YOU MARRY A WORK-IN-PROGRESS, BUT HE NEVER MAKES ANY PROGRESS.

⊗

Carol's Story

"I take full responsibility for knowing that Jack was a fixer-upper. It's just that I thought I could fix him up. Jack was a lot like Kramer on *Seinfeld* when I met him. Jack had a trust fund that was just enough to pay the rent and buy some groceries and some new clothes once in a while. Like Kramer, Jack always had these ideas for businesses he was going to start. But that's never how you think about it starting out. You think, 'Oh, he's this really sweet, nice, wonderful guy, and he's smart, and he can do anything he wants, and I'm what's been missing. I'll be the difference between his staying in a rut and his zooming to the top.'

"Maybe I should've known what I was getting into, but Jack gave me a very mixed message at the beginning. He told me, 'I am what I am,' and that was my clue. But he also kept telling me about his hopes and dreams and plans. Then when we were falling in love he'd say things to me like, 'With you I know I can do anything.'

"I don't know how to describe what it was like. Every day I'd go to work. I'd come home. Some days Jack watched TV all day. Sometimes he'd spend a week at the library researching some idea he was trying to get going. When we got on the Internet he'd surf the web all day like there was a million bucks waiting for him on the web. To be fair, he did develop a couple of business plans. They seemed kooky to me. But Jack would do such a good job of selling them to me that it renewed my faith in him.

"Now here's where my problem came from. Jack never gave me a reason to stop loving him. So you love this guy and when do you say, 'Okay, that's it, he's never going anywhere'? And then when do you say, 'Okay that's it, he's never going anywhere *and for my own sake I've got to get out of this*'?

"But you know how it is. Sometimes love is like a balloon that floats above a world of pins. There's always something waiting to pop it. Things go along but guys like this always fuck up badly. Anyway, Jack got this idea for a web site that was going to make a ton of money. It was going to be a site you visit to get vicarious travel experiences. You know, you'd click on a link to some ongoing expedition to the North Pole or the Congo or something and all these travel companies would advertise like crazy on it.

"It was typical Jack. A great idea that he had nothing to offer in terms of the experience and savvy needed to develop it. But that wasn't the problem. The problem was that he took money from me without asking me to develop his idea.

"I'm glad he did, actually. That was the pin I needed to pop my balloon. I was still young enough to have babies, but I was way too old to stay married to a baby. I'm sorry I wasted so much of my time with him, but he cured me of my need to be needed. I'm with a great guy now. And we have a great life. And there's none of that stress from spending every day trying to roll a boulder up a hill."

The emotional hallmarks of this experience. To understand what it's like to be in a relationship like this emotionally, just think of the premise it's based on. There's this guy who's an underachiever or who's got problems but you think there's something special inside him that you'll be able to bring forth. You keep trying to bring it forth. It keeps not coming forth.

How else would you feel? You're mad, you're constantly disappointed. Worst of all, you're kept on the edge of your seat as if you're at some incredibly suspenseful movie. It's this constantly stimulated, teased, tantalized state you're kept in, hoping for change. And the thing is that to acknowledge he's failed you've got to acknowledge that you've failed. So you're always scared of connecting to a hopeless place inside you.

Diagnosis and prescription. If this feels like your story, here's what you should watch out for as you move into the future, because these are the ways women who've gone through a similar experience have gotten into trouble.

• *Where you might get stuck:* Love sucks. Just think about it. This whole experience was so exhausting, so frustrating, so disappointing, and wasted so much of your time and energy, that it's easy to conclude that love just ain't worth it. You'd have loved for things to work out. But they didn't. And the one thing you know is that you're not going to put yourself through this again. It's easy to see all guys as fixer-uppers to some degree. So why bother anymore? Plus you're angry. You had so much to give, and it all went to waste. Why put yourself through this again?

Prescription. What women suffering from a bad case of *love sucks* do is take themselves out of circulation. And that's the danger. Normally what would happen is that you'd need time to lick your wounds, but then your faith in love would reassert itself. But by taking yourself out of circulation, it gets harder and harder to overcome the mind-set that says you're better off living without love.

So what you have to do is this. Meet people. Go out with people. Get involved with people. Assume inside yourself that you won't get into a relationship. You're not looking for someone now. You're just staying in circulation because it's healthy, because isolation is a recipe for disaster. You don't have to get involved with anyone you don't want to.

There is one thing to watch out for. Some of us are really stubborn. We feel, okay, I couldn't help this guy but maybe I'll be able to help the next guy. All I can say is that if you get involved with two fixer-upper guys who both turn out to be major disappointments, run, don't walk to the best therapist you can find and get whatever help you need to never make this mistake again.

• *Where you might get stuck:* "I'm poison." If you come through a situation of trying to help a partner who just won't benefit from what you have to offer, it's common to conclude that it was your fault. You thought you were good for him. You intended to be good for him. But you were really bad for him. You're poison! you think.

Prescription. This one is easy. Your partner was a grown man capable of making his own decisions. He did make decisions. Plenty of them. And obviously far too many of those decisions were bad. But he made the decisions, not you. The point is that you were *present* during your partner's failure to make progress, but that doesn't mean that you were *responsible* for his failure to make progress. So unless you made all the bad decisions, you're not poison.

What you need is an outside opinion you respect. You need someone you can tell your story to who could point out your mistakes, if you made any—things you did that hurt your partner. Someone who would be in a position to know if those mistakes were normal errors anyone might've made, or if they came from real problems you have that'll cause you to make the same mistakes over and over.

It sounds like I'm talking about seeing a therapist—and that might be just the thing for you. But what you really need is someone wise, experienced, and objective. And that could be a clergy person, an aunt, an old sorority sister, your actual sister, or indeed a therapist. Anyone who would be in a position to say, "Here's what you did wrong, here's how these were perfectly natural mistakes, and here's where these mistakes came from."

Breakup Experience #5:

YOU'VE BEEN SHIT ON AND TOLD YOU'RE SHIT.

☙

Sally's Story

"I just wanted a little respect, but I could never do anything right as far as he was concerned. Forget things like how I parked the car or how I paid the bills. Let's just talk about girl stuff. I bought the wrong makeup, according to him. I didn't dress right. I bought the wrong bras. *He thought I was stupid for using tampons.* Do you understand what I'm saying? He was a bigger expert than I was on feminine hygiene.

"For a long time the whole situation was very confusing. For one thing, a lot of the time he was a really nice guy. He was a big present buyer, you know, he'd come home with flowers or jewelry. But even then there was an undercurrent of, I don't know, it was like look at how wonderful I am for buying you presents.

"He was also a really smart guy. And a lot of his criticisms were valid, I guess. I might as well just say it—he was a lot smarter than I was, or am. So you could look at our relationship and say, well, I had a lot to learn and he was there to teach me. That was what hooked me. I kept thinking that if I hung in there I'd finally 'get it' and then he'd think I was wonderful and I'd probably be close to perfect at that point. I don't know, I was young and you just want to please your husband.

"What tore it for me was when our kids got to be school age. That's when I realized that Duncan was putting me down in front of my kids. He was putting me down *to* my kids. He'd explain to them why they should listen to him, not to me. He once said to them, 'Your mother's a good person but she's not very smart'—and I'll never forget to my dying day how I felt when I heard him say that. I mean it was one thing for him to destroy my self-respect. But to destroy my children's ability to respect their mother . . .

"Thank God for my job. This whole time I was supposed to be so stupid I was working at the animal hospital where I'd started out as a billing clerk and I eventually became business manager of the entire hospital, and it's a big one. I basically run the whole thing except for the veterinarian side of it. And I'd be sitting around the office and of course we'd all complain about our husbands but believe me I was the only woman who *everyone* told, 'Honey, you've got to get out of that relationship.'

"So being the stupid klutz that I am I got this really smart lawyer and I got a really good deal on my divorce. It was funny because my ex-husband would complain about how he got shafted and his friends would say how could you have gotten shafted if your wife was so stupid? And he'd say, well she had a smart lawyer, but it looked very lame.

"I'm in a good place now. Believe me, I'm in no rush to get married again. But I'm lucky, I date a lot. And I just won't put up with any guy who doesn't treat me very well. But it's been hard. You're sort of brainwashed. You've sort of got to believe that all the ways you're being criticized are true, because if they're not true, then why aren't you getting out of there immediately? So you stay because you believe they're true, and you believe they're true because you stay. I guess the point is that you really don't know who you are. Going through something like this is like you've been broken up into little pieces and you've got to find a way to put yourself back together again. I know who I am now, and I like myself, but it's been hard."

The emotional hallmarks of this experience. Self-esteem is an overworked word. But this experience strikes at the heart of your self-esteem. When you're told you're stupid, it makes you very anxious, like when you were in the fourth grade and got called up in front of the class to do math problems on the blackboard. You're constantly afraid you're going to make some mistake.

Then you start believing there's something wrong with you. And that creates a sense of despair. It's easy to feel you're just not worth much.

But of course most women come through this and survive it intact. Once you reclaim the knowledge that you're someone worthwhile, you can feel your worth in a positive way that most women just take for granted. You actually get the opportunity to savor how much you have going for you.

Diagnosis and prescription. If this feels like your story, here's what you should watch out for as you move into the future, because it's how women who've gone through a similar experience have gotten into trouble.

• *Where you might get stuck:* The incredible shrinking woman. When you've been relentlessly criticized, you shrink. That's what I've seen for twenty-five years of working with women whose parents or boyfriends or husbands subjected them to merciless criticisms. If he's making you a target, make yourself a smaller target, and maybe you won't be hit so often.

This shrinking of yourself takes place in parts of life you might've called your own. If you'd been called stupid for your political opinions, for example, you'll stop issuing forth your political opinions. If you'd been criticized for the way you are in bed during lovemaking, where will you get the sexual confidence necessary to make love with someone else?

Every part of you that's been criticized is at risk of disappearing. I've seen women who were kind, smart, loving mothers get to the point where they couldn't make decisions for their kids because they're told they're stupid.

Now you might say, "How can this happen? Just because someone puts you down doesn't mean you have to believe it. You don't give in. You fight back." Theoretically that's true. And most women do that in some ways. My husband thinks I'm a bad driver, but I think I'm a good driver, so screw him. Sometimes it's that simple.

You have the problem because you stayed in the relationship. Why did you stay? You thought there was something there for you. You thought he had something to offer. You wanted to believe he had something to offer. And that's how psychologically you'd been led to feel there must be truth somewhere in his criticisms. Because if some of his criticisms were true, your world made sense. Yeah he made you feel bad by telling you how stupid you were, but you were stupid in a lot of ways, you thought. At least he was telling the truth.

Women get out of these relationships only when they realize that their husband wasn't really interested in telling the truth. Instead he was interested in power, in putdowns, in making himself feel good by making you look bad.

The best way to diagnose this problem, I've found, is to make a list of the parts of your life that are important to you— for example, your job, being a mother, being a friend, being a sister, being some guy's girlfriend. Now for each of these items write down three or four things that you think someone who does it needs to do well.

For example, you might put down that to be a good mother you have to be a good disciplinarian, and you have to be able to help them with their homework. And to be good on your job you have to be able to plan ahead, pay attention to details, and keep everyone happy.

Okay, now look at your list of all the things in your life that are important to you that you need to do well. Here's the critical question: *How many of these things do you feel you actually do well?* You should feel you do the majority of them quite well indeed. Sure, maybe there are one or two or even three things you don't feel you do well. That's okay. But if, for example, you don't feel that you can do well half the things you should be doing well in your life, and you're coming out of one of these relationships where you've been made to feel like crap, then I think you're suffering from the incredible shrinking woman syndrome.

If it looks like that to you too, do a check to confirm it. Have you actually started to shrink your life because of your sense that you don't do things very well? If so, that's just more evidence.

Prescription. Rebuilding your self-esteem is a lot easier than you might think. There are three ingredients: new feedback, a new attitude, and new growth. Let's take these one at a time:

1. *New feedback.* Those parts of your life you think you're not so good at—maybe you're better than you think. You'd be amazed at how many women think they're bad at this or bad at that and then they talk to their friends or coworkers and find that they're perfectly okay.

I knew one woman who constantly complained about how disorganized she was, particularly at work, although she had a responsible job as an executive assistant to a senior vice president of a big downtown bank. It's true that her desk was a mess. And she did give the impression of being a juggler with just one ball too many up in the air. But at my urging she went to her boss for an evaluation.

He told her, "My job is too important to keep you on if you couldn't do your job. I have to tell you that at first you scared me because watching you work is like watching someone roller skate around the rim of a volcano. But you've got it all together. You do what needs to be done, you do it on time, and you do it right. And you know, that desk of yours. I was going to ask you to clean it up, but people think I'm incredibly busy when they see what your desk looks like, and so in a crazy way it makes me look good."

So check it out. You might be doing a lot better than you think.

2. *New attitude.* Okay, so maybe some people would think that the way you do things isn't perfect. So what? Sometimes the self-esteem problem can be solved by taking on a whole new attitude. This attitude is based on a what I call the Sinatra Principle: "Hey, you do things your way. I'll do things mine." You know, "I did it my way."

All those criticisms you've gotten? It's just a matter of style. You've been criticized for not helping the kids more with their homework? Hey, your style is to help them learn to be responsible for themselves. You've been criticized for being illogical? Hey, you're an intuitive person.

So maybe you're not perfect, but the way you do things is just fine. Not the wrong way, just your way. And this is important because a lot of women coming out of a relationship with an overly critical partner were put down for the crime of having a different opinion on how to do things. And that's no crime at all.

3. *New growth.* The reason you become the incredible shrinking woman is that for all his criticisms your partner made you feel that you really couldn't do any better than you're doing. You shrank from doing an activity because you gave up on it. Now if you really do need to improve in some area, and you can't get away with saying that it's just "your style," then you'll have to do better. Well, what's wrong with that? Thinking that you don't do something well is not a psychiatric disease, it's an opportunity to do it better. Your ex-partner's crime wasn't so much criticizing you as making you think you couldn't do better. So do better!

I'm not going to insult your intelligence by giving you examples. There is no area of existence where you and I can't do better if we decide to do better. There are just two necessary ingredients: You have to decide that you need to do better; you have to be open to feedback. That's it. And by "feedback" I don't mean criticism. Criticism is "The way you do it sucks." Feedback is "Here's a better way to do it."

Here's what you have to watch out for if you're going to choose the new growth option. Growth means accepting that your way of doing things in a specific area is not good enough. But if you feel very badly about yourself you might have an unconscious agenda to turn every situation into one where you end up feeling that your way is the right way. You say you want growth, but you really want attitude. Fine, but you've

got to make up your mind. An openness, a humility is necessary for the growth option. A willingness to do things differently. If you're going to be open to growth, you have to be
willing to change.

Breakup Experience #6:

WE JUST GREW APART.

☙

Gloria's Story

It happens. It's sad. But it's not necessarily tragic. People do
grow. Growth is complicated. So growing in sync is hard.

Growing apart is not inevitable because there are also forces
in a relationship which pull you together, which drive you to
coordinate things. One of you moves in a certain direction
because the other has moved in that direction. So any two people starting out on a relationship that can last a lifetime can
be very hopeful about the possibility of growing together. But
sometimes you do grow apart and it's no one's fault.

"I'm a furniture restorer and I see it in my work how you
can replace one thing on a piece of furniture and then another
thing and then another thing and then at some point you cross
some line and it's no longer the original piece of furniture. The
original piece is completely gone. That's what happened with
my lover and me. We started out so much the same. You know
how you're sometimes attracted to someone because she's so
different and sometimes you're attracted because you're totally
in sync with each other and you like all the same things.

"That's how it was with us. We met at one of these wom-
en's music concerts which, let's face it, can be big Lesbian meat
markets, but they're great for meeting someone. I was really
into the music and there was Jenny, and she was really into it
too. We started talking and we were just the same about so
many things. There's all this talk about being your own person

and having your own space, but Jenny and I were totally into finding a soulmate. And that's what we found in each other.

"I don't know where to begin. Okay, you could begin with the way our day begins. We both like getting up and grinding our coffee fresh. We like making a big hearty breakfast. The kind nobody makes anymore—pancakes, sausages, scrambled eggs, berries in a bowl. We'd do that every day.

"Okay, that's superficial. Much more important I thought we both had this big belief in craftsmanship. We were so similar, I thought. I restore furniture, Jenny did landscape design. It wasn't supposed to be about money. And it wasn't supposed to be about work—I mean in the sense of work, work, work, all day long, nothing but. It's not like we didn't talk about this. Jenny was the one who said a day should be like a work of art, with everything in balance, and that's of course exactly how I felt.

"I used to blame Jenny for our growing apart. But it was me too. I really do see that now. But it's still sad. Anyway, it doesn't matter who started it. We just got so out of sync. I started getting into historically accurate furniture restoration because I wanted to get into museum work. So I had to do a lot of studying, and I admit that I started making less money. It's just that it wasn't supposed to be about the money.

"But maybe I scared Jenny when my income fell. I take responsibility for that. Anyway she's busy with her landscape work, and so she gets these ideas for making money in real estate. It started with this one house that was okay but had terrible grounds. Jenny had this inheritance. It wasn't a lot but it was enough to put a down payment on the house and pay expenses while she was redoing the landscape. I guess the real estate market took a good bounce at the right time for her, and she made a lot of money from that one house and she just kind of went *boinggg!* at the idea of making money.

"I say this now but back then for Jenny it was more like oh, this is fun, and I get to make houses really beautiful and I have more control, so it was cool. Okay, look, this is painful for me to talk about because it was like death from a thousand paper cuts for us. At first nothing had changed, but everything had changed. Next thing you know I'm becoming like this poor, dedicated furniture scholar and Jenny's like this wheeling dealing real estate developer and it's all just money, money, money with her. There were so many things. I'd get in the car and turn on the radio after she'd driven it and it would be turned to these junky AM talk radio stations. What else? Suddenly Jenny's got to look good. So our food has to change. It had been such an important point for us not to fall into that women-having-to-diet thing. But now Jenny won't look at a pancake.

"I could go on and on. At some point you look at your partner and you say if I'd just met this person today I wouldn't even talk to her, much less fall in love with her and everything."

The emotional hallmarks of this experience. People have two very different experiences of this. Usually both people change, but one of you has usually changed more than the other, sometimes a lot more.

If you're the person who's done most of the changing, you're apt to have a sense of impatience and disappointment. You were moving forward, growing. Your partner stayed stuck. You kept trying to get him to keep up with you. He wouldn't, or couldn't. By the time it was all over you may have wondered what in the world you saw in that person in the first place.

If your partner's the one who's done most of the changing, you probably feel betrayed and abandoned. Adultery isn't the only form of betrayal. And walking out isn't the only form of abandonment. New interests, new philosophies, new lifestyles, new friends are all ways of leaving you for someone or something else.

Diagnosis and prescription. If growing apart like this feels like your story, here's what you should watch out for as you move into the future, because it's how women who've gone through a similar experience have gotten into trouble.

• *Where you might get stuck:* "It's hard for me to really believe we're similar." If you felt incredibly connected to someone and then you mysteriously grew apart, it's easy to become very wary next time out. There you are dating and you meet someone with whom you seem especially in sync, why won't you and this new person grow apart too? Usually this condition of suspecting you'll never find the right person doesn't kick in the first time you break up with someone because the two of you grew apart, but if it's happened a couple of times, then it's easy to not get turned on by the sense of connection that's so important in launching a new relationship.

A lot of women who make a big deal about wanting to go slowly when a relationship's starting have been hurt by the experience of growing apart in a previous relationship. You can recognize that this applies to you by gauging your sense of suspicion and distance, your disbelief at whatever connections you happen to feel with a new person.

Prescription. The solution to the problem is to check each other out much more carefully than you did before. Let me tell you something I think is pretty important. All those "surprising" ways people grow apart: the clues are there from the beginning. For example, over the past fifteen years my husband's gotten increasingly involved in studying medieval history. Who is this strange man studying medieval history in my house?

But you know, all the clues were there. Way back at the beginning, he'd told me stories about how some history course or project had been the most important thing to him in high school or even elementary school. He'd told me about a conversation he'd had with a professor in college about majoring in history. And all I have to do is look into our library to see evidence of history books he's read during every one of the more than thirty years we've been together. Even in the field of psychology and psychotherapy which we share, he's had an unusual interest in the history of various approaches to mental illness.

Now here's where I made a mistake. And here's where you

have to avoid making a mistake. I wasn't all that interested in history. So I conveniently formed an image of my husband that left out that part of his personality. We don't see what we don't want to see.

So as you start meeting new people be open to everything they have to tell you about themselves. Find out all different kinds of things about them. Don't dismiss some aspect of who they are because it doesn't fit in with who you are. Look for all the seeds. Assume any seed you find today could sprout tomorrow. If you can't live with its sprouting, this is not a relationship you want to be in. *That's* how to prevent the two of you from growing apart once you get going.

Think of it like this: what you don't pay attention to is what will haunt you later. There's no guarantee that the person you get involved with won't change and grow and zig and zag. It's not "growing apart" if you understand and welcome those changes, and if you're not surprised by them. You'll be able to welcome the changes if you know about them from the beginning. *And you will know about them from the beginning if you listen carefully to what your future partner has to tell you.*

Breakup Experience #7:

SOMETHING HAPPENED TO TURN YOUR WORLD UPSIDE DOWN.

&

Zoe's Story

"I'm okay now. I always say that these days because I know that I really scared all the people who care about me. I basically tried to kill myself when I took all those pills. I'll never know how serious I really was—I'd like to think I wasn't all that serious. But I was playing Russian roulette with three bullets in the gun.

"It's funny how back then I didn't think there was anything else I could do. My world was perfect. We'd been married for twenty-four years. The youngest kid was away at college. I'd spent years looking forward to the time when we could be lovebirds again. Now it was our time, I thought.

"I was realistic. Harvey had always been busy with his law practice. Actually, he'd never been home all that much. But he'd always been incredibly nice to me. None of the other husbands in my circle were as nice to their wives. And he'd always talked vaguely of slowing down and cutting back. Thanks to all his hard work taking time for ourselves was something I thought we could afford to do.

"Here's how I first found out. My daughter was home from college for a long weekend and we'd gone clothes shopping. We'd gotten back to the car and I was about to pull out of the spot when my daughter said, 'Wait a second. Before we go. I've wanted to ask you this. Who's that woman Daddy sees?'

"I just couldn't take in her question. I mean I just didn't know what those words meant. What woman does 'Daddy see'? He sees his secretary. He sees clients. He sees our friends. I felt it was very hard to breathe. I knew Cindy was telling me something that was going to ruin my life. It's like someone hands you a pink slip and says, 'Here, your life is destroyed now.' I just felt all that immediately. It's bizarre, isn't it? I would've bet my life that everything was perfect. But when my daughter said, 'Who's that woman Daddy sees?' I knew it was all over.

"I didn't think I could let my daughter see me deal with this. So I said, 'Oh, she's a woman your father helps.' That was it. He was a helper.

"I didn't say a word to Harvey about this for two weeks. Those two weeks of silence, of being in the dark, of knowing everything but knowing nothing—those were the worst two weeks of my life. All because I simply didn't know the words to use to talk to Harvey about this.

"Finally, it was a Saturday night and we went out for dinner and we went to a movie like a normal couple, although that was something we almost never did. When we got home he went to the den to watch TV while he was waiting for me to get ready for bed. I looked at myself for a minute in the bathroom mirror and I remember looking at my face and saying to myself, 'What a pretty woman.' It broke my heart. I'm looking in the mirror and I'm thinking I'm so pretty, and I have nothing. I walked down to the den, turned off the TV, and said to Harvey, 'I know about that woman.'

"Of course he goes, 'What woman?' and I go, 'Come on, Harvey. The woman. I know about it. Just tell me the whole story.' I was acting like I just wanted to know the truth, like I was strong and our being honest with each other was what was really important. But it wasn't really like that. I wanted Harvey to lie. I wanted Harvey to tell me I was pretty and there never was any other woman, and never would be. I'm probably kidding myself but I think if Harvey had done a really good job of lying everything would've been fine. All I wanted was to get back what I'd thought I'd had.

"I guess I meant so little to him that he told me the whole story right then and there. He didn't leave out anything to spare my feelings. It was so, so much worse than I could possibly have imagined.

"I really don't want to go into the details. Basically he'd been with this other woman for over twenty years. She had a child that was his. I even knew her. I saw her in church on Sundays. She sat in the back. I'd always thought of her as this struggling single mother who was a secretary at the high school. I'd always wondered how she managed. Harvey'd first known her because she'd worked as a secretary for his law firm when they started getting involved. She was his emotional wife. I was his social wife. No wonder he was so nice to me. He'd always had very good manners.

"I should've thrown him out, and I would've been entitled to, but somehow the whole story made me feel homeless, like even my own house didn't belong to me. So I went to a hotel, and just like in those short stories, that's where I tried to kill myself.

"When I say I'm okay now, the pluses are that I'm still close to my children and I managed to get a very good divorce settlement. I was very clear about wanting to take Harvey to the cleaners, and I think I did, although I never went back to our house.

"I like my life now. I just don't think I'll ever get married again."

The emotional hallmarks of this experience. Intense emotions. Devastation. A sense that the world no longer makes sense and you no longer have the ability to figure it out. Imagine someone deliberately pulling the rug out from under you. That's what this sensation feels like. Except the pain is deeper. The anger is bigger. The fear is broader. And the person who did it to you is the person you trusted most to take care of you.

Diagnosis and prescription. If this feels like your story, here's what you should watch out for as you move into the future, because it's how women who've gone through a similar experience have gotten into trouble.

• *Where you might get stuck:* Hidden depression. When you've been as royally and profoundly dumped as Zoe was, of course you're going to be thrown into a terrible grief. In a way losing your husband the way Zoe did is worse than losing your husband to death. When your husband dies, you lose the future, but you've still got the past. Zoe was robbed of her future in a way that stole her past as well. Her husband snatched from her all her happy memories.

But at least intense grief is visible. What I'm worried about here is hidden depression. Hidden depression occurs when you're among the walking wounded. You get up in the morning and get dressed and go to work and come home and go to bed. You talk to the people you have to talk to. You say the things you're expected to say. If you're expected to sound chipper, you'll sound chipper, because paradoxically enough you're too depressed to take the risk of revealing how depressed you really are. It's as if you're watching TV and for some reason the color goes out and the sound goes off and suddenly, your favorite show is silent and in black and white. Everyone is there as before, but they're just going through the motions and it's all gray to you.

Here are some signs that you may be suffering from hidden depression. For each one of these ask yourself, "Does this apply to me?"

- "I just can't make up my mind about things anymore. When faced with a decision I just don't decide."
- "I'm really not interested in the things I used to be interested in."
- "There were things I was working toward at work or in my personal life, but I've pretty much given up on them."
- "My sleeping patterns have been completely different for the last several weeks from the way they've been before."
- "My eating patterns have been completely different for the last several weeks from the way they've been before."
- "When people I cared about call, I talk to them but I'm not interested."
- "I've recently started drinking to excess or taking drugs."
- "I'm restless much of the time. Things I used to be able to sit still for, like reading or watching TV or doing the crosswords, I can't concentrate on anymore. It's as if the things that used to satisfy me just annoy me now."

If *two or more* of the above apply to you, and if it's been more than eight weeks since your relationship fell apart, then you are very likely suffering from hidden depression.

Prescription. You need help. You may be in serious trouble. Yes, the state you're in might disappear all by itself. That could happen. In the same way, that lump you discover in your breast could dissolve all by itself too. *But are you willing to take the risk?*

You must get help immediately. Call your doctor right now and tell her that you need a referral to a psychiatrist or psychotherapist. If you already know the name of a psychiatrist or psychotherapist because of a previous recommendation or because you've had a good experience with that therapist, call up that person immediately and make an appointment.

The good news about depression is that it's overwhelmingly likely that treatment will be successful. You can't count on getting better by yourself. You will get better if you get help.

Moving On

There are two ways to look at the death of a relationship. Before it happens, you want to look at it as a tragedy you'll do anything to avoid. Because, make no mistake about it, the *unnecessary* death of love is a tragedy.

And after the death of a relationship, the only way to look at it is as part of nature's plan. It's a way of clearing the decks. It's a way of liberating you from stress and pain and difficulty. It's a way of opening up a world of new options to you.

The only thing worse than the death of love is getting so stuck that you can't move on to enjoy the world of opportunity that lies in front of you. This is the time when old wounds get restimulated. Old angers cause women to get inappropriately angry now and spoil a good thing. Old fears can lead women to run away from something wonderful. They can even lead you to run into the arms of someone dreadful. But if you understand how you've gotten stuck and what there is to do about it, none of this is necessary.

If all the women in the world who've been through what you're going through now could raise their voices in chorus, they'd say: yes, you cry; yes, you rub your wounds; yes, you work through your fears; but ultimately you open your life to the wonderful new things that are in store for you that you would never have known otherwise.

SEVEN

I Feel the Earth Move

Make-or-Break Experience #5:
Getting the Best Out of Both Love and Sex

We all hope for the same thing. We want true love and good sex to come together, so to speak. A full *91 percent of women today say they'd be disappointed if they fell in love with someone and then it turned out that sex with the person wasn't good.* Well, good for you. You're right to want the best when it comes to love. And you understand that "good sex" isn't some abstract thing. It's all about being true to yourself, your needs, your feelings, the way you work as a sexual being.

But how do you make it happen?

The myth about women is that love and sex always go hand-in-glove. You know: "I can't sleep with someone unless I have feelings for him, and then love makes everything good." The truth about women is that we'd like love and sex to go together, but sometimes they're not in sync at all.

Deeply entwined as they are, love and sex are different. Sometimes you want to be loved. Sometimes you want to get laid. Sometimes sex is a wild card, sometimes it's the main card. Sometimes it's a delicious accompaniment to love, sometimes it's the hidden reason for love. Sometimes it keeps the ship of love afloat, sometimes it torpedoes the ship of love.

You're not always the same person either. Day to day, year
to year, your priorities shift. Most of us can look back on that
one year when we slept around too much.

So let's talk about that turf where romantic needs and sexual needs collide in the night. As one woman put it, "The man
you love is supposed to be the man who meets your needs
sexually. But what if it's not so simple?" Usually it's not so
simple. There are people who are great in your bed who somehow can't find their way into your heart. *I asked women, "Did
you ever have this experience: there was a guy you really wanted
to sleep with—but you didn't love him or even want to love him?"
Sixty-two percent of women acknowledged they'd felt this way.
More than half of the women who'd had this experience said
they'd not only felt that way but actually slept with the guy.*

There are people you let into your heart who don't work all
that well in your bed. *I asked women if this had ever happened to
them: "Were you ever in a relationship where you loved the guy,
but the sexual chemistry between you wasn't so great?" Seventy-
four percent of women said that had happened to them.*

But just think about what this does to the battle between
hope and discouragement in the land of love. Love is hard
enough. Sex is hard. Now you want to fit the two together!
Here's the make-or-break part of this experience. Will you end
up concluding that it's just too much to hope for real love and
good sex together? Or will you find a way to keep alive your
hope that real love can be filled with great sex?

It's like going to a restaurant that's supposed to have great
food and expecting you'll get great service too. But wait a minute—you *can* get great food and get great service at a lot of
restaurants. It happens every day. And it happens every day
that you get what you're looking for when it comes to both
love and sex in the same relationship.

Hitting the Jackpot

As I've talked to women over the years, I've learned that there
are two things we need here. We need a sense of sharing and

perspective, a way of fitting our own experience into the experiences of other women. We need to know we're not alone and that there's nothing wrong with us.

And we need answers. To the extent that we can't make love and sex work together, we need a way to diagnose how we've gotten into trouble, and then we need directions for how to get back on track. You see, because it's so easy for love and lust to pull us in different directions, it's easy to fall into traps. It's easy to get lost. And that's too bad because most of us can be doing a lot better than we are. We care about love and want more of it in our lives. We want more good sex too. Why shouldn't we have both?

The Three Permissions

For once I'm going to give you the solution before I help you figure out exactly what the problem is. You're going to discover something amazing. Whatever problem you've had that's prevented love and sex from coming together for you in the same relationship—all these problems arise because we think something is forbidden to us that is actually permitted us.

I'd like to present to you what the Chinese might call The Three Permissions. These are attitudes or feelings or approaches to life that women today *desperately* need to give themselves permission to hold on to. If you've been struggling with love and sex, it's because you haven't given yourself one of The Three Permissions.

THE THREE PERMISSIONS

1. "I give myself permission to desire sex and feel satisfied with sex even when it occurs outside of a committed relationship, even when it occurs with a relative stranger, even when I have no intention of ever seeing this person again. Wanting sex doesn't make me a bad person, nor does it mean I won't be a loving, faithful person when I'm ready."

The First Permission says that sex is important in and of itself. And it says that you have a right to make decisions about your sexuality. And it says that if you act thoughtfully you have a right to trust the decisions you make on the basis of your sexuality.

2. "I give myself permission to accept that love is real and true and permanent even if the sex isn't all I'd like it to be. Good sex enhances love, but good sex doesn't confirm love."

     The Second Permission says that sex and love are different. You can make whatever decisions you want about a relationship, but love stands on its own. Love doesn't need sex to validate love.

3. "I give myself permission to find love, to be loved, to feel love—no matter what I think is wrong with me, no matter what I've missed out on, no matter how much bad luck I've had. I'm entitled to all the love in the world, even with my imperfections."

     The Third Permission says that you're not defined by your past. You're not trapped by your past. You're not condemned to endlessly repeat your past. You're entitled to love and capable of love, even though your past might seem to condemn you.

Reread each of these. Ask yourself, "Do I really, deeply, truly in my heart of hearts, give myself each of these Three Permissions?" *You need to say* yes *to this question.*

Here's how to know you've given yourself The Three Permissions.

1. *Do you feel it?* Let's take the first permission, for example. I know you're not a slut, and you don't want to be a slut. That's not what you're giving yourself permission for here. But suppose it should happen that you wanted to have sex with someone—maybe even did have sex with someone—you might

not ever see again. Can you feel inside yourself, "Look, I've got to trust myself. I can feel okay about doing this."

Let's be clear about what you're actually giving yourself permission to do. You're not saying it's okay to cheat on your lover. You're not saying it's okay to run around like a tramp. You're not saying it's okay to be used and abused. You're not saying you would sleep with any scummy guy just because you felt horny.

What you *are* saying is that you can feel that it *would* be okay—if the situation were right, if you freely chose to do it— to have sex with someone just because you wanted to have sex with him.

If you really *feel* that *yes* this is okay for you, then that's one sign that you've given yourself The First Permission. The same with the other two.

2. *Do you live it?* This is a check on whether you're kidding yourself when you say you feel it. For example, you may feel you've given yourself permission to accept that love can be real, true, and permanent even if sex isn't all you'd like it to be—The Second Permission—but that's only a theory if the minute you're disappointed in sex you begin to doubt your love.

Now let's see how you might've gotten stuck somewhere with this make-or-break experience.

The Five Dilemmas of Sex and Love

In our attempt to strike some sort of balance between our sexual needs and our love needs, we keep falling into the same dilemmas. The good news is that there is a way out of all of these sex-love dilemmas. You just have to see which dilemma you've been wrestling with and then follow the prescription I offer.

Dilemma #1:

**IF I'M INVOLVED BECAUSE OF THE SEX, I MUST BE FEELING LOVE TOO,
BECAUSE OTHERWISE I'M JUST A TRAMP.**

Tracy's Story

Many women, at some point, go through a period, maybe a
long period, of having too much sex with too many people they
don't really know. Sometimes this can create serious problems.

Tracy's thirty-six now, and her promiscuous days ended a
long time ago, but it's taken her years to recover from the
repercussions. Lust would lead her into a guy's bed. Much
sweating and moaning and crying out would take place. Orgasms would blossom in the night. But then, wide awake in
the darkness, when everything was still except the thoughts
racing in her brain, Tracy would start playing cat's cradle with
the feelings in her heart, and out of a mere thread of nothing
she would convince herself that she loved this guy with whom
she'd just had sex she'd thought was meaningless. Like eating
potato chips and falling in love with the empty bag.

It was simply that she couldn't allow herself to feel lust
without thinking it was love. The guy had gone to bed with
what he'd thought was this cool chick who just wanted to get
laid. But the woman he woke up with had fallen in love with
him. She'd say things like, "Hey, you know you're great." Or,
"You know, I think maybe we've got something going here."
Or, "Listen, do you like me?"

If he was a "nice guy," maybe he'd play out the string a
little, go along with it, appease her, get a little more sex out of
her. If he wasn't such a "nice guy," he'd say, "What the hell's
wrong with you?" and throw her out.

Either way Tracy kept getting badly hurt, over and over.
Just because what started out as an arrangement based on lust
turned into a conviction that if she's feeling all this lust, then
it must be love.

How could she keep on making this mistake? When the lust that brought her to the guy's bed had been satisfied and she was left lying there in the wet spot next to some stranger, she started feeling like a horny tramp, just the way you feel hungry before you eat that first Oreo and like a total piece of crap a minute after you've polished off the last one in the package. And it's a horrible feeling.

You've been caught in Dilemma #1 if you keep having experiences like Tracy's. Your willingness or eagerness to have sex hooks you up with guys, and whenever you start having sex with a guy you start thinking you are in love with him. He might like you a little, but he barely knows you. You might like him a little, but you certainly like him way less than you think you do. Again and again you crash through into the icy water of rejection and abandonment.

Does this scenario seem familiar to you? If you're still not sure, the key is this. Too many sexual encounters with too many men, too many experiences where you hoped you'd found love but didn't. You look for love but you keep ending up with sex.

If this applies to you, then you fall into the group of women who are struggling with Dilemma #1.

Prescription. Why would a woman feel that if she had sex with a guy, she must love him? Because she's not given herself The First Permission. That's why they're falling in love with the guys they have sex with. They feel it's not permitted to have sex without love. Check it out. Ask yourself *Do I feel it?* and *Do I live it?* when it comes to The First Permission.

Probably not. Just think about it. Why else would you be feeling you have to love someone just because you've had sex with him?

You can see how dangerous it is not to give yourself The First Permission. It means you're letting your genitals, not your heart, choose your soulmate for you. *The First Permission means that your genitals can be busy whatever way they want to, but your heart still can and will take its time to find the right person for you.*

The First Permission is important even if your religious beliefs make you feel it's wrong to have sex outside of marriage. By all means stay true to your religious convictions. But let's tell the truth to each other as women. Good little Catholic girls, born-again Christians, and Orthodox Jewish women can be just as horny as anyone else. Suppose we should happen to have sex without love? We would need as much if not more protection than any other woman from feeling we've got to fall in love with a guy just because we slept with him. Don't add to the sin of fornication the even worse sin of concocting a love that's really a lie.

To feel safe accepting your sexuality, pledge not to do anything that will make you feel ashamed of yourself. Never sleep with a guy you'd feel ashamed showing off to your friends. Never do anything when you sleep with a guy you'd be ashamed to tell your friends about. This way you'll draw a line. You can accept your sexuality and at the same time reject anything self-destructive about your sexuality. If you refuse to let yourself be trampled, then you're not a tramp.

Dilemma #2:

I'M IN LOVE BUT I DON'T FEEL TURNED ON.
SO IT CAN'T REALLY BE LOVE, CAN IT?

&

Pamela's Story

At twenty-nine Pamela is in the most committed, serious relationship of her life so far. It was shortly after she moved to Paris to work in the office of an American fashion magazine that Pamela met Madeleine, a brilliant young geneticist at the Sorbonne and the daughter of an important French politician.

She was the best woman Pamela had ever gotten involved

with, and she felt she could truly love Madeleine. They moved
in together and within a year had the unspoken sense that they
could be a couple forever. They even talked about having a
marriage ceremony. Madeleine's parents liked Pamela very
much. Their only fear was that Pamela would take their daughter back to America at some point.

It all sounds nice, but there's a bug in this salad. Madeleine
is a nerd. A rich, French Lesbian nerd, but a nerd nonetheless.
Pamela's girlfriends up until now had all been glamour cakes.
Runway model types. Tough, pantherlike lipstick Lesbians in
motorcycle jackets. And so Madeleine just didn't make Pamela
hot. Sex was okay, but it wasn't great. And this was weird:
sex had always been very important to Pamela, but with the
woman who was possibly the love of her life sex meant little.
All the other women she'd been with treated sex like it was
the big moment. The payoff. Madeleine treated sex like an
unwelcome afterthought to the cuddling that she craved.

This put Pamela in a terrible dilemma. Where had her sexual feelings gone to? Sex and love had always been tied together. Deep down she wondered, "If she doesn't do anything
for me sexually, how can I say I really love her? Maybe I'm
just kidding myself. Maybe I've been so hungry to have a smart
rich woman think I'm great and want to take care of me that I
just tell myself it's love. My heart says it's love, but my libido's
whispering that my heart is lying."

Pamela's story had a happy ending. And there's an important moral here for everyone: You're never as stuck as you
feel. Even when you feel completely trapped, rescue may be
just around the corner.

Here's what happened to Pamela. She made friends with a
more savvy woman than the friend she'd been talking to all
winter. An older woman from work. This woman asked Pamela some very simple questions:

"The other women you remember so fondly and that poor
Madeleine compares to so badly—was your sex with them
really so wonderful? Maybe they were just sexier-type women.
And maybe you're not really comparing Madeleine to them at

all. Is it possible that because she's the one for you and you've always been so free you're just facing the possibility of settling down with one woman forever and that scares you shitless? And you're putting all your fears on the issue of sex, because that's a little easier to face than thinking you're afraid of commitment itself. What about *that,* my poor confused little American girl?"

If only all of us had friends as wise as that French woman. Maybe we do, but we just don't listen to them. Anyway, these comments turned things around for Pamela. She realized her friend was right. Precommitment jitters. It wasn't much more complicated than that.

The same answer won't work for every woman facing Dilemma #2. But perhaps I'm moving too quickly.

Diagnosis. Are you wondering if you're really in love because you don't feel turned on enough by your partner?

You have to look at two simple things. (1) Are you upset because in fact you don't desire your partner all that much? You don't need for sex to be bad to feel this way. This is just about not feeling so horny for your partner. (2) And does your lack of interest in sex with him lead you to doubt your love? A yes answer to both questions means that you fall into the group of women who are struggling with Dilemma #2.

Prescription. Don't you think we need to avoid driving ourselves crazy? I think so. That's why The Second Permission is so important. A lot of times when we fall in love the relationship is less than perfect, and there are things missing from it. But, hey, if you go to a restaurant, just because the waiter was rude to you doesn't mean you don't walk out nice and full.

If you're not getting your needs met in a relationship, find a way to get them met or decide if you can live without their being met or move on. But don't deprive yourself of an experience of real love just because there's something missing from the sex part.

You can also work at directly making sex better. Let me zero in on three ideas that can give you a lot of help fast.

1.   *Have more appropriate expectations.* I'm not talking about lowered expectations. I'm just saying that every woman who's found a way to feel better about sex in her relationship has had to make adjustments in what she expects. So do this. Write down your secret dreams, fantasies, yearnings, and sexy scenarios. What you want to do is drag into the light the expectations you've been bringing to sex.

Then look at your expectations in the light of day. Expose them to the sunlight. If they're all about what excellent sex means to you, hold on to them. If they're all about being true to yourself in sex, hold on to them. But if you realize that your expectation is more habit than anything else, then this is an expectation that's hurting you, and you'll be better off letting it go. Empty dreams are contaminating what could be a rich reality.

2.   *Throw yourself open to new ways of doing things.* Every time someone is stuck here, there's some preconception preventing her from finding the good sex she's looking for. I'm not talking about wild experimentation. This is not about "Let's have sex in public," or "Let's have sex with other people." This is about discovering the hidden barriers in your mind and heart that without your even knowing it are keeping you in a sexual jail.

Do this. Write down your top three completions of the following: "When it comes to sex, I could never_____."

Now write down your top three completions of the following: "When it comes to sex, I always have to_____."

These are what are keeping you trapped in your old way of doing things. Now you don't have to throw all of these overboard. But I guarantee that one of them—I don't know which one—is a huge and important barrier between you and sexual satisfaction. Think about them. Talk about them to your best friend. Most important, talk about them to your sexual partner.

Then throw overboard that one old way of doing things that's preventing you from making the changes you need to make.

3. *Get some new ideas.* People who've successfully journeyed down the path you're about to take say the same things. I read books. I talked to experts. I realized I didn't know it all. I gained new understanding and in the process I got what I needed for sex to become great.

Sex is like cooking chicken. It's easy to get stuck only knowing one way to prepare it—roast chicken—and always having the same problem—it's too dry. What would you do if you were in that situation? You'd read a book that gave you ideas about new ways to cook chicken that also offered a lot of insight on how to make your chicken come out moist. It's the same with sex. Find the best book you can filled with good new ideas for how to have great sex.

Let me show you how simple it can be. To prime the pump and spare you the agony of yet one more trip to the bookstore, here are some easy-to-use, fast-working ideas.

THE TOP TEN WAYS TO LUST UP YOUR RELATIONSHIP

1. Give your partner a *full* body massage. Do every part of his body. Omit no part. Then the next day make sure he does the same for you.

2. Sit on your sofa and make out like teenagers hoping that your parents won't barge in on you.

3. Each of you write on separate slips of paper three adventurous things you'd like your partner to do while you're in bed, one "thing" per slip. Pull them out of a hat and do them one at a time.

4. Teach each other one new thing about your sexuality—something you like or don't like in sex.

5. Have your partner lick you down one side, from the neck to the back to the rear end to the feet, turn you over and

lick you all the way up the front side. Then do the same for him.

6. Play sex slaves (but only if you each get a full turn). The way you do it is make love and have one of you be in complete charge, deciding who does what to whom, for how long, everything. The next time you make love the other is in complete charge.

7. Have a let's see how long we can kiss on the mouth without either of us breaking it off contest. Whoever stops the kiss . . . well, there are just no losers here.

8. Make a tape of music to slow dance to. You know what to do with it.

9. Make a meal of bite-size food like rigatoni primavera or steak tips and mushrooms or pieces of fruit and feed it to each other.

10. Take a bath or shower together. Pretend you're both very dirty and in tremendous need of being washed head to toe by the other.

Dilemma #3:

I WANT TO FEEL LOVED. BUT THINGS HAVE HAPPENED TO MAKE ME GIVE UP HOPE OF FEELING LOVED. MAYBE SEX CAN BE A SUBSTITUTE FOR LOVE.

Tori's Story

Some women embrace what other women run from. Most women are horrified to be thought of as sluts. Some women find salvation in sluthood. Tori, twenty-five, was one of these women.

Back around age fifteen, Tori remembers feeling deeply unlovable. It was a mystery where that feeling came from, but she felt it with utter conviction. At the same time, more and more of Tori's friends were telling her about their having sex with guys. They bragged of their conquests, just the way we imagine guys bragging. They were in the full flush of their sense of sexual power. It hit Tori like a ton of bricks.

At a party one Saturday night, Tori went up to the most popular boy and said, "I have a surprise for you, come with me." He went to a bedroom with her, she closed the door, and promptly got down to the business of giving the delighted kid a hand job. Tori says she actually amazed herself by the words that came out of her mouth when she was done. "There's more where that came from," she told him, "but you've got to play ball with me. There are things I want and you've got to help me get them."

You use what you've got. Imagine that, only fifteen and Tori saw how to use her raw sexual power as a shortcut to getting what she wanted from the guys who had it all. Tori had never done well in school. But, without brains or beauty, without being aware that she had any other talent, she seized on one thing she had to offer and determined that she would use it to get what she wanted.

She was amazed at how emotionally gratifying it was, having given up on the possibility of feeling loved, to feel she could get from lust what other girls were still hoping to get from love. "They don't want you for you," we would've said to her. "But none of the girls I know," Tori would've said, "feel they're wanted for themselves. At least I know I'm wanted for something."

For the next ten years Tori offered men quick, dirty, uninvolved sex as her part of a series of escalating deals that got her into college, into prestigious Wall Street internships, and into a cool postcollege job coordinating top-level meetings, where she got to "interface" with even more powerful men, many of whom appreciated what Tori had to offer. She wasn't a particularly good meeting planner but she was excellent at demonstrating how sorry she was for her screw-ups.

I'd like to say Tori's strategy ended badly. We can't hold her up as a role model. But outwardly she's fine. Inside, though, she's not so fine. For the past few years depression's been sneaking up on her. She calls it boredom. It's what Holly Golightly in *Breakfast at Tiffany's* called the Mean Reds.

Things have been getting worse, not better. Women feel betrayed by her once they understand how she lives, and then they have no compunction about betraying her themselves. The men she ingratiates herself with have no loyalty to her. No one asks her how she feels. No one buys her flowers.

Diagnosis. You don't have to be a total slut to be stuck in Tori's dilemma. You don't have to be a Tori to feel unloved. You don't have to do what Tori did to feel you have to do something to tide you over until real love walks through the door. That's how you diagnose being stuck in Dilemma #3: You recognize that you've had too many sexual encounters with too many men, too many experiences where you hoped you'd found love but didn't. Just to tide you over. Just to get something for yourself. Just to speed up the process a little as you look for someone to love you.

If you recognize yourself in this, then you fall into the group of women who are struggling with Dilemma #3.

Seventy-eight percent of women say that at some point in their lives they used sex to get someone interested in them or to just keep from feeling lonely. Just to put those of us struggling with this dilemma into perspective.

Prescription. Women like Tori who feel they don't deserve to be loved are echoing a judgment they heard from voices around them. These voices could come from a parent who told them how worthless they were when they were growing up. It could come from an influential older sibling always putting them down. It could even come from society as a whole, as it does for some women who feel they've been written out of the social fabric because they don't look like models.

So why would anyone be crazy enough to believe this shit? It's simple really. We want to believe that the world makes sense. We want to believe that authority is authoritative. We want to believe that the voices we hear are telling us the truth. We *don't* want to feel we're so incredibly lost and alone that the passionate messages of the people who mean the most to us are empty nonsense. But in return for believing the world makes sense, we're forced to accept the idea that we don't deserve to be loved.

But please remember this: It's better to believe the world is a kaleidoscope of meaningless chaos than to believe you don't deserve to be loved. The fact that you deserve all the love in the world is the first truth, even if it means that your mother and father and sister and friends never told the truth about what was possible in love.

At the beginning of this book I said that women who care about love are the lynchpins of this world. You are what holds this world together. Believing that you deserve love is at the heart of believing that love matters. So I guess I'm saying that you damned well better believe in The Third Permission. Otherwise the whole world will fall apart. It's up to you.

Then do this. Become friends with guys. Get to know guys not as sexual partners, not as people you might fall in love with, but as buddies. As people you like, who like you, and who hang out with you—just because you're comfortable with one another. If you focus on friendship, love will come and it will be much easier for you to accept.

Dilemma #4:

I GET SO MUCH FROM SEX ALONE. AND LOVE'S A LOT OF TROUBLE. SO WHY BOTHER WITH LOVE?

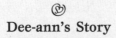

Dee-ann's Story

Looked at superficially, Tori's and Dee-ann's stories might look the same. Too much meaningless sex. Too few meaningful relationships. But psychologically they are two different stories.

The Toris of this world lead psychologically with their despair of ever feeling loved. They seek sex but the Toris aren't really sexual—they are after the benefits sex can bring them.

The Dee-anns lead with their sense that they can get most of their desires satisfied through the real lust they feel, so why bother with love? The Dee-anns are very sexual—in fact they get so much from sex that they wonder why bother with anything else.

Dee-ann, thirty-four, is doing well for herself as a sales rep for a popular local radio station. Why don't we let Dee-ann tell her story.

I don't know, this idea "Ooohh, she's just a tramp," doesn't really get to me. Maybe it should. I mean, I don't want people I know to think that's who I am, but I know how I live and I know what kinds of conclusions people could draw. It doesn't bother me. I meet a lot of guys. If I meet a guy I like, even if I meet a guy who just strikes my fancy a little bit—you know there's just something about him—so I'll bring him home and we'll sleep together. I'm absolutely, totally so not expecting anything will come of it.

It's not that I don't want to find some completely great guy who'll fall madly in love with me and me with him. But unless it would just be perfect I think it would be horrible— the love stuff. You like him but he doesn't like you. He likes you but you don't like him. I just don't think two people are ever in sync.

I like having a man in my bed—I guess I'm pretty easily satisfied—but I just as much like being able to throw him out the next morning. They always say, "I'll call," but I always say, "Whatever," and that's the best part for me. The sex was good. It was what it was. It's over. And I don't care.

So what's Dee-ann's dilemma? It's the dilemma everyone faces who gets almost everything they want the easy way: why work a lot harder and risk a lot of pain for barely any more benefit? At least that's the way someone like Dee-ann sees her dilemma. But in fact she stacked the deck to make herself comfortable with her trampy status quo.

People like Dee-ann are the biggest romantics of them all. She really wants love to be perfect. Or nothing. The pain of real, imperfect love is too much for her to bear. Dee-ann was one of the women who said straight out, "Love sucks." She left out, "and I want as much of it as possible." Some women play hard to get with men. Dee-ann played hard to get with love.

But love got her. She met a good-looking guy—the son of a man who owned a popular downtown dance club—and brought him home. Routine so far. But he wouldn't sleep with her. At first she was furious. But quickly she collapsed into total amazement. She was a girl guys couldn't say *no* to. So why would this guy say *no?*

"Because I like you too much," he said. "I know the deal. You'll kick me out tomorrow morning, or some tomorrow morning. Because there's nothing between us. But we'll have made there be nothing between us. I don't know, there's just something about you. I don't want to throw it away before I give us a chance."

They're a cute couple, and they're married. But she still won't let him say I love you. She isn't looking anymore. But she just doesn't want to say she isn't looking.

Diagnosis. Having that feeling in the pit of your stomach that you've slept with more than your share of guys doesn't mean that you're struggling with Dilemma #4. What's key here is the sense that you like sex, and you like guys, but you've never found one you want to keep and you don't have IN-CREDIBLY high hopes that you will find one like that. You feel safest thinking about a man as a sex object. Even if you claim you're looking for Mr. Right, you're more than willing to settle for Mr. Right Now.

Prescription. The issue is *why* you're basically saying that lust is enough for you so why bother with love. Is it because you're still young and you feel there's a world of guys out there? If that's how you feel, and if you really do have time and opportunity on your side, then maybe you don't have to do anything. You're just doing the chick equivalent of a guy sowing his wild oats. The only danger you face is that you'll put off too long the time when you need to get serious. So make a promise to yourself that by the time you turn twenty-eight or thirty-three or whatever age you choose, you'll start looking for someone to settle down with.

You could also take seriously the possibility that you never really want to settle down. A lot of women don't. There's something about being tangled up with a man, a mortgage, kids, and a bunch of other shackles that's wildly unattractive to you. If you really feel this way, fine. But just don't kid yourself. Don't claim that you don't want to settle down just because you're discouraged about ever finding someone to settle down with.

Or it may be that you haven't been able to give yourself The Third Permission. It would be tragic if you said that lust was enough simply because you were scared to give yourself permission to look for love.

Dilemma #5:

IF I'M FEELING LUST WITHOUT LOVE, THERE MUST BE SOMETHING WRONG WITH ME.

Carla's Story

Many women share Carla's dilemma. It's very hard for us to accept ourselves as purely sexual creatures. Carla's story ends in an unusual, surprising way. Few of us will share that ending. But most women struggling with this dilemma find they wake up in one dramatic form or another.

Carla's forty-three now and like most women who've struggled with her dilemma she decided there was something wrong with her a long time ago. Carla went to college in Boston after growing up in a small town in New Hampshire. She went from an over-supervised world where everyone knew everyone to a wide open world where it felt like no one knew anyone and no one cared about anyone.

She graduated from high school a virgin. But the summer before she went to college her boyfriend finally persuaded her to have sex with him. He tried every argument he could think of, including "I love you," which he thought would be surefire. But what finally convinced Carla was his saying, "Isn't there going to be a lot less pressure if you show up at college having gotten your first time out of the way?" Good point. Carla caved.

Sex was a revelation. Almost like a religious transfiguration. Most of us get hooked on something the first time we try it— pepperoni pizza, lying on the beach, surfing the web. Carla got hooked on sex.

Wow! For a lot of women, the first time isn't so great. Carla's was fantastic. And the explosion of satisfaction she felt was immediately followed by an explosion of desire. I know from twenty-five years of clinical practice that there really are women who want sex five times a day. Carla saw that she was like this, except that she started feeling she wanted to have sex with different guys, and she felt she was the only woman in the world who felt this way.

Her first night at college she slept with someone. Her second night she found someone else. She was consistently finding one, sometimes two, occasionally three guys a day to sleep with. It wasn't until Thanksgiving that Carla realized that just about every guy at the college knew about her, and a lot of the woman hated her. But it was easy to pretend she didn't care.

If you followed Carla through her twenties, you'd see why she'd be confused. Sure she had a lot of sex with a lot of different guys. But there was that three-year period starting with her last year in college when she was with one guy. The relationship ended when Carla had to have an abortion. Carla had told herself that she'd never get an abortion. She wasn't against it for other women, but she just didn't feel right doing it herself.

But two years out of college this guy was getting ready to dump her, because she couldn't really stand him except for sex, and she let him know it. The career she was trying to jump-start—managing new rock and roll bands—wasn't bringing in any money. No husband, no money—no baby.

And no more sex. That was her resolution after her abortion. She was lying on a table. Some woman, a nurse or something, was holding her hand. Carla kept squeezing the woman's hand. She wasn't supposed to be feeling pain, but she was. She wasn't supposed to be feeling regret, but she was. The woman held her hand and patted it and stroked it. It was the first time a woman had been nice to her in years. Guilt and loneliness overwhelmed her. She just wanted to hold hands with a woman for the rest of her life. And so she resolved to stop being the superslut tramp whore she felt she'd been for her whole life.

A new beginning. Celibacy lasted for about four-and-a-half months. But it was hard for Carla to make friends with women. And there were so many hot men on the Boston music scene. Eventually there was another steady guy. Carla didn't love him but he seemed like the kind of guy she should love. A solid guy. He owned his own recording studio, and he had money and connections. They had the same taste in music. And he was so incredibly convincing when he said he'd leave his wife for Carla.

Nine months into their relationship this guy must've gotten the word from some of the guys Carla had slept with. "What kind of fucking whore are you?" he asked. Carla remembers taking his question literally. She started wondering as she stared at him, "Gee, what *are* the different kinds of fucking whores?" It was like deep inside at that moment that's what she really wanted to know. Like the guy had asked a really good question.

They were sitting in his car in front of her apartment building. Finally, without saying a word, she just got out of his car and slammed the door behind her. As she stood in the slow-moving trembling elevator taking her to her floor, she thought, "I'm the kind of fucking whore who's completely all alone in the world at twenty-eight. I'm one *sick* fuck."

By the time she fell asleep that night, her pillow squishy from all her tears, she'd decided to become a nun. "I'll pray, and I'll help people, and I won't screw around anymore. And all the women there will be my friends."

She went to the neighborhood church the first thing the next morning. She was stunned when the priest explained that before she could become a nun she'd have to become a Catholic. "Are you a Catholic?" he'd said. No. "What are you?" he'd said. "I'm a nothing, I guess," she'd said. "You don't have to be a nothing anymore," he said, "because no one's a nothing here."

Carla made it all the way to full membership in a religious order. She's as passionately celibate now as she was passionate about screwing around. She's open about her past, and brings it up when she talks to young women who've gotten into trouble, any kind of trouble. "Sometimes some of us have a sickness inside ourselves so powerful and so destructive that only God or death can heal it," Carla says. "Better God." She's dedicated her life to saving herself from herself. And she's found a world of Sisters.

Diagnosis. Here are three telltale signs that you've been struggling with Dilemma #5:

1. *You've had more than your share of sex for the sake of sex with men you don't care about.* I'd better be clear about this: simply having a very strong libido is not a sign that you're stuck in Dilemma #5. Some women who feel they've "gotta have it" three times a day wouldn't dream of "having it" with anyone but their current committed lover. No, the sign here is feeling that you've "gotta have it" but not caring what your relationship with the guy is. As long as you "have it," you're happy.

2. *You're not happy.* Maybe you have orgasms, but you hate
    yourself and your life. If you're not coming from a particu-
    larly moralistic place, you're still convinced you have psy-
    chological problems. When you look at the way you live,
    your gut tells you this is not right for you. You want sex
    too much, you feel, and even worse it seems as though you
    want love too little.

3. *You have a lack of balance.* It's as if the drive you bring to
    your life has completely soaked up all your sexuality, to
    the point where you have no sexuality left.

Now you know the three signs. Does any one of them apply
to you? If even one of these signs applies to you, then you fall
into the group of women who are struggling with Dilemma #5.

Prescription. You don't have to become a nun to find a
solution to this dilemma. That's a pretty extreme solution. For
you, things will probably be a lot simpler.

You're really scared of two things. Your capacity for sex
without love. And the possibility that you'll never find love,
perhaps because you feel you don't deserve it. So you need to
give yourself The First and Third Permissions. Bottom line:
you need to give yourself permission for both sex and love.
You feel shut out of both. But you deserve both.

So why don't you think you deserve both? I've asked many
women struggling with Dilemma #5 this question. One answer
kept coming through loud and clear: "If someone really knew
the real me, they'd be horrified."

Take a look at the people in your life right now. I'll bet
there is at least one person in your life who knows you and
thinks you're just fine. What you and Carla share is the need
for acceptance. *Strengthen your relationship with the person who
believes in you.* If there's no one in your life like that, find
someone fast—a friend, a clergyperson, a therapist. Someone
who will accept the real you with open arms.

A New Self-Image for Horny Women

I think what we need is new ways of thinking about ourselves. Let's face it, we haven't had a lot of good choices. How many kinds of women are there? Nuts. Sluts. Mutts. And the occasional klutz. Bimbos and Lesbos. Bitches and witches. Do you see a pattern here? These are all ways of putting us down as women. Janet Reno? A mutt. So much for Janet Reno. Mother Theresa? Another mutt. Hillary Rodham Clinton? A bitch, a witch, maybe a Lesbo too. *No* woman—no matter how talented, accomplished, beautiful, or devoted to helping others—is more than one word away from being demolished as a human being.

It's just like when you were in high school. There's one narrow, tiny way of being the right kind of girl. And dozens of ways of screwing up horribly and being hit with some label that you're afraid will doom you forever.

It's time this stopped. I've worked with more than my share of women who've gotten themselves into trouble. And I've been lucky enough to talk to far more than my share of women who are doing just fine. And I've found that there are hundreds of ways of being a strong, healthy woman. It's bad enough that we put each other into straitjackets and create categories to judge each other—or, even worse, use the categories men have created to judge each other. But when we judge ourselves with these same categories—that's where the real psychological damage occurs.

Use The Three Permissions to lift yourself out of whatever crippling categories you've gotten stuffed into. It's the only way to be true to yourself and find excellence when it comes to making peace between those two huge, complex areas of love and sex.

EIGHT

How Sweet It Is
to Be Loved by You

Make-or-Break Experience #6:
Being Truly Yourself While You Find a Home for Your Love

It's one thing to fall in love. That's where you get to taste a dream. It's something completely different to start to live together. That's where you get to see if you can make your dream a reality. It's where the rubber of love hits the road of real life. This is where you get to experience what it will really be like to make a life with this new person. Then what will happen? What can you do to make sure that living your love confirms your love?

I want to let you know where we're headed, you and I. This is the time for me to make a passionate plea for profound honesty in love. As honest and open a person as you are, it's a challenge to be even more so. You don't have to be stupid about it. You don't have to be a pill. But grown-up women are committed to real honesty, and only that kind of honesty will make you feel your love is your emotional home.

The period of settling in together is a surprising turning point in the story of love. As women told me about their experiences with love, this was a big surprise for them. And it was a big surprise for me, too, how common it is that your whole relationship with someone is thrown into question at just the point when you'd thought all your questions were answered.

☙ Connie's Story

At thirty-two, Connie had worked hard to get where she was: a midwife with a glowing, growing reputation. She's been bringing up a child, now age ten, who was the result of a one-night stand back when she was young and crazy. Paradoxically, for someone who was as hardworking and responsible as Connie was, she loved partying and dancing and going to the beach. And the kinds of guys she met tended to like the same things. But Connie was looking for something more. She desperately wanted to feel a real connection with the guy she'd get serious about. She wanted a soulmate.

Then she met Simon. They seemed to click together. They had similar backgrounds. Their fathers were both high school teachers. They both wanted to help people. They both felt there were a lot of problems with traditional medicine. It felt strange to Connie that Simon was three years younger than she was, and she was a little uncomfortable with some of his New Age beliefs, as well as with his situation in life—he was just starting out and struggling to establish himself. But, hey, nothing's perfect. Connie never really confronted Simon with how she felt about what she saw in him. She never got a chance to see how he'd show himself if she did confront him.

Other than a long weekend here and there they didn't see that much of each other because they worked so hard, although they soon got to the point where they spent whatever free time they had with each other. Finally after long, happy, hopeful conversations they decided to give up their old apartments, rent a new one, and move in together. It was like getting married.

Moving in together was, Connie hoped, the beginning of a lifelong relationship. Her days of looking for someone were over. Her signature on the lease meant more to her than a gold ring on her finger. This was it. Finally. Little did she know.

Discovering the truth. Here's what living with Simon revealed. Simon was weird. Simon was bad with money. And Simon was willing to make a big issue about every little thing he thought was important.

It wasn't his New Age beliefs that made him weird. Simon prayed all the time. Connie gradually realized that Simon actually believed himself to be in communication with a variety of spiritual entities. He'd pray instead of act. He'd pray instead of think. He'd pray instead of getting information. The more stuck he was, the more he'd pray. And Connie could never challenge or question the answers Simon got from the spirits he prayed to.

They'd been in agreement that you don't enter medicine to make money. For Connie this meant you don't get rich on the backs of your patients. It turned out that for Simon this meant you forget to charge your patients and you rack up all kinds of expenses. Simon was a bankruptcy looking for a place to happen.

All this would've been workable if she'd been able to talk to him. Since they'd agreed about so much and were so in sync during their falling-in-love days Connie was unable to see that she couldn't tell Simon a damn thing. He really wouldn't listen to her, and if she did manage to get through to him, he didn't want to compromise. He just wanted to win. He could never be wrong about anything.

It doesn't take much. A lot of us go through a painful experience like Connie's. *When I asked women, "What was your worst experience in the story of love in your life so far?" the most common answer wasn't some kind of betrayal. That came in second. The most common "worst experience" was some form of what happened to Connie. Where you pass through the sacred membrane of commitment because you're sure you've checked each other out but then you find in the new light of living together that your dream has subtly turned into a nightmare.*

An ounce of prevention is worth a pound of cure. That's what we'll focus on here: saving yourself from having to deal with a situation like Connie's. Then, at the end of this chapter, I'll show you what to do if you're wondering whether you're another Connie right now.

An Ounce of Prevention

You're making a nest. This is the honeymoon period in the broadest sense—the months when you feel that you've found a home for your love. It's the time when your relationship still has the new car smell about it, and no major glitches or rattles have shown up.

That's when you go from how you think you'll be together to how you really are together. It's the shakedown cruise, where you work out the kinks. It's a transition *from* the time when everything's wonderful but there's an unreal, holiday-for-love flavor to your relationship *to* the time when everyday life kicks in and you're too stressed, too tired, too distracted to do anything but let the unlovely parts of you shine through.

It happens a little differently for everyone. Here's a strong, graphic example, but it makes a point. Some proper ladies will never ever *ever* let their husbands hear them fart. Some rocker chicks will fart out loud on a first date. But for most of us, unless you're going to hold it in forever, *settling in* is the time when your partner gets to know what your farts smell like. It's when you let your partner know how you really feel about his farts. I'm sure you understand that I'm not literally talking about just farts. I'm talking about all the vapors of the body and mind and soul that only come out when we settle in for real.

And then we discover how our partners feel about them. And about us for letting them out. "How free can we be to be ourselves?" That's the make-or-break part of this experience of love. How are you going to end up feeling about love if you feel you can't be your true self in love?

Confronting reality. Even if you were the most open, honest person in the world, that honesty still had to fight with your basic shyness, your fear of confrontations, your hope that things would be easy, and your simply not knowing how you're going to feel about some things until you've lived with them for a while.

Imagine feeling safe enough to show your true self. That's what we're all hoping for. And it's possible for most of us to achieve this. That's what it means to feel at home in your love—you feel safe enough, and you really are safe enough, to be who you really are. And when the real you emerges, what's important for your happiness is whether your partner sees these new facets of you as a betrayal of everything you meant to him, of everything he feels you promised him, or whether he sees what he pretty much expected all along.

Love Me Tender, Love Me True, Love Me Naked

It's funny. There you were, falling in love, and you saw each other naked a lot. But then you start settling in. And you start getting naked all over again. In a whole new way. For the very first time. Adam and Eve—no longer in Eden, but living with each other in the real world. Getting in each other's way. Telling the same story over and over. Revealing what bores you. Showing how you respond to stress. Getting in touch with your real ambitions and the price you're willing to pay to achieve them.

It happens to everyone. It happened to Maxine.

⊛

Maxine's Story

As a twenty-seven-year-old associate producer for a local public-affairs program, Maxine had been married to Kevin for a full year and things were still going great. But sometimes it pays not to look too closely. What do you do when you notice chips and cracks on your teacup of perfection? Do you speak up or shut up? Do you make a stink or live with the stink? Do you look for safety by revealing what's really going on for you or do you look for safety by hiding your truth?

The problem for Maxine wasn't a minor issue. Things were great when they were together. But actually, if you kept a time clock, they weren't together that much. Maxine almost did keep a time clock one week when she started wondering if she was going crazy. Kevin had told her, "Honey, we are together a lot. I mean, I work, but I come home as early as I can and then we're together."

This had made Maxine feel crazy because it was totally not what she'd been experiencing. During the week when she kept a record, Kevin came home on average at about 7:30, which he probably thought was early because that gave him a whole half hour before there was something good to watch on TV. But when they weren't watching TV together he always had stuff to do on his computer for work. There was work on Saturdays too. There was family, friends, more work on Sundays.

During that week when she kept tabs, Maxine had a total of *three and a half hours* face time with her husband. But most of this was spent talking about how was your day and did you call your mother and who's going to pick up the dry cleaning, not talking about anything intimate. Their talk was that of roommates. It's true they had sex almost every night before going to sleep. And sex was good. But it didn't feel like face time, and that in itself made Maxine feel a sense of loss.

What's the real truth? So she didn't know what to believe. Were they still two newlyweds madly in love, because that's the way Kevin saw them, bringing home presents from work and calling her pet names? Or was their "togetherness" merely an empty token of something that no longer existed, which was Maxine's worst fear. Whose label should she trust?

Maxine had trouble trusting herself. Three guys in her young life had told her she was too intense, blew things out of proportion, made too big a deal about things. "Do I drive men away?" was the question she'd tearfully asked her best friend the day before she'd met Kevin. Her friend had supported her, saying she was right to stick up for herself. So why had Maxine gotten off the phone thinking that her friend was really thinking, "Yeah, you do drive men away"?

The way it had been, living through previous relationships, was that her honesty was like a supersensitive smoke detector that went off whenever you made toast. Who needs that hassle? So maybe with Kevin, Maxine was doing what a lot of us do—because the smoke detector keeps going off, you take it down and put it in a drawer. No more hassles. The world will be a better place if there's just a little less of you in it. Sssshhhhhhhhh.

But your house can burn down that way. And now Maxine was feeling that she was living in a burning house. So she'd *have* to say something. And yet her smoke detector had driven all her other boyfriends away. So she'd better *beware* of saying something. And that left Maxine still sailing through her honeymoon, wondering if accommodation and denial were really the secrets of a happy marriage.

As she thought about it, she faced echoes that reverberated all the way into the darkness of her future years. What empty shell of a nothing marriage, where *love* was only a word, awaited her if she kept on saying nothing to Kevin and denying her need now for *more love*? But would there be any marriage at all if she did say something?

Almost exactly two-thirds of women—67 percent—say that issues came up in the first year of marriage that they hadn't foreseen and that made them wonder if they'd made a serious mistake.

Working with what you've got. Maxine was smart enough to realize what a lot of people never figure out for their own relationships. Kevin loved her in the sense that he'd chop off

his arm for her if a chopping-off-your-arm situation ever came
up. But he hadn't signed on for a high-maintenance marriage.
Love for him was a foundation that enabled him to go on with
his life; he didn't want to live all that close to the foundation.

Here was Maxine's problem. Would she be wise enough to
avoid complaining so much she'd drive her husband away? And
at the same time would she be wise enough to avoid destroying
her own hope of love, which is what would happen if she said
nothing about what she really felt?

Maxine was a smart cookie. She understood there's no way
she'd be able to stay silent forever. She could speak now, before
she was filled with rage and panic, or she could speak later in
the grip of even more desperate emotions. She spoke now.

Maxine was not just smart, she was lucky. She spoke up as
soon as she realized she was heading for an incredibly lonely,
miserable existence if nothing changed. And she was lucky
because Kevin deep down shared her vision for how two people
in love should be together.

He might not have. Which is why a constant theme here is
that it's got to come out, it's got to come out, it's got to come
out in the morning of your relationship. At the crack of dawn.
The sooner the better. So that when you take that perilous step
from the experience of falling in love to the experience of settling in, there are no bad surprises. Of course it can't all come
out so early. Which is why most of us end up like Maxine,
having to face a world of unfinished business as we settle into
living with love.

Transitions. Maybe you're going through the experience of
settling in right now. If so, understanding how you get into
trouble will help you see what to do to prevent trouble.

Maybe you're between relationships. Understanding what
goes wrong with the process of settling in will help you set
things up right with the next person you fall in love with. Let's
face it, on some level settling in is the easiest thing in the
world. No surprises—no problems. The trick is how to set
things up so there are no surprises.

And maybe you're coming out of a relationship. If it didn't work out, it's probably because of problems that first emerged when the two of you were settling in. You probably have all kinds of fears because of your experience with these problems. If you understand where they come from, and how to prevent them, there's less to be afraid of.

Barbara's Story

It happened fourteen years ago, one evening about a month after their honeymoon. Barbara, now thirty-eight, had worked hard all day as a freelance graphics designer. But she'd made time to get the house looking just right and add some special touches, like starting a potpourri pot simmering. Getting a special dinner ready. Then she waited and waited for her husband the writer to come home.

Danny finally showed up hours late. Barbara hated his coming home late and was disappointed. It was her nightmare vision of what marriage would be—two people whose lives didn't connect. But Barbara understood. After all Danny always had people to see for the articles he was working on, and Barbara was comforted by the thought—the guess, really—that Danny was disappointed too. Barbara was one of these well-brought-up women who believed that the road to chaos starts with showing how you really feel about things. "Make things nice, and they will *be* nice" was her motto.

So instead of expressing her annoyance and disappointment, Barbara held Danny's face in her hands and said, "You're my blue sky." It was supposed to be an expression of love.

But Danny heard different music in these words. He stepped back. "I'm not your blue sky. I never want to be your blue sky. I can't be that for you. I'm just me. I can't be part of what you need to be happy."

Barbara's world turned gray immediately, all the colors fading out of it. She still loved Danny. But the hope of happiness, that their lives together would be a special place for their love, was gone. It was like the scene in Tennessee Williams's *The Glass Menagerie,* when all the little glass animals were smashed. A terrible moment of devastated hope.

How could his words have so much power? You're right to be suspicious. Other stuff was going on.

Isn't it romantic . . . ? One problem Barbara had . . . look, I love Barbara. The more I got to know her, the more I respected how sweet she was and how much she had to give. If you valued people by how much they had to give to a relationship, and how hard they tried, Barbara would win a prize. But Barbara was a fool for love. She had a load of romantic crap in her head. She walked into marriage as if there were an imaginary bundle of mistletoe eternally hanging over her, as if every day were Valentine's Day.

Somehow, she thought, the vows of marriage and their love for each other would make everything wonderful.

That's the first way women get into the situation where something goes wrong with the process of settling in. They have the wrong idea about what it's actually going to be like to live with their partners.

Here's what Barbara would've needed:

> You've got to be able to picture what your everyday life with the person you've fallen in love with will be. Because that's what you're actually settling into.

This might sound obvious to you, but you have to be aware of your ability to kid yourself, even if you're convinced that you're much less of a romantic than Barbara was. Women who think they know exactly what they're getting into when they hook up with some poor, dumb guy somehow often simultaneously think that rubbing up against him will turn the guy on. Not to sex, but to romance. Not in a minute, but in a year or two.

When Danny said he could never be Barbara's blue sky, he dashed her hope that her love would be her home. She'd built a castle in the air and had gone to live in it, but when he showed her there was nothing in the sky, just the solid ground under their feet, Barbara felt incredibly lonely. She tells me that the very sounds in the house were different from that moment on. There was an echo. As if someone had stripped the house emotionally of drapes and carpets. There was an empty sound to it, like a house no one lived in.

Millions of women have this experience. Because things are so different from their romantic vision, they have the sense they've lost everything.

But in fact there was plenty of hope for Barbara. She could've talked to Danny about what she needed. They could've groped their way back to the vision they shared of two people who loved each other and were willing to demonstrate it. Millions of women save themselves from post-romantic stress disorder by doing this. But this would have required absolute honesty, the willingness to deal with conflict and face a confrontation, and the patience to work through to a solution.

But when these women really show what's been missing, their partners usually step up to the plate. "I'm so sorry, honey," their guys say to them, throwing their arms around them. This proves that their love has what it takes to provide a home for them.

Piercing the veil of dreams. Barbara had other problems. She was also blind to who Danny really was. Barbara had grown up in a world of prosperous, powerful men who took care of their women. We all take things for granted when we first step out onto the stage of adulthood, and what Barbara took for granted was that she'd feel safe because her husband would provide a world of financial and emotional security for her. The way her father had for her mother, her grandfather for her grandmother, her older brother for her sister-in-law.

Of course all these guys were boring to Barbara. Law, finance, stuff like that. Danny wrote about sports and entertainment. He was always around people with a lot of money, and he was always filled with ideas about how some of that money was going to rub off on him. The big book. The event he'd promote. The network gig that he could nail down with just one more trip to New York.

But her dream Danny had never been the real Danny. Somehow Barbara had gotten it all wrong. Danny wasn't a guy who'd make a lot of money having fun with plenty of time left over to be with her, which was, she'd thought, his real priority. Danny was a guy who for ten years never managed to make much money, didn't have much fun either, and wasn't interested in spending much time with her. It was the worst of all possible worlds. Danny was a workaholic failure. He was somehow so busy with his unlaunchable writing career that they rarely managed even to spend Christmas or Thanksgiving together. Something so unthinkable for Barbara that she could barely see or admit it.

So that's another way women get into this situation, where something goes wrong with the process of settling in. They didn't let themselves know the truth about their partners from the very beginning.

> You've got to be able to see who the other person really is. Not your hope for who he can be. Not your most charitable assessment of who he is. But the kind of clear vision of the other person that leaves you safe from surprise and disappointment.

Why would you have trouble doing this? It's not because you're stupid, or inexperienced. Come on—we all know women who are savvy as hell but who are blind as moles to how jerky their guys are. Women are wonderfully complex and diverse, but to the extent that we're blind to who this guy is that we're settling in with we're all suffering from the same problem. It's that love hunger again. Hunger for love and fear of not finding it.

My research tells me that millions of young women eighteen to thirty are literally traumatized by the overwhelming jerki-

ness of the guys they run into. The selfishness of one guy. The
drunken irresponsibility of another guy. The sexual promiscu-
ity of another. The way another guy has no time for them.
Then of course woven through these experiences are the nice,
sensitive guys who either bore you to hell or who make you feel
they could take care of you just about as well as an umbrella in
a hurricane.

These are real experiences. No wonder millions of women
are scared they'll never find the love they're looking for. In
this environment blindness seems to be self-protective. It pre-
vents you from getting discouraged.

Not so fast. But the real problem here isn't the guys, and
that's why I feel very hopeful. After all, I have two daughters
in their late twenties and I feel very hopeful for them. In fact
there are plenty of good guys. And the guy who's a jerk at
twenty-three can be terrific at twenty-seven or thirty-three. The
real reason we get so scared is that we're in a rush.

Partly because of our biological clocks, which women hear
even in their mid-twenties. Partly it's competition. There are
always those one or two friends who hook up with great guys
early on and quickly make us feel we're behind the eight ball.

And then there's loneliness. Of course we're not really al-
lowed to say this word because it sounds too pathetic. But let's
face it—we want to be with somebody. It's not just that we
want someone to share our lives today and tomorrow. A room-
mate can do that. But there's a kind of loneliness that comes
from feeling you have no one to share a future with. Without
a future the present can feel meaningless.

All these factors make us panic. And that's a recipe for
disaster. If you're still at that point where you have not yet
made a commitment to a guy, get up right now, fix your hair,
freshen your makeup, and then, while you're looking damned
fine, gaze at yourself in the mirror and say out loud,

"I've got plenty of time to find a good guy, a solid guy, the
kind of guy who's right for me. I'm not so scared of being
alone that I need to be blind to who I'm really getting."

And the reason you have to do this is that *women who make choices blinded by fear take seven, ten, fifteen years or more to finally see who they've gotten*. That's what happened to Barbara. And it's worth paying attention to how this happened to her, because it happens this way to a lot of women.

Almost at the beginning Danny said he never wanted to be her "blue sky" and the period of terrible loneliness set in. When she should've been settling in to love she was settling in to loneliness. Years of being alone in the evening and on weekends. Years of eating by herself. Years of having to find a way at the last minute to have Christmas or Thanksgiving with some relative or other. Barbara *felt* all this as keenly as you feel a shoe that doesn't fit. But she couldn't see any of it because she had an image of Danny that told her that none of this should be happening.

The way to prevent this is to put a stop to that panicky feeling that you won't find someone to love you. *Because it's fear that you won't be loved that will push you into a relationship where you won't feel loved.*

Getting what you need. What do you do if you're in Barbara's situation and the settling in experience has already started?

You have to face what's really at stake, and you have to make your partner face it. Stop living in la-la land. What's at stake is the death of your love. What's at stake is a lifetime of loneliness. You've got to make all this clear to your partner. Figure out for yourself what you need not to feel lonely living with him.

Here are the top six reasons why women who are settling in feel lonely. Write *yes* after any of these that apply to you. If more than one applies, pick the one that hurts the most:

1.   Is it that he's never there?

2.   Is it that he puts you down?

3.   Is it that he never listens to you?

4. Is it that he's always busy with something else besides you?

5. Is it that the two of you don't have anything in common?

6. Is it that a wall of anger has built up between you?

Now you have a top candidate for what to deal with, now that the blinders are off. Notice that none of these are about what's wrong with him (or about what's wrong with you for that matter). That's because when you stop being blind it's easy to be distracted by all the little things you see wrong with your partner. And that's how relationships plunge into a pit of criticisms and negativity. What you have to focus on is working with him to address the issue that's making you feel lonely. If you can do that, none of the little things you find wrong with him will matter.

What you have to do is have a "the future of our relationship is at stake" meeting. Let him know that because he doesn't make you feel he listens to you (or whichever one you said most applies to you) you feel terribly lonely and that means the relationship essentially has a fatal disease. He can start listening to you and save the relationship. He can continue not listening to you and kill it. Tell him exactly what you need for him to do so that you'll feel he's listening or whatever your issue is.

You've got to focus on the one issue that's most responsible for your feeling lonely. *And you've got to care enough about the future health of your relationship to make a big deal about it right now.* Every single day hundreds of women save their love because they find a focus and because they act on their caring. Every day relationships die because some women never found an issue to focus on and didn't really care enough to take their loneliness seriously.

When my kids were little they had a pair of gerbils. I thought they were old enough to take care of the gerbils. They promised me they'd be responsible. But they were just kids.

They got distracted by school and friends. They forgot to give the gerbils food and water. The gerbils died. It was so easy to kill them. It would've been so easy to keep the gerbils alive.

It's the same with your love.

I always believe happy endings are possible. And the thing about love is that there are many more happy endings than you'd think. It's just that in the soap opera of our lives it's often darkest before the dawn, and you have to go through a very stormy night before you get to the dawn. Barbara cried the tears of any woman who feels she's thrown away the best years of her life on a guy who was never right for her. Who was so *obviously* not right as soon as she saw him for who he really was.

But you'll never be any younger than you are right now. You'll never have more options than you do today. And spilt milk is just water under the bridge, or something. Anyway, Barbara saw that she could never feel at home with the real Danny. She decided to leave. Most of all, she made the decision that's all-important for making settling in an experience of discovering you've found a home for your love. She made the decision that while she was going through the experience of looking for someone to love, she'd show everything there was to show about herself. So that the person she was with would have no surprises. And she'd see everything there was to see about the person she was falling in love with so that she'd have no surprises.

Barbara was still a romantic. She still thought that love was wonderful. She still wanted to find a guy who could be her blue sky. But she decided that she'd no longer let her fear of not finding someone stampede her into finding someone who couldn't make her feel loved. She lived the lesson more single women need to know. There is a worse loneliness than being on your own. There's the loneliness of being married to a stranger.

Honesty is the best policy. What happened was predictable. Why is it that we always achieve our dreams when we find a

way to stop needing our dreams? There was a guy Barbara had
known for years. A lawyer. A friend of the family. They talked
to each other with an honesty that shocked both of them. The
kind of honesty that inside makes you gasp with the certainty
that you've driven the person away. But amazingly the more
she bombarded him with honesty, the more his respect and
admiration grew.

Scariest of all for her had been coming clean about the
biological clock issue. How do you say to a guy you've barely
gone on a date with that you're thirty-eight, you're desperate
to have kids, you ain't gonna have kids without getting married, and so you have no time to waste with guys who aren't
serious prospects? And how do you say it while still conveying
the fact that you're very romantic?

She just said it. He was relieved. What kind of an idiot
would he have been not to have known it anyway? So instead
of her revealing this horrible deep secret, she let him know that
he'd get what he needed to feel at home in this relationship: an
honest woman who didn't play games and wasn't silly. By
showing him what she thought was worst about her, she let
him see what he felt was best about her. He fell for her big
time.

One woman hearing the story said, "Oh that was such
luck." Not really. Earth to women: healthy guys want to see
you naked. You don't want a guy who doesn't want to see you
naked, physically and emotionally. This is a no-lose situation.
Barbara tells the guy the truth, so he knows exactly what he's
getting into. If he likes the truth, then he falls in love with her
for telling it. If he doesn't like what she has to reveal when
she stands naked in front of him, *then she's saved from a horrible experience of loneliness if they should ever get to the point of
settling in.* When Barbara told the truth, she could've gotten
the guy or not. But she would've won either way.

But there are more ways you can save yourself from problems during the experience of settling in.

(ℬ)

Nicole's Story

Nicole, thirty-one, had the kind of job most women would kill for, but for many years she'd had the kind of love life most women would run from. Her love life had been a desert. Her professional life, though, had been a celebrity-filled party. Literally.

She worked for a PR firm that basically threw together shindigs that connected the three C's: celebrities, charities, and corporations. You know, something like Elton John and Sharon Stone come together to raise money for AIDS research under the sponsorship of whatever bank happens to be the biggest one in Boston at the time. And Nicole gets to pull it all together, and makes a ton of money doing it.

Nicole's not just some glorified gofer either. She's the lady of the moment, the gal everyone thanks "for making all this possible."

The reasons her love life is a disaster are endless. She desperately wants that great guy. But she's too picky. She's too busy. And she's afraid that the kind of serious, solid guy she wants won't really think she's much of anything. She's afraid of getting hurt.

Then she meets Whit. He's not her kind of guy, she thinks. He's a doctor, doing the kind of research her celebrities, charities, and companies raise money for. He's got a personality a little bit like Robin Williams in *Awakenings*—he's kind of a driven dreamer. Oh, but he also has the looks of a Tom Cruise. Tom Cruise in a lab coat with a faraway look in his eye.

Now here's what Nicole thinks is true about herself: if Whit knew it he wouldn't be interested in her. She thinks she's stupid. Not IQ stupid. But smart only about dumb, practical details. Shallow stupid. And she thinks she's a ball buster. A cold, basically not-nice woman who has to call the shots to have any peace of mind at all.

Nicole hated thinking this about herself. She was afraid no

one could love her. Who *could* love her? "Only some poor
pussy-whipped fool I wouldn't want anyway," she said to me.

But Nicole wanted Whit, the way you see a necklace in the
window of Tiffany's and you've just got to have it no matter
what. Nicole did what a lot of us do. She was as open and
honest as she knew how to be but she hid from herself and
from Whit who she really was. She presented herself as somehow very sensitive and thoughtful and vulnerable. Not really
at home in the party-planning world. Yearning for a man to
make her feel safe by taking from her the burden of having to
make tough decisions.

She wasn't being phony. Phony is when you know who you
are and pretend you're something else. Nicole was someone
who hoped so desperately she was someone else she started to
believe it.

Living the lie. After three dates Whit felt he'd come across
this warm, wise soul, fragile as an Alpine flower, who couldn't
cope without him. Nicole needed a new couch for her apartment and asked Whit to help her pick one out. At the furniture
store she acted as if buying a couch were something like buying
a carburetor, as if she were completely out of her element.
They looked at dozens of couches and finally Nicole buried her
face in his chest, moistening his shirt with her hot tears, as
she confessed that she needed him to choose a couch for her
because she was overwhelmed. Besides, she moaned, why do
people need furniture anyway? Why can't we live in bare
rooms? And wasn't it wrong to buy a couch when there were
people in the world who didn't have floors?

Nicole somehow managed to convey to Whit, as he told me
later, that she was simultaneously too weak and yet too intelligent to go about the business of buying a couch.

Whit, of course, fell for it like a ton of bricks. Plus Nicole
had the biggest breasts of any pretty woman he knew.

What happened next for Nicole was what happens to a lot
of women. Whit fell in love with the woman she was showing
him, and Nicole fell in love with that woman too. That's who

she wanted to be when she grew up. But it wasn't who she was. Only her breasts were real.

Marriage. Honeymoon. Then settling in. Suddenly here's Nicole feeling that she's going to go out of her mind if she has to take part for another minute in one of Whit's bullshit intellectual conversations. Here's Nicole discovering that outside of work Whit is one of the biggest idiots she'd ever run into. And that she'll go out of her mind if she has to defer to his defective judgment one more time. Nicole can throw a party for two thousand people. Whit can screw up an order for Chinese takeout.

You can run but you can't hide. Like an embezzler who knows he's going to be caught by the company auditors, Nicole waited for the day when the lie would come crashing down around her. She watched her true self leak out. Whit told her some story about a conversation he'd had with the director of the hospital about funding for his research and, boom, Nicole told him he'd handled it all wrong. Then she went on to tell him what he'd have to do the next day to correct the impression he'd left that his project didn't need any more money because he wasn't really getting the results he was looking for. "Whit, sweetie, he's got to think you need a lot more money because the results you were looking for are just starting to pour in."

Working things out. After Nicole outlined what he had to do she pretended that she really didn't know what she was talking about, but clearly she did. Of course Whit felt hurt and angry as if Nicole had attacked him for being an idiot. That's of course exactly what she'd done.

He started acting cold and distant toward her, but if he wasn't going to be nice to her, she felt less motivated to hide her real self from him. Whit started talking about some theory of how poverty causes disease. Nicole blurted out, "Look it's all just blah, blah, blah. You don't cure people with words." Whit felt as if he'd been slapped in the face.

His anger and their distance escalated. It started feeling to both of them as if their marriage was a terrible mistake, as if someone had gotten the crazy idea he could keep a Great Dane in a one-room apartment.

It's got to be obvious to you that the third way women get themselves into this situation of terrible loneliness as they try to settle in is that they hide who they really are.

What Nicole should've done of course is this:

Show who you are. Show as much as there is about who you are as soon as possible. It's much better to show who you are after twenty minutes of dating than after twenty years of marriage. But if you've been married for twenty years and you're still in hiding, come out of hiding now.

Nicole had trouble showing herself because she was inexperienced. Sure, there'd been a lot of men in her life, and she probably had enough know-how to run the entire country. But how many of us actually have a lot of experience with falling in love with that perfect person and then holding on to him past the honeymoon and on into the settling-in period? Even Madonna has not had very much experience with this.

This inexperience is another way women get themselves into trouble when it comes to settling in. They think they can get away with not showing who they really are.

Understand that it's all going to come out eventually, and the bigger the gap between what you thought was real and what is truly real, the more difficult it's going to be.

It should've destroyed their marriage. The real Nicole and the one Whit had fallen in love with were like night and day. I don't want to tell you how their story turned out, because I'm afraid it will give you the wrong impression. Once at the height of a hurricane in which people were killed I saw two guys out playing golf. That was less stupid than what Nicole did, and less dangerous. It's just that the guys playing golf survived, and so did Nicole and Whit.

Whit had grown up with three brilliant older sisters, and yet he was expected to beat their brains out at every academic challenge. Whit was haunted by the sense that the only reason he got as far as he did was hard work and motivation, not any real gifts. He suffered from stress and the sense that he was in over his head. It was exhausting and terrifying. Plus he felt he was just a big old nerd and that no one would like him if he didn't talk about a lot of important sounding intellectual bullshit. He was deeply afraid that he really had nothing to say.

So, weird as it is, Whit was an accident waiting for a Nicole to happen. Once he got past feeling hurt by Nicole's acting like he was an idiot, he loved the idea of her taking charge. Once he got past his terror of her thinking he was empty, he loved the idea that he could stop talking about the dumb stuff he talked about to impress her. They saw that they needed to talk.

"Let me choose the restaurant," Nicole said, "because you don't know how to choose a restaurant."

"Fine. Great," Whit said.

They sat down in the restaurant and as they were waiting for the easy-to-eat food she said, "Look, I don't need you to take care of me. You need me to take care of you, and I need to do that. I was afraid you'd hate me if you knew that what I really wanted was to run your life the way I run everything. But I think you've been yearning for someone to run your life and make all the decisions. I can't do science. But you can't do anything else."

Whit's head disappeared beneath the table as he went to look for his napkin which he'd somehow misplaced. He came up, sighed, and said, "When you're right, you're right."

You're not as bad as you think. But ask yourself this. What are the odds of all this happening: you're in hiding, the person your partner falls in love with isn't the real you, then the real you emerges, and your partner falls even more in love with the real you? Come on. It's hard enough for two people to fall in love the first time.

Yes, you say, but if Nicole had shown herself as the manage-

rial type she really is, Whit wouldn't have been interested in
her. But look again. Nicole was *afraid* she was a ball buster.
But she wasn't really. She was a sweet, affectionate person
highly tolerant of human frailty as long as she had a reason
for respecting someone. And she was even sweeter when she
was the boss. If she'd shown Whit her true self, he would've
seen a take-charge woman who offered him the love and attention his sisters had given him.

After the honeymoon there was a moment of terrible loneliness for Nicole. She saw the world of lies she'd created for
herself and realized there was a real possibility she'd spend her
life hiding from the man she loved. So she'd never get to feel
that the person she loved loved her. Not the real her. It was
like spending your life as a spy. And who's lonelier than a spy?

There are two outcomes to the settling-in experience. Terrible loneliness or a wonderful sense of at-homeness. There are
two ways to be. You can see what's real and show what's real.
Or you can hide yourself and hide from seeing who the other
person really is. There are very few parts of life or of the
complex story of love in our lives that are as clear as this.

Bottom line, how do women say they were protected against
finding themselves strangers from their partners when they settled in?

- Show everything there is to show about yourself at the beginning—this is the best option. It's scary, but it's the way
  to go.
- Know what to expect, so when your partner comes out of
  hiding, it's no surprise. Have experiences that will give you
  realistic expectations.

Puppy love is for puppies. Real love is for real women.

A Pound of Cure

Suppose you're way past the honeymoon stage. You should've checked things out better, but you didn't. Okay, so you were like most of us, including me. You wouldn't have said it at the time, but looking back you'd have to say now that you just figured everything would be okay and, what the hell, if there were any problems you'd deal with them.

But things turned out to be so different from the way you'd thought they'd be. You knew your guy was "serious," but you didn't realize what an incredible, irredeemable, unstoppable bore he'd be. You knew he was a little "casual" about things, but you never dreamed how irresponsible he'd show himself to be. You knew he wasn't the horniest guy in the world, but you never expected a guy could find a beautiful naked woman like you rubbing up against him every night and still not want you.

The problem comes when things are bad enough to make you think about leaving but not so bad that it's crystal clear leaving is the only choice.

How do you know what to do? Stay or leave?

Here are some quick guidelines. I asked women what had worked for them. Here, in their own words, are the best words of wisdom I've found.

• "If this is just hitting you, give it some time, but not too much time." Three months was the consensus for seeing if you can get used to something you don't like about your new life mate. One wise woman added that it's great to keep a journal during this period. Write down how you feel about your partner every day. That way you can see if it's getting worse, or better, over time. You might find out that whatever is bothering you is only a problem for one or two days, and the rest of the time it's no problem at all, but you only remember the bad days.

• "Some things can change, some things can be fixed, some things are hopeless. Check out which it is." Take a guy who's bad with money. This can be a terrible albatross around your neck. But if a guy can admit he's got a lot to learn about handling money and is willing to learn, or if he's willing to let you take over the financial chores he's so bad with, it's not hopeless. But if he's convinced he knows everything, he's set himself up as someone who can't and won't learn. This can't change, and it can't be fixed. Nor can any other problem if you're with someone who doesn't think he needs to change or isn't able to change.

• "Don't be confused by spillover effects, like how you get mad because you can't talk to each other, and then that makes sex bad and then you think everything is terrible." This one's important, but tricky. It can lead you to make a big deal out of nothing, or to ignore something that's really a big deal. Let's say your guy always comes home late from work, doesn't call, and doesn't like to apologize either. He just wants you to "loosen up" about it. But instead of loosening up, you get up-tight and then sex is bad and then you're just generally mad at each other. The whole relationship seems terrible but the initial germ of the problem is really something you should be able to deal with. But let's say your guy lies to you. Same result—no sex, anger, etc. And you say, "Well things really aren't as bad as they seem, it's just the spillover from that little lying problem." But lying isn't a little problem you can over-look. It's infected your whole relationship.

• "You may be disappointed but if all he's showing you is that he's pretty much like every other guy, then what are you going to do—dump someone with his good points for someone else with the same bad points but fewer good points?" You've got to be careful with this. I trust the basic wisdom in this guideline, because so many women have said it, but if you and I believe that love should be real and wonderful, this could just be a backdoor way of settling for far less than you deserve. Here's how to protect yourself. Don't confuse "pretty much like *every* other guy" with "pretty much like *a lot* of guys." For example, a lot of guys have nothing to say and don't want to hear anything you have to say. But the majority of guys aren't like this.

• "You're not stupid—think about how this is going to play

out for you if you live with it year after year." Right now you guys are basically in your honeymoon period. It ain't gonna get better than this. Ask yourself this question: this thing about your partner that bothers you, is it like a pebble in your shoe that's going to feel bigger and bigger and get more and more painful over time? Or is it like a tampon—it was kind of a big deal to wear a tampon when you were thirteen, but most of us are completely used to it within a few years. Come on: force yourself—is it going to get more and more annoying, or less and less? If you go back and forth, take a vote every single day for a month. Majority rules. If most days you said this problem is going to get more annoying with time, then the handwriting's on the wall.

• "We all have two kinds of dreams for when we find the right person. The big dream—'I'd love to meet a man who has a house on the beach,' for example. The minimum dream— 'Any man I marry has got to be physically affectionate.' So you've started settling in and your guy's disappointed you. But which dream has he dashed? The big one? You shouldn't have counted on it. The minimum dream? You have a right to that and you should never let it go." This woman's advice speaks for itself. Write down your big dreams and your minimum dreams. If based on what you've discovered your minimum dreams are not going to come true, that's a good place to draw the line.

A Home for Your Love

That golden period when you settle in with someone after making a commitment is sort of like being given a gift of a new house. What a wonderful gift. So you move into your gift house, hoping to love it. There's one thing you have to do though. You've got to make that house your home. You've got to see if it can be your home.

In the same way, your hope of love is the home for your

heart. The relationship you happen to be in right now embodies your hope. But you've got to take care of your heart. Now that you've moved into your new house of love you've got to do what's necessary to make sure it's a home for your love. The kind of home you need for your love to feel like home.

I've had many women talk about the relationship they're in, list many good things about the relationship, and then go on to tell me they were completely miserable. These women aren't crazy. They know what it means to find a home for their love. You could live in a house that had dozens of things to brag about and yet never feel comfortable or happy there. You could live in a house that had some things wrong with it and yet it could feel like a perfect home.

So as you settle into this relationship, listen to what your heart says: "I need to know you'll find me a good home. I don't need this particular relationship to have hope of love. I just need to know that whatever relationship you place me in will feel like a home for love."

Write down what it means to you to find a home for your love. Forget all the stuff you've ever read about what it means to have a "good relationship." This is not the time for some therapist to tell you what's good or bad. This is your moment. "I'd feel at home in a relationship if . . ."

Write down ten things. This is your personal top ten list for what you need to feel at home in your relationship. Take it seriously. As your relationship is on its shakedown cruise, *this* is what you need to have to be happy.

Love Takes Time

Make-or-Break Experience #7:
Making Sure Your Love Survives the Test of Time

This is the experience of love that can last the longest. That's the miracle of it. That's the challenge of it. This is the experience—seeing what happens to love over time—where all the really big prizes lie. Here's where you work through problems and feel the triumph that comes from your love enduring. Every woman who feels like a success in love has gone through this experience.

But it's so huge. How do we begin to think about it?

The Gift of Creativity

Imagine that you were given a great artistic gift. The ability to paint wonderful pictures. The ability to make people laugh. The ability to write beautiful songs. Wouldn't that be great? But you wouldn't want to have that gift for only a couple of years. Once you'd tasted the ripe juicy fruit of creativity, you'd want to keep it going. How terrible to feel your creative juices dry up. How fantastic to feel them flowing for as long as you live.

To have a life full of love you need the hope that love can last for a lifetime. Nothing damages hope more than the experience of one relationship after another that starts out full of promise, that shows its promise for a year or two, and then fades. Sure keeping love alive over many years is hard, but so is having a life as an artist. You don't expect it to simply happen. All you want—*and you have every right to expect it*—is that your creative juices won't dry up. All you want, when it comes to love, is the confidence that you'll never give up and you'll always have something to offer.

Creativity is the secret of keeping love alive through time.

Here's the make-or-break part of this experience. Hope is the lifeblood of creativity. Of course things won't be perfect over the course of a long relationship. But will you feel that you're getting the kinds of results—will you feel smart and strong and effective enough—to feel the love you're making is high quality? So that your hope stays alive? So that your creativity stays alive? So that you're able to keep feeding your relationship and keep making it high quality?

Love in Time

The settling-in experience for me took less than a year. I met my husband in the summer. By the following summer I'd discovered pretty much everything bad about him that there was to discover. So I've spent over thirty years hanging in there, being in it for the long haul.

The essence of the experience is time. Time always plays an enormous role in the story of love. Remember when you were dating and maybe you'd seen a guy a few times and really gotten along with him? You'd never spent more than a few hours together. Suddenly you had the possibility of spending a three-day weekend alone together in a cabin by a lake. No TV. No phone. Just you and this guy that you'd only experienced in small doses.

And you were terrified. Endless hours with someone who was basically a stranger. What if the alchemy of time made all the good things about him unimportant and heightened all the ways you annoyed each other?

Compared to this experience, all the others can happen really fast. Falling in love can take a minute. Making a commitment can happen in the blink of an eye. Five minutes later you can be settling in and getting your first glimpse of who the two of you *really* are together. And now you're going to have to figure out how to spend years and years together.

I've got good news for you. It's easier, and simpler, than you might think. The shelfloads of relationship books you'll find at the bookstore might make you think you need to be a rocket scientist to keep love alive over time. I'll let you in on a secret. If you keep your creative spark alive, those books can help a lot, but they're rarely necessary. If your creative spark is lost, all the books in the world won't help you.

And the good news just keeps on coming. You're not a helpless victim, when it comes to the life and death of the creative spark of love. I now know something I didn't believe was true when I first started working on this project: There are things you can do to keep your creative spark alive.

The Miracle of Creativity

But we have to solve a mystery. How do some women manage to maintain a lively, creative connection to their relationship—which is its creative spark—and others seem to get bored, lose interest, and stop caring?

Some women faced with the normal problems that pop up

in a relationship over time continue to maintain their sense of creativity and commitment. They stay involved and caring.

Other women lose the creative spark. If having a marriage were like being a novelist, these women would be like the hack writer who's found a formula and spends the rest of her life just phoning it in. Going through the motions. Present in body, but not in spirit.

So that's what I care about right here, right now: What keeps your creativity, caring, and commitment alive, and what makes them die?

Your job might be an incredibly creative outlet for you, or it might be that you express your full creativity in some hobby or sideline. But whatever you have going for you, keeping love alive through time is an important creative challenge for most of us. Things don't always turn out the way we've planned, but imagine being an old lady one day and looking back over the story of love in your life, and being able to say, "Once we were in it for the long haul, I'm proud that I was able to keep on giving to my love."

Let's meet a woman who could've said just that. Buried within this story are the four ingredients that work to keep our creativity in love alive.

☙

Nancy's Story

Nancy, fifty-eight, has been married for thirty-five years to Gordon, a professional gambler. A *real* pro. The kind of guy who can show up in Las Vegas with fifty thousand bucks, find some high-stakes poker game, and walk away three nights later with two hundred thousand dollars. Or a lot more.

Or he might walk away with nothing. And when that happened Gordon would go back to California where he had a real estate license and would start trying to turn over some properties to generate cash. Once the money started accumulating he would be back to looking for a high-stakes game to get into.

You can guess what life was like for them. Ups and downs. Periods of being broke, shorter but happier periods of having suitcases stuffed with cash.

Nancy remembers one night sitting in a hotel room high above the lights of Las Vegas. The curtains were drawn. The beckoning neon meant nothing to her. Sitting on the coffee table was a leather bag with $550,000 in it. And she remembers thinking to herself, "That's not real. It's just a temporary visitor. A week from now it might be gone. A week from now it might be doubled. And *then* two weeks from now it might be gone. I'd probably go insane if I paid much attention to it one way or the other."

It may not be for everyone, but . . . Now get this. These are not words you hear very often: Nancy loved being Gordon's wife. Why? *Not* because Gordon was such a gem of a husband or because their relationship was so great. Gordon was an unreliable, oversensitive worrywart. They spent a lot of time apart, and a lot of the time when they were together Gordon didn't want anyone talking to him. But Nancy felt that being Gordon's wife kept her creative juices flowing.

As you can imagine, it was hard for me to understand at first how it could keep Nancy's creative juices flowing. "On the surface, it doesn't sound so great," I said. "Show me what I'm not seeing."

Nancy sighed, stood up, and walked to the window. She was silent for a while, seeming to stare intently at a man mowing the lawn across the way. Finally she spoke.

"He's no bargain, but he needs me. I make a difference. Being a professional gambler is who he is, but without me he couldn't function, and one of the good things about Gordon is that he often lets me know how important I am to him. How I keep him going. He doesn't fight my attempts to be his partner. I know that he'll always let me influence him.

"A couple of years ago Gordon had managed to scrape together, I don't know, maybe three hundred thousand dollars to enter a private game with some rich guys in New York. These

guys weren't professionals, but they weren't suckers either. I
mean they could play high-stakes poker. Next thing I know
Gordon's down to $20,000 and I figure that's going to go too.
It just wasn't his table. So I just basically take his money away
from him and insist that we go down to this island that's so
out of the way that you can't get a game going. Just so we can
be together."

Taking charge. "Gordon is pissed, but I can see in his eyes
that he's grateful too. I left him alone the first couple of days
down there, just long enough for him to start getting bored,
and then I started insisting on our doing things together. Not
that there was so much to do, but when I decide we're going
to act like newlyweds, we just do it. Gordon goes along, because he knows I'm taking care of him.

"You know how women get into trouble, I think? We get
this idea that a relationship should be fifty-fifty. Then it's like
we won't ante up until the guy antes up his half. But most
guys never do. So instead of being there for the relationship,
women are just waiting. I think that if I'd gotten it into my
head that Gordon was going to take care of our marriage, I'd
have spent the last thirty years being mad at him. But that
would be as stupid as spending thirty years waiting for some
guy to come up with decorating ideas for your house. Ain't
gonna happen.

"I've always worked and I've always had money of my own
I'd never let Gordon get his hands on. The thing is, I'm a
feminist. Big time. I mean I would really like it if women ran
the world. The world would be a better place. And I think the
average woman can do everything the average man can, and
can do it better. I'll go even further. I don't think women need
to get married and have children to be happy. Some do, but
plenty don't.

"But for Christ's sake you've got to face facts. A guy will
work his butt off to get a woman, but he just doesn't know
what to do with her once he gets her. If I've been a happy
woman in this marriage—and I have been, in spite of the crazy

life we've led—it's because I told myself and I told Gordon this is *my* marriage and I'm going to fix it up and make it work the way I want it."

And then she charged in . . . Nancy went silent for a while. I started to ask her a question but she raised her hand to stop me. I could tell she was getting ready to say something that was hard for her. Finally she sighed. "You've got be able to get through the catastrophes. Ten years ago I thought it was all over. I'd had this really good nursing assignment and Gordon went to St. Bart's for some game he'd heard about. It was the kind of thing I usually would've gone along with him for, but I couldn't because of my job.

"Then my job suddenly ended early and I thought I'd zip down and surprise him. It was always okay with him if I was with him when he was gambling. Well, I surprised him all right. He'd hooked up with this cocktail-pianist dame I guess he'd run into a number of times over the years, so they knew each other, but I found them sleeping together. Literally. I go up to his room, I get the maid on the floor to let me in, and there's Gordon fast asleep with this naked woman next to him snoring away like she didn't have a care in the world.

"You know, you think you're going to go nuts at a time like that. But I just stood there watching them sleep. I wanted to cry, I wanted to kill, I wanted to just go to bed and stay there forever. But where did I want to come down? I knew I wasn't the type to just cry and be the victim. I don't know, but I took another look at that woman, and you know she looked like me. The same kind of dyed black hair. The same kind of pointy chin. An Elizabeth Taylor kind of look. There was just something about her looking like me that made me feel competitive. Now don't misunderstand me. This is the first time I'd ever caught him cheating. I would never let myself be one of these women whose husband's had one girlfriend after another. I just figured, okay, mister, this is your first time and it's your last time.

"So they're lying there snoring and I strip down to my bra

and panties and I climb into bed next to him on the other side
from her. And I start sort of snuggling up to him and he starts
cuddling up with me. Maybe he's thinking I'm her. Maybe he's
thinking I'm me and he's too sleepy to realize that I shouldn't
be there. Anyway, he's kind of nuzzling me and moving
around. She wakes up. She sees me. She screams, like a . . .
like a bad horror movie actress. Anyway, she screams and then
Gordon screams like a girl.

"I'm still lying there in bed and I pick up my bag off the
floor and put my hand inside it and I tell Miss Droopy Tits—
the bigger they are the harder they fall—I have a gun and I'm
going to kill her if she doesn't get out in the time it takes to
throw your clothes on real fast. And the poor shithead believes
me, and Gordon believes me, which helps me understand why
he wasn't a better poker player. He just didn't have an instinct
for the bluff.

"Anyway she's gone and believe it or not I'm *this close*,"
putting her thumb and forefinger very close together, "to enjoying myself. I looked at Gordon and said, 'If you think she'll
be a better wife than I've been, say so right now. Otherwise if
I ever catch you with her or anyone else ever again you might
as well just hand me divorce papers. And a razor blade.'

"I must've scared him very badly, because he started crying.
Gordon's a tough guy, but I think he felt very guilty. Anyway
he's promising me, in between these big gulping man-sobs, that
he's very sorry and very stupid and the woman didn't mean
anything to him and she just sort of seduced him and he'll
never do it again. You know, blah, blah, blah. But the strongest
feeling I had inside was that I was feeling very competitive.
Like that chick had got her hooks in him somehow, but I was
going to be the chick he went home with, so to speak."

No one, least of all Nancy, would recommend marriage to
a Gordon. But look at what it did for Nancy. For some crazy
reason it kept her creativity on the boil. And it was the creative
spark staying alive that meant everything for the long-term
viability of that relationship. Even though most of us aren't in
a relationship with a professional gambler, most of our lives

have their share of uncertainty, difficulties, and the occasional crisis. And what's nice about Nancy's story is that it contains, based on my research, what works for most women if they want to keep alive their creative connection to their relationship.

Here are the four ingredients.

1. YOU KEEP YOUR CREATIVE SPARK ALIVE WHEN YOU KNOW THAT WHO YOU ARE AND WHAT YOU DO MAKE A REAL DIFFERENCE TO YOUR PARTNER.

What do you think happens to a woman who's in an okay relationship with an okay guy but the guy doesn't need her at all for anything, not to get ahead at work, not to have someone to talk to after work, not to have someone to have fun with on the weekends, nothing? You lose any sense of having a reason for being involved with each other. It's like hiring a plumber to do work in your bathroom and you hang around for a few minutes in case you have to get him something or answer a question, but he doesn't need you and so you walk away.

There have been many studies showing that when a person loses the sense that she matters, she goes dead inside. When a teenager doesn't feel she matters to her parents, she loses the sense that she has to take care of herself. When an old lady feels she no longer matters to her family, her risk of death skyrockets. We need to be needed. And what's wonderful about being needed is the way it stimulates every creative bone in your body.

Now if you're going through this experience of trying to make your love survive the test of time right now, you might say, "Yeah, but my husband *doesn't* need me. That's what's real. Okay, he needs me for sex. And he needs me if we have people over. But that's it."

This is why the movie *It's a Wonderful Life* has taken such a hold on our psyches. It's the story of a guy who didn't feel he was needed. The question is, what would the story have shown the wife in the movie to make her feel she was needed?

And what about you? What do you do if you look at your relationship and don't feel needed at all?

Based on my experience talking to hundreds of women like you, I'd bet anything that you make a huge difference in your partner's life and are in fact needed very much.

He needs you to make things special. For one thing, he may not need you for him to just jog along in his life in a boring kind of way. But he might need you very much to make things special. Do things *feel* special between you right now? If not, he needs you.

He needs you in ways you may not realize. Maybe you haven't taken the time to look carefully through your lives together and inventory all the places where you make a big difference. It's not that he takes you for granted. It's that you take yourself for granted. I dare you to take up this challenge. See if you can come up with ten important ways you make a difference in your partner's life. You might have a tough time coming up with the first one but once you break the ice, I bet all ten will be clear to you.

I've asked women who are in the situation you might be in—where they're wondering if they really make a difference in their partner's life—to take up this challenge. Based on their answers, here are the most common, important ways women make all the difference in the world to their partners. Maybe some of the items on this list apply to you. Maybe you can use some of these items to prime the pump and come up with your own reasons.

THE TOP TEN REASONS YOU MAKE A DIFFERENCE TO YOUR PARTNER

1. "My husband would be a very sad, lonely man without me to talk to."

2. "Well, I don't know anyone else who laughs at his corny jokes. And I'm glad I do, because would I want to live with a guy who'd been convinced he had no sense of humor?"

3. "I'm the only person in my husband's life who knows how to make him feel he's worthwhile. Everyone else complains and asks him for stuff."

4. "I make nice things happen. Special things. Unusual things. Without me he'd fall into a rut so deep you couldn't see him."

5. "It's simple. With me around there are all kinds of really neat people in our lives. Fun, interesting friends. Without me he'd be a dried-out couch potato."

6. "Without me there'd be no one in the world who really loved him."

7. "Whenever he has an important decision to make about his life, he's lost without me."

8. "Look, every woman in the world has a vagina, but I just think there's something special about the way we work together as lovers—our sexual chemistry, I guess—that he couldn't get anywhere else."

9. "I guess my husband's pretty eccentric, and he has to keep that hidden. I'm the only person who accepts him for who he really is, who makes him feel good for being who he really is."

10. "A guy's not supposed to be like this, but my husband's scared of taking risks, and I think a lot of guys are really like that. If it weren't for me, I think he'd still have the same low-paying job that he had when we first met and

he'd feel terrible about himself. Because of me, he's been able to take the risks that have made him feel he has a life."

Do any of these things start you thinking? Remember, what's important is that you come up with your own list of ways you make a difference to your partner.

Let him tell you how he needs you. If you're really having trouble coming up with ways you make a difference to your partner, I'm going to ask you to take a risk. Talk to him. Ask him to tell you the ways you make an important difference in his life. Give him time to think about it. One guy couldn't think of anything at first, and his wife was getting furious when he suddenly said, "Remember that time when you went to stay with your mother for ten days? I'd get out of work and I didn't feel I had any particular reason to come home. Then when I was home it was like that painting where the clocks are melting—time went soft. Nothing seemed to matter. You make a difference because you give my life meaning."

Wow. She'd had no idea.

Bottom line: feeling you don't make a difference deadens your creativity. Women who feel a creative connection throughout this experience of love over the long haul are women who first connect to the ways they make a difference.

Diagnosis. Can you point to a specific, important way you make a difference in your partner's life?

YES_____ NO_____

Prescription. If you answered *no,* help is on the way. I've already given you some ideas about what to do. Think about ways you make a difference in his life. Ask him how you make a difference. Don't rest until you do it. You need to make your experience of love satisfying.

Perhaps you need more help. Here's another way we can get at this. Write down ten things you like about yourself. I don't mean physical things, like having nice hair or nice hands. I mean things about who you are as a person that make you respect yourself. Things like honesty, kindness, intelligence, people skills, being a good negotiator, being a good friend, having a lot of common sense, having a good sense of humor . . . you get the idea. Things about you that would make you happy if someone praised them, while deep inside you knew that you really deserved their praise.

Then for each item on your list write down one way that that good quality of yours makes a positive difference for your partner. For example, you might prize your solid common sense, and it's a good thing too because your partner's smart but he's a bit of a dreamer, and your common sense has more than once saved him from going way out there and getting into trouble.

This is your *good-things-about-me-that-are-good-for-my-partner* list.

Most women won't have much trouble coming up with things they respect about themselves and then connecting these things with ways their partner needs them. This should give you a surge of appreciation of how important you really are. Now you'll see: that feeling will nurture your sense of creative engagement.

2. YOU KEEP YOUR CREATIVE SPARK ALIVE WHEN YOU LIKE THE PERSON YOU BECOME IN RESPONSE TO THE CHALLENGES YOUR PARTNER PRESENTS YOU.

People talk endlessly about fit in relationships. But, you know, it's not such a big deal if you both like anchovy pizza. The *most* important kind of fit is the one most often overlooked. It's the fit that grows out of the ways your partner's needs bring out the best in you.

What good is it if your partner's needs don't bring out the best in you? Suppose that your husband's biggest need is for you to be pretty. Well, unless you're some airhead who thinks, yeah, I like the idea of being a decoration, there's likely to be a war between what your husband needs from you and what you need to feel proud of yourself. If my husband needed me to be an expert gourmet cook for him to function. . . . oh boy, would we be in trouble. Julia Child I could never be. It would be like needing your dog to sing opera. I couldn't do it. I wouldn't want to do it. Thank goodness he's happy eating the most god-awful crap he makes for himself while being scared to death of the health food I make for myself. Now you know the darkest secret of my marriage.

Now let me tell you a happy, hopeful secret about the great majority of relationships. Men have a deep hunger and need for smart wives. Women like themselves when they're smart. *Women being as smart as we can be* not only makes relationships feel good, but makes women feel good about being in them. And that keeps your creative spark alive.

Now you're probably the kind of women who doesn't need to hear this. But believe it or not, every once in a while I still run into a woman who thinks that she's got to act dumb to make her guy feel smart, or who's afraid that when she does show her intelligence it makes her seem bitchy or bossy. In other words, a lot of women feel that their intelligence causes trouble.

Well, being bitchy probably will cause trouble. And being in a relationship with a guy with a fragile ego is a recipe for a bad relationship. But let me make clear what's at stake. Not only are you a smart cookie, but your smarts are one of the best things about you, and if your partner doesn't elicit your smarts then this make-or-break experience of trying to survive the test of time will ultimately result in your going dead in the relationship.

This is really good news for you though. It's always good news when what's best about you is best for the life you're living.

Diagnosis. Ask yourself what are the top three challenges

your partner presents you. Obviously for Nancy the challenges were financial, emotional, and practical. But be specific for yourself.

Then for each of these three challenges ask yourself, "Are there things I like about myself that I can use to meet this challenge?" Were you able to say *yes* to each one?

YES_____ NO_____

Prescription. The danger here is that when we don't feel we have what it takes to meet a challenge, we lose interest. We sort of wander off emotionally. And that can be fatal for love.

The solution is to realize there are many different ways of responding to a challenging situation, and there are many different things you can like about yourself. No matter what challenge your partner presents you, there is some part of you that you like that can respond to the challenge. What you must do is think about your situation in a new way, one that gives you hope, that restimulates your creative energies. Here's an example.

Rosemary's Story

One woman I know worked for a number of years as a bookkeeper in the trucking company her husband Ernie started. At the beginning they had very little money and frankly Ernie didn't know much about the business. But Rosemary was an experienced bookkeeper and they were really full partners. She loved feeling she ran the business alongside him. But then she got busy having kids and he got busy as the company started to grow and grow and grow.

Before she knew what was happening Ernie started bringing home business problems that were out of her depth. Where once she'd felt smart about the problems they discussed, now Rosemary felt ignorant and stupid. Of course this was a recipe for her to go dead inside, since she no longer felt she had anything to contribute. How could she compete with the high-level consultants her husband brought in sometimes?

But it wasn't only as a businesswoman that Rosemary liked herself. She also liked herself in the role of amateur psychologist. She felt she understood how to help people understand and help themselves. So she said to herself, "Look, Ernie doesn't need me anymore as a business adviser. But he's got so many stresses and worries to deal with. What he needs desperately is someone to help him sort things out and put them in perspective. I don't need to know a damn thing about the trucking business to help him do that. Anyway, I'm more interested in psychology than I am in trucking."

Rosemary's story makes it clear that there are always many ways to connect with a situation. If you can't feel good about yourself for connecting one way, find another way to connect so that you can feel good about yourself. Perhaps you can connect in a more focused way. In Rosemary's case, instead of advising her husband on all parts of his business, she might have concentrated on advising him on important personnel issues, like who to hire, who to fire, who to promote. Just don't make the mistake so many women make of losing a way to connect—the way Rosemary lost her business adviser role—and then just give up. There are always alternative ways.

3. YOU KEEP YOUR CREATIVE SPARK ALIVE WHEN YOU STAY OUT OF RUTS.

You know, there's something that happens to couples in the bedroom that's a kind of microcosm of what happens to couples over the course of their whole relationship. Sex is supposed to be an area where you exercise your creativity, among other things. But we hate stress and we hate disasters. And so couples who make love to each other more than a few times quickly start zeroing in on what works. For example, when you're on top things go fine, but when he's on top you have problems. So you end up always being on top. When he initiates everyone's happy. When you initiate, there's something not right about the experience. So he always initiates. It's safer and less stressful that way. The comfort factor is higher.

But sex then eventually becomes boring and predictable, the creative juices stop flowing, and the bedroom becomes a sexual dead zone.

The same thing happens to love when you're in it for the long haul. The more you learn about how to feel safe with each other, the more you tread a narrow groove where you always do the same things and say the same things and respond in the same ways.

Nancy benefited in one way from the crazy life Gordon led. Things never stayed the same for them. Because things kept changing she never went stale. They'd be broke, they'd be rich. They'd live here, they'd live there. Gordon would be around twenty-four hours a day, Gordon would have disappeared. They'd have to reinvent their relationship every three months. It led to fights. It led to discomfort as they often had to face ways in which they were strangers to each other. But in the process of reconnecting they kept forming slightly different patterns. There was no groove to fall into.

You and I aren't so lucky. I know in my case, my husband and I work incredibly hard during the week and try to leave as much free time on the weekends as possible, where we both pretty much just collapse. It's a good, safe routine that helps us recharge our batteries. The problem is that it's a routine that leaves surprisingly little room for having fun together. Work during the week, collapse on the weekend. Because fun isn't part of the routine, it doesn't happen as often as we'd like.

If you're sharp-eyed, you probably notice how we get trapped in this rut. No one says, "Oh boy, I'm jumping into a rut." What we say is, "Oh boy, this is what I have to do to take care of myself." It's the things we do to take care of ourselves that get us into our ruts. Like having sex in a certain way every single time. Now you see where the power of routine comes from: We're held there because of the things we do to take care of ourselves.

This is really the most dangerous aspect of the ruts we fall into: they're invisible. What we see is that we're just doing whatever it is we have to do. It feels right and inevitable. How *else* would you make love other than first he does this then you do that? How *else* would my husband and I organize our lives other than working to the point of collapse? So we think.

If the road to hell is paved with good intentions, the road to relationship death is paved with sensible ideas for how to live your life. But what's the alternative?

Prescription. What you have to do is *fight it*. I'm talking to myself as well as to you. I'm not even going to bother with the diagnosis here. Almost all couples are working themselves into a rut, and they're convinced they can't do anything about it.

There is only one solution. Permanent revolution. You and I aren't as lucky as Nancy, in the sense that your life and mine aren't revolutionized for us by being with a partner who's a professional gambler. It's strange to call that lucky, isn't it, because Nancy has lived with a tremendous amount of stress and insecurity, which takes a toll.

But this is our dilemma: There are sources of stress and insecurity in all of our lives and we seek routine as a way of coping. Routine *is* a way of coping. I'm not knocking it. I'm just saying that it's medicine for life that has deadly side effects if it's overused. And that's why we have to force ourselves out of our routines. Otherwise our emotional spark goes dead.

Here's how you institute a program of permanent revolution.

• *Don't take anything for granted about how you live.* For example, almost everyone gets up in the morning, goes to work, comes home, and has an evening. Most of the time we're damned tired in the evening. But it's possible that you would come home in the evening, go to bed as soon as possible, get up very early, and have a morning together before you go to work. I know, I should be locked up for proposing something so crazy. Most people can't do this. *But I can name three rela-*

tionships I've saved just because I got the couple to do this when there was no other way for them to have a life together.

Let's not get carried away by this example. There are dozens and dozens of ways you can shake up your life. If you analyze your routine and refuse to take anything for granted, you will find an amazing number of opportunities for shaking things up.

• *Make a routine out of destroying routine.* This just means you put yourselves on a schedule for destroying your schedule.

Once a week you do one little thing different from the way you've been doing it. Or you do one little new thing every week. Go out for breakfast together. Get into bed early one night. Talk about something that you've never talked about before.

Once a month, do something very different. Play hooky from work together and spend the day on the town. Go out together where one of you plans the date as a surprise for the other. Sign up for dance classes. Do something you've never done before, like going to a tractor pull or a fashion show or a performance of Shakespeare. You may not like it, but at least you'll be able to say, "We're people who try new things."

Once a year, institute a major shake-up in some aspect of your lives. Take a course together, like at the extension division of a university. Reverse responsibilities in the household—you be the one in charge of initiating sex, while your partner becomes the one who pays the bills. Decide that this year you'll go for a walk together every single day. Reverse roles: you know how you're convinced that you're the practical one and your partner's the romantic? Well, switch. You be in charge of making all the romantic stuff happen, and let your partner be in charge of the practical stuff. Just to see what happens, for better or for worse, just to shake things up.

You probably won't do these new roles as well as you did the old ones. But that's why we fall into ruts. If ease and comfort are your priorities, routine will rule and the experience of love for the long haul will become an experience of creative death.

But if you keep shaking things up, breaking out of the shackles of routine, trying new things and sometimes failing with the things you try, you'll keep that creative spark alive and you'll be giving yourself a gift. It's the gift of hope. Love is a feeling, not a fact. And keeping the spark alive means having the hope inside you that you can keep the feeling alive.

You need this gift of hope that you can keep your creativity alive no matter what happens to your relationship. Suppose the worst happens, and the relationship you're in ends. Maybe because your partner dies or dumps you or does something awful and you dump him. These are painful catastrophes. But when you come out the other side and find yourself having love adventures and looking for someone to love, the fact that you were able to hold on to that creative spark in yourself before will give you the confidence to recreate what you once had, and that it will be worthwhile. All of this because of the creativity you know you have in you.

4. YOU KEEP YOUR CREATIVE SPARK ALIVE WHEN YOU ACCEPT RESPONSIBILITY FOR THE RELATIONSHIP.

This is a very controversial point and I could get into big trouble for making it. Both partners are supposed to be equally responsible for the relationship. That's what the books and courses tell us. That's the ideal. And here I am saying that *you* have to accept full responsibility for the relationship. I'm not a traditionalist and most of my friends are not traditionalists either, and I don't want to lose any friends. But I've spent my life trying to figure out how love works, and I've got to tell the truth about love even if it makes some people mad.

What I've found is that the creative spark stays alive for women when they accept and welcome taking most of the responsibility for the relationship. If you wait for the guy to shoulder his half of the burden, you'll get pissed, you'll get discouraged, and you'll wait forever.

It shouldn't be women's work. I'm not any happier about it being this way than you are. But we will have a woman president and men who leap up to wash the dishes long before we have men feeling it is their responsibility to take care of the relationship. If a woman doesn't see the relationship as her work, the guy will never see it as his work. And if you think you can mobilize him by just sort of acting unhappy, all he'll do is bug you about what's wrong with you and try to fix *you*.

Why we give up. Here's how we get into trouble with this. Believe me, I know because I've gotten into trouble with it myself. We start out gung ho for taking care of the relationship. We monitor what's going on. We have ideas for how things should be between us and our partners. We do creative things to try to raise what goes on in our relationship to a higher level. You know: we try to have more, better, richer, deeper intimacy.

But of course it's not smooth sailing. What makes it worse, though, is that when you try to work on the relationship the guy acts like you're taking him shopping to buy drapes. He just doesn't seem interested in the whole thing. Now here's where your creative spark dies. You say to yourself, naturally enough, that if he's not going to work at it, why should you. You're tired, and it just doesn't feel fair. You're sick of it always being you with the whole responsibility for saving your love life from falling into a terrible slump.

What happened to me. I got into this in a bad way with my husband. Remember, I wasn't only taking care of my own marriage but I was seeing couples who came to me for therapy and so I was taking care of a whole bunch of other marriages too. Plus—and this is what really galled me—my husband also worked with couples, so he didn't even have the excuse of being a bricklayer or a gas station owner whom you might not expect to know much about relationships. It felt like the height of unfairness that he wouldn't eagerly, actively, try to seize oh, say, 60 percent of the responsibility. Fifty percent. Something.

I remember one Sunday morning. We were enjoying the luxury of a Sunday morning in bed. Now it had been my pattern to use a time like this to bring up problems I'd noticed in our relationship.

Anyway I had this incredible suspicion that if *I* didn't say anything, *he* wouldn't say anything. I guessed that if it were up to him we would live this Sunday morning as if we had no past and no future. Sure, he'd talk to me about something he remembered that interested him and he might suggest his getting us something to eat, but he lived the philosophy that if you ignored problems, they'd go away, like if you ignored a sinkful of dirty dishes, they'd clean themselves.

Anyway, I'm always making experiments, so as I lay in bed next to my poor, ignorant, fool of a husband, I thought, *If I never bring up anything about our relationship—no complaints, no problems, no needs—how long will it be before he brings something up?*

When Stubborn meets Stupid. Most women reported similar experiences to mine. And they find what I found.

The only possible problem there could be in the relationship from my husband's point of view was that *I would think* there's a problem with the relationship. His philosophy was, If you're happy, then I'm happy. If you're not happy, get happy.

I'm an incredibly stubborn person. So when I went on strike with my husband that morning and stopped "working on the relationship," I really could've gone on that way for a long time. I didn't bring up anything that Sunday morning, or the next week, or for many weeks. A lot of women do this kind of thing when it comes to housework, and it's often effective. They stop cleaning up after a meal they have prepared on the theory that it's only fair that if one cooks, the other cleans. Their partner gets the point and picks up the slack.

But from my husband's point of view, my not bringing up

issues about our relationship was a wonderful gift. He thought it meant everything was okay.

Then came our anniversary. My husband arranged for us to go to a new, upscale Thai restaurant that we'd heard good things about. I was looking forward to it. We sat down, and the waiter immediately came over with the menus. So we talked about what to order, which is always a big deal at a brand-new restaurant. Then we talked about what the place looked like, and how it seemed more like a French restaurant than a Thai restaurant. Then we talked about the waiter. Then we gossiped about some of the people in the place whom we thought we knew. Then we talked about the food. Then we talked about how much the food cost.

We left the restaurant, and we hadn't talked about anything. My anniversary dinner had been about nothing. If we'd been strangers, we might've talked about more interesting, important, and personal things.

Don't get me wrong. My husband has a lot of important, interesting things to talk about. But an anniversary dinner shouldn't feel so empty.

I felt I was being strangled. My husband was acting as if everything was fine, because for him it was fine. It was crystal clear to me that leaving him in charge of our relationship would be like leaving my cat in charge of the laundry. It just wouldn't get done. And I felt it was killing my caring.

I just couldn't take it anymore. So what was I to do? I knew *how* to charge back in there and find problems and figure out solutions. The problem was to get over my sense of the unfairness. Just think about it: I do all the work and then I get labeled a troublemaker for my efforts. But something simple stared me in the face. My little experiment had made my relationship worse, not better. Unhappy relationships are unacceptable, but I was making my relationship worse.

I just couldn't stand it anymore. I noticed that at some point every single day my husband was asking me how I was. "How are you feeling?" "How are you doing?" "Is everything okay?"

And I'd just say, "I'm fine," or, "I'm preoccupied because I have a lot to do today," or, "I'm getting my period." And he'd be happy.

What I realized was that when I went on strike and stopped taking care of our relationship, my husband dimly realized that something was different. Those stupid questions were his version of doing the job of taking care of the relationship. Someone was doing the job. But instead of my doing it well, he was doing it badly. *That's* what got to me.

I'm going dead inside and he thinks he's taking care of things, I thought. It's like a ship headed for an iceberg because no one's steering it.

So I said the hell with it. Lots of things are unfair. But you've got to have fun and enjoy yourself and make things be the way you want them to be anyway. *This relationship was my home.* The more deeply I understood that, and appreciated it, the more my creative energies would be engaged. Who is so stupid that she'll let her home go to hell?

Besides, if he didn't like the way I was working on our relationship, let him come up with his own ideas.

I went back to work. Noticing things, commenting on things, asking for things. And it didn't feel like I was participating in something unfair. It felt like I was alive again. My creative juices started flowing again. And that's the magic thing about creativity. The more you express it, the more of it you have. And then I started feeling my caring again.

Diagnosis. I think I'm going to leave it to your honesty and integrity to decide this. Most women are wonderfully in tune with themselves. So which is it? Do you act like someone who feels she's responsible for her relationship? Or are you just sitting there, your arms folded, waiting?

Prescription. There are two reasons you might have abandoned your sense that your relationship was your responsibility: (1) feeling that it was unfair for you to do all the work;

(2) feeling discouraged because all your work didn't get you anywhere.

It's interesting, isn't it, that the make-or-break aspect of this experience is all about what happens to your creative spark? And the sense of unfairness and discouragement are the two things that squelch creativity in artists of all kinds. Every painter, poet, musician, filmmaker, short-story writer who's given up has done so because she's just stopped having the hope that anything will happen as a result of what she does. And this is often made worse if she somehow develops the sense that it's those people with connections or money or politically correct opinions or the right kind of school background who get ahead in the art world.

Every artist who gives up is exactly the same inside as every woman who gives up on her relationship.

But what do artists who have struggled with these feelings say when instead of giving up, they have hung in there and managed to fill the world with meaning and beauty? We can learn a lot from them. Here are some quotes from some of the most successful artists in America:

- "It was a matter of pride. I simply told myself I'd never give up."
- "I decided to stop trying to please other people and instead just worry about pleasing myself."
- "I realized I can't control how things turn out, but I can control what I do."
- "I just had this vision of how things should be and I felt I couldn't quit until I'd expressed this vision."
- "You know, if we all sit around waiting for things to be fair, nothing will get done. It's only when they silence you that things are really unfair."
- "There was nothing heroic about it. I liked doing this, and I made sure to keep on focusing on what I liked about it."

These are the voices of artists. What's amazing is that these are also the voices of women going through this make-or-break experience of love. It's largely a matter of attitude and nourishment. I don't have to tell you the attitude to have. Just reread these quotes.

But I would like to say something about nourishment, because when it comes to the story of love in our lives, particularly when you're in it for the long haul, too many of us are running on empty. And every artist needs nourishment to keep the creative spark alive. What about *you*?

Finding Nourishment

Every creative artist and every woman who is successful with this experience will tell you that she gets two main kinds of nourishment. From Picasso and Madonna to your Aunt Tillie, the creative spark is kept alive with *ideas* and *inspiration*.

Creative ideas for long-haul lovers. Ideas don't come to you. You have to look for them. Every great singer ruthlessly exploits singers and musicians of today and yesterday. You know Picasso's *Guernica*? It's a masterpiece of passion and creative intensity. Well get this. Every image in it is closely derived from images going back hundreds of years in the history of art. His painting is really a painting of the massacre of the innocents. Many of the images in his painting come from other paintings of the massacre of the innocents, like Poussin's.

So here's this genius ruthlessly exploiting the geniuses of the past, and here you and I are sort of shuffling through our relationships in broken-down slippers and ratty bathrobes waiting for ideas to come to us.

If you want good ideas you've got to go out and look for them. Read couples' books, starting with my own *Our Love Is Too Good to Feel So Bad*. But I hope you'll read many couples' books. There are a lot of good ones out there. Read the women's magazines. Whoever heard of a woman's magazine without an article on relationships? Read other material on relationship-type issues. A book on negotiation. A book on dealing with difficult people. A book on how to have more openness and honesty in your relationship, like Dr. Charles Foster's wonderful *Truth Without Fear* or *There's Something I Have to Tell You*. If you're sick of reading, get ideas from friends, from sitcoms on TV, from movies.

The point is that the world is full of ideas for people who turn to the world and say, "I'm looking for something new. Can you help me?"

Inspiration. Different people get inspired in different ways. Think about times you've been inspired in any part of your life—work, hobbies, or whatever. What did your inspiration do for you then? Look for the same things now. Based on what women have told me, here are the main sources of inspiration:

• *Success stories.* You're watching TV and you see some human interest item about this couple who've been married for fifty years and seem to still love each other today as much as when they first met. That's an example of the kind of story that inspires many women to renew their creative commitment to their relationship.

• *Competition.* Most women with a creative spark are surprisingly competitive, and I think we might as well just admit this. The annual county fair inspired Aunt Bea on the old *Andy Griffith Show* to heights of creativity when it came to her pickles. Most of us are no different. A sister, a friend, a movie star you read about—these people can all stimulate your competitive juices when it comes to your creative spark.

• *Idealism.* Everyday life wears away our sense of what's most important, which is why many of us go to church or synagogue. Some inspiring clergyperson stands up and blows the dust off of our forgotten ideals. We're reminded of how things should be. As artists in love, this experience of reconnecting with our ideals is essential. It's the main reason I've written this book: my idealistic belief that I deeply want to convey to you that love can be and should be excellent and true and real, as well as being something that enables you to realize what's best about yourself. Plus my belief that love like this holds the world together.

• *Memory*. You are the repository of the best sources of inspiration. You remember how things were when they were at their best? You remember what it was like to fall in love? Why not let your memories inspire you now? I remember a couple who'd fallen into that common pattern of distance and anger. I asked them to describe their best day. I couldn't believe it. Their best day had more ingredients than a Chinese Caesar salad. There was a beautiful field with wildflowers. There was a dog, a pig, an old swing hanging from a limb of a tree, a brook and a leaky rowboat, an old lady who sold pies from her house, a book of poems, sex in the field of wildflowers under the tree with the pig and the dog looking on. The point is that their best day, like all of our best days, was a treasure trove of memories to use for inspiration.

I know you know how to find nourishment. It's just that you forget to do it. You wouldn't forget to eat—not for long anyway. Well, don't forget to fuel the creative energy you need to keep love going over the long haul.

So creative people find ways to nourish themselves, and now you have some ideas for how to do it when it comes to creativity in your relationship. But they have another, perhaps deeper, secret. They also find ways to prevent the nourishment they do get from leaking out.

Stopping the Nourishment Sappers

Imagine Picasso, filled with ideas for a wonderful painting he's going to do. But then a voice whispers, "What if you're not good enough? What if no one likes it? What if you screw up?" Picasso could have the greatest ideas in the world, but this voice would kill those ideas. If he let it.

It's always fear of something that destroys our creative spark. But what do you do about it? There are two ineffective ways of responding to these fears in a relationship. Freezing and fleeing.

Let's take them one at a time. You decide for yourself which of these has been deadening your creativity (and therefore making your love go dead). Then I'll give you a way to deal with it so it'll lose its hold over you.

Freezing. *"I've tried so many things that don't work. Now I'm afraid that if I do anything different I'll make things worse."* This fear has a strange hold on us because we feel we've earned it through hard work. It's almost like we point to this fear and say, "See, aren't I right to be paralyzed?"

For example, you've tried many things to spice up your sex life; every time your partner's responded negatively. So why not give in to the fear that will lock you into a routine? Or you've tried to talk about new and different topics and your partner has responded with all the bounce of a dropped meatball, if you haven't actually started a fight. So why fight your fear?

What to do if this applies to you. I understand how you feel. But I've worked with hundreds of women suffering from this fear, and I've learned something, damn it. We think we've tried everything and that nothing else will work. In reality, we've tried only a narrow range of things, and we haven't used our partners as a source of help for what will work.

So do this. Wherever you're stuck, ask your partner, "What do you think would work to get us to . . ." Then fill in whatever it is you feel stuck with. For instance, have sex more often, talk about money without fighting, do something that's fun once a week. Listen to what he says.

And then—I know this is hard—ask yourself if you have really tried everything. I know you haven't. I know that there are many different kinds of things you could try. Every woman who's come to me for help who's said, "I've tried everything," has been astonished when I've offered her dozens of new ideas. It's not that I'm so clever. It's just that I refuse to be beaten down by those smug words, "I've tried everything." Sorry, kid. You haven't begun to try everything. You just haven't.

Let me add some psychological depth to this. You and I need to feel smart and capable. We need to feel that if there's a problem, we can handle it. It's painful for us when things happen that we can't cope with. So if some kind of bug attacks the tomatoes you're trying to grow, you not only want to save your tomatoes, you need to feel effective at dealing with the problem. There's so much research to support the idea that we get depressed when we lose the sense that we can cope effectively with our problems.

But we're clever psychologically, too. If we can't cope one way, we try to cope another way. If you're bad at stopping those tomato-eating bugs, maybe you can be good at predicting when and how those tomato-eating bugs are going to attack. After several damp, rainy days you look outside and say in a strangely satisfied way, "Those bugs will get those tomatoes now." You've gained your sense of self-efficacy through your ability to predict rather than through your ability to fix things.

I'm sure you can see why this applies to keeping your creative spark alive. When we convince ourselves we've tried everything, and that nothing works when it comes to dealing with some aspect of our relationship, it should be more depressing than it is for most of us. We save ourselves from depression by becoming good at predicting how the dumb jerk we've been with for so long will respond. "I knew he'd do that," we say to ourselves.

Can you see what the psychological danger here is? *The more your sense of effectiveness comes from predicting how nothing will change, the more you get locked into nothing changing as a way to save yourself from depression.* "Nothing changing" is depressing, but being good at predicting exactly how "nothing changes" makes you feel better.

But it also makes you go dead inside. You stop caring about the relationship. Your creative connection to the relationship dries up. You might have a gay old time talking to your friends about your relationship, but your relationship itself becomes a desert. So watch out for this trap of being "the good predictor." It's something you do when you're afraid that if you do anything different you'll make things worse. I've shown you how to overcome this fear. Predicting how things will stay the same is not the way out.

Fleeing. *"Harry will never leave me. And I have a nice life. So what if we don't have a marriage anymore? I have a lot of other things to do with my creative energy than try to be happy in love."* There are so many ways to run in response to the fears that sap your creative energy. You're afraid nothing you do will make a difference? Well, you're busy anyway. So why not limit contact as much as possible and blame it on your schedule. You probably have a lot of love to give. Why not give it to someone who will appreciate it? A child or a grandchild. Friends. What the hell, have a love adventure. Or give your energy to some *thing* that will benefit from it. You might find a creative outlet. Do charity work. Further your career.

But it's important to understand what you're doing. Let's say you have two gardens. One gets a lot of sun. One is in the shade. You love the shade garden but you have some problems with it and start putting more and more of your energy into the sun garden. The shade garden's neglected. Every day it stands as a more and more visible testimony to the fruitlessness of working on it. The sun garden is so easy. Anyway, you're tired after working on the sun garden, and now when you look at it the shade garden overwhelms you with the sense of how hopeless you feel.

That's what happens sometimes to love. The creative spark goes out of love because we neglect the relationship because we put energy somewhere else. And because we put energy somewhere else, the relationship deteriorates and then we feel less and less able to do anything but neglect it.

What to do if this applies to you. If you remember, I said that nourishment comes from ideas and inspiration. This is a nourishment sapper because it makes you lose your desire for ideas and inspiration. You just have to understand the trap you're in. The more you flee by putting your energy into the easy outlets, the more you stop bothering with the ideas and inspiration you need to keep your love alive.

But there's another issue too. My hunch is that one reason you've withdrawn energy from your relationship is that part of you isn't even sure if you want to be in it. It's like that neglected shade garden: If you're thinking of selling the house in a year, all the more reason not to bother with it. Well, you've got to make a decision. Are you in? Or are you out? You can survive the death of a relationship. But I don't know if you can really survive the death of the spark of love inside you. I'm talking about your psychological survival as a woman for whom love is truly important.

If your relationship is too bad to stay in, it's time to move on. But if you'd have to say that your relationship is too good to leave, well for God's sake, fish or cut bait. If you're not going to get out of it, be in it. This tactic of pouring your creative energy elsewhere is destroying your love. It's destroying the creative spark in you that's necessary to keep your love alive.

Get a divorce or give it your best. Kill it or cure it. But love is too important to be half-assed about it.

We've Only Just Begun

Make-or-Break Experience #8:
Finding the Right Balance Between Love
and the Rest of Your Life

We spend our lives trying to give love a place that feels right to us. We started doing this when we were junior high school girls torn between whether to do our homework or talk to some boy on the phone. But finding a balance between life and love is never completed once and for all—the tightrope walker can never completely relax. Women in their twenties and forties and sixties are all struggling—each in her own way, each with the unique realities of her life—to find a place for love that feels right.

You Be the Judge

Which one of these three women found a way to give love a place in her life that felt right to her?

Anna's Story

" 'She could never find a man,' is what they said about me. But that's absolutely not true. Lots of guys wanted me. I had lots of relationships. A whole bunch of guys asked me to marry them. So most of the time there was some guy somewhere in my life. But ultimately I said *no* to all of them. And most of the time I lived on my own. Why? Because I knew what I was looking for. There are so many compromises you have to make sharing your life with someone. I didn't want to make those compromises unless I found the perfect guy. And I just haven't found him yet."

Bettina's Story

"When I was starting out becoming an artist—in my twenties basically—it's weird how completely uninterested in love and relationships I was. There were absolutely no guys in my life. And I didn't miss them. Things were going great for me without love, but then suddenly there I was thirty-one and I met Frank. Everything changed. We fell madly in love. He had money, and he had those travel books he wrote, so for, I don't know, five years we had this nonstop love affair that took us around and around and around the world. I don't think I paid much attention to where I was, though.

"Then maybe I felt something was starting to change, but I got pregnant, had my first baby, then a year later had my second. It's weird how suddenly Frank meant little to me. Like I'd suddenly gotten very tired of him. For ten years or more my girls were my life. Then they started having lives of their own and I was completely absorbed by my painting again."

Lily's Story

"I've always felt that having balance in life is the goal you've got to strive for. I start my day thinking about what I'm going to eat that day, and it's got to include all the basics. Why should it be any different when it comes to love? When I met Mark and we dated and fell in love, I decided this relationship was going to be part of my life forever. And that meant doing it right. That meant having dinner together every day. It meant sitting together in the living room after dinner and talking. It meant going out once a week. It meant having people over at least once a month. Maybe different people would do it differently, but if love was going to be like eating and breathing—and shouldn't it be?—then you've got to be absolutely consistent. I hope this doesn't make me sound too rigid."

Which of these three women found a way to give love a place in her life that felt right to her?

Well, it's a trick question. I bet you were going to say it was Lily.

But in fact *it's all three of them.* Love had a different role in each of their lives. Anna hasn't given love much play yet. Bettina was completely absorbed by it for one five-year period. Lily had what she thought was just the right dosage day after day for most of her adult life. But each had found the place for love in her life that felt right for her.

The Task of a Lifetime

Love may be an incredibly important story in your life, but it isn't the only story, even if you sometimes feel it's the heart of all the other stories. There are things you care about besides love. We find ourselves struggling to figure out how much room love should have in our lives. Everything? Barely any room? The center? The periphery? And of course we come up with different answers depending upon everything else that's going on in our lives. But no matter what answer we come up with, we all feel that our overall happiness depends on our finding the right balance for us. That's what makes this a make-or-break experience.

There are only two unacceptable answers. We don't want to give up on love. And we don't want to put ourselves in a position where we end up sacrificing everything for love.

What's Right for You?

It's not enough to say that we need love, that we care about love, that love is fundamental. Sure, but so is food. And yet some of us eat to live while others of us live to eat. I've talked to many women about this. And I now know that there is no one right answer to the question, *"How do I give love a place in my life that feels right?"*

The mystery is discovering what's right for you at this point in your life. I've got a news flash for you:

> Many women aren't able to find a place for love that feels right to them because they limit themselves to one option. They think there's only one place love should have in a normal, healthy woman's life. If the place they think is right isn't right for them, they suffer.

The one option more women subscribe to than any other is Lily's: the idea that every day has got to be balanced, as if there were some Minimum Daily Requirement of love you had to get in every day. But we've got to be open to the idea that there are other options.

⊛

Millie's Story

Millie's had three big relationships. The first was a fairy tale love affair with a tragic ending. She was a beautiful young nurse. He was a handsome, charismatic young doctor dedicated to working with poor mothers and their children in a neighborhood clinic. They worked together and also had a lot of time to revel in each other and their love. Millie knew that this was a once-in-a-lifetime relationship. But it felt so right she was sure it would last forever. And it probably would have if he hadn't been killed in a completely stupid, wasteful car accident. They hadn't even had a chance to get married.

She mourned him for a year. During that period the men she met repulsed her. Then she made a radical turning. She was suddenly hit with how lonely she felt. It didn't feel right not to have a man. That's what she said to her best friend: "I've got to get a man." And her friend supported her because she saw how devastated Millie had been and she thought "normalcy" would be good for Millie.

The first guy she actually married was also a doctor. He was both more of a big shot in the medical community and yet less committed to grass-roots medicine. But Millie thought he was maybe a little more substantial, more settled. So she'd be safer. What Millie discovered was that he was a compulsive cheating womanizer. Why had he even married her? Had he thought she was too stupid to catch him? Had he thought she wouldn't care?

Once she got sick of trying to find a way to blame herself, and once she accepted that she'd have to go through another loss, she dumped him, and good riddance to bad rubbish.

But Millie still had this sense that she had to get married. Maybe it was because things had been ultimately so out of control in her other relationships that she felt the need for control in the next one. So she found a nice, but boring guy at her church—there were no fireworks here, but fireworks had proven dangerous. And he seemed to love her.

So they got married. And he did turn out to be a nice guy. But he was so boring and Millie's life with him was so empty that she almost felt she'd go out of her mind if she stayed with him very long. That was the end of her third relationship.

Now what? Millie realized that if she kept up with this "I've got to have a man" approach to finding a place for love in her life, she'd go emotionally bankrupt. She was one of the first women I interviewed for this book and she clued me into the idea that there are many ways of finding balance. Here's what she said to me:

It's taken me years and years and a lot of heartache to get to this place. But I'm happy now. And I want to share with other women why I'm happy. I had a great, great love affair when I was a young woman. I think it would've been wonderful if it had lasted, but it was taken away from me far too early. Somehow I made the mistake of thinking that great love like that was normal. I expected to find it again. And it hurt so much to lose it I made the mistake of thinking that I needed it again, or something close to it, or else I just wouldn't be able to go on. So I gave myself an extra decade of pain and misery trying to do things "the right way," at least as I saw it.

I could've saved myself a lot of pain if I'd realized there are different paths for different women. Once upon a time I had something great. I didn't have to run around like a crazy woman trying to get something just to make up for my no longer having that great thing. Maybe it was time for me to accept the kind of love story my life was. You know, I give love to people every day. And even though they're sick and it's hard for them, they give love back to me. All right then, I've had my big love affair. My once-in-a-lifetime kind of thing. Now my life is filled with love every day. I don't need a man waiting for me in bed at night for the love story of my life to be a happy, healthy story. The love of my life died, but even so I've had more than most women. If I should be so incredibly lucky as to find that again, I'll embrace it. But I don't need any lesser kind of relationship to feel I've got love in my life.

Don't draw the wrong conclusion from what I'm saying. I'm not telling anyone what to do. I've finally found a way to have love in my life that works for me. I'd thought I'd found a way, but it was wrong for me. But those are only two ways. I don't know how many ways there are. But if you're going to help women with love in their lives, tell them don't copy Millie. Don't copy anyone. Don't fall victim to some idea that there's only one option. Find a way to have love in your life that's right for you. Just don't think that it's the way you've automatically assumed would be right for you. It's your life. Give it some thought. Then do it your own way.

The Balance That's Right for You

Millie put her finger on it. Do it your own way. That's exactly right. We have too few images of how love is supposed to fit into our lives. But the good news is that that there are a lot of options. Women have come up with a surprisingly varied range of answers to the question of how to find the right balance between love and the other parts of your life. What this means for you—if you've been having trouble finding an answer—is that you have many more options than you may have known about.

As I talked to women about their attempts to give love a place in their lives that felt right to them, I saw something interesting. I saw some women whose love lives were very unbalanced in the moment. And yet they were happy. And I saw some women whose love lives were perfectly balanced— they seemed to have to all. And yet they were miserable.

The stories here are an attempt to unravel that mystery. But I'll let you in on something. Perfect balance by itself is not what makes women feel that love has the place in their lives that's right for them. What does give us this feeling is our sense of ourselves as moving, growing, learning, and generally staying alive.

So when it comes to finding the right place for love in your life, you must understand that what's most important is the dynamic, changing quality of your life and your own uniqueness. There is no single, perfect formula for having love in your life.

How do you know if you need help with this? There's a secret to diagnosing whether or not you've found the place for love that's right for you. Just ask yourself this: Does getting love right feel like one of those mystery problems to you? You might be stuck here if you've examined and re-examined and *re*-re-examined the course of love in your life and you just can't make sense of why you feel so bad.

That's a sign that you've gotten stuck in the process of finding a place for love in your life that's right for you.

It turns out that as women today struggle to give love a place in their lives that feels right to them, certain solutions keep emerging over and over that women find particularly satisfying. So let me tell you some stories of women who've found solutions to the problem of finding harmony between life and love.

I can't tell you which solution is right for you. For many women different solutions make sense at different stages of their lives. But if you understand the solutions other women have found, maybe you'll get a better sense of what you've been looking for.

You see, that's what's most important. As we struggle to give love a place in our lives that feels right to us, we often don't know what we're looking for, which makes our search much harder. These stories will help you see what you've been looking for without even realizing it. Think of these almost as a series of landscapes. I'll paint the pictures. You decide which landscape you want to be in.

All you have to do is give yourself permission to take a whole new approach to balancing love with the rest of your life. You feel stuck because the approach you've been taking isn't right for you, no matter how strongly you feel it should be right. Give yourself permission to let one of these women provide a new and better option for you.

Option 1:

LOVE AS FRIENDSHIP.

❧

Jackie's Story

"I couldn't give love a place in my life that felt right until I realized that as long as I focused on romantic love—and whatever became of romantic love over the course of a marriage—I'd always feel frustrated and uncentered.

"After my second divorce I started talking to my first husband again. I'd always felt badly that things hadn't worked out between us, although I'd never regretted the divorce. Suddenly Hank and I were talking, hanging out together, and actually helping each other. Romance was something neither of us would've touched with a ten-foot pole. In a way it was the miracle of my life: the way I 'fell in like' with my ex–first husband. It was so right. A straight man-pal with whom there was no danger of the complications of romance rearing their ugly heads."

Like most women, Jackie fell into her solution pretty much by accident. She started out at twenty-one wanting to eventually fall in love—the real thing—and then for love to turn into one of those great marriages. But she didn't know how many surprises would be in store for her. She didn't know how easily she'd fall in love. She didn't know how easily love would fizzle.

Then when she got married the two times, she didn't realize how sometimes when love turned sour it turns into a raging beast of anger and disappointment, so that you can't wait to get out. And she didn't realize how relieved she'd be to get out, because it was just too much for her. Too distracting. Too overwhelming. Jackie in love felt like a small child in a large amusement park— she always got lost, and that was no fun at all.

The turning point for Jackie came one evening when she was sitting in a bar with her ex-husband Hank. They'd been talking about this and that. There was a period of silence, and he suddenly turned to her and said, "This is fun, you know?" And he was right. It was fun, shooting the breeze, talking to someone you cared about without being obsessed by thoughts of what you weren't getting. The timing of Hank's comment was amazing. During the silence, Jackie—a twice-divorced woman now in her late thirties—had been wondering if she'd ever again hear a man say how much he loved her.

But what had that ever given her? Hank's saying, "This is fun, you know?" felt like the most authentic words she'd ever heard. No pressure. No expectations. Just the sense that she was safe, because friendship was low key, and that meant it wouldn't collapse under its own weight. She wanted to stay best friends with him for life, and that's what she's done, so far anyway.

A lot of women are like Jackie. Lots of women try love and then come home to one great friend. Unfortunately a lot of women go through hell to get to this solution. A lot of women, for example, stay stuck for years in a bad marriage in an exhausting attempt to hold on to love—and then they realize years later that the friend they stayed connected to was the real source of love in their lives. They'd thought that that love wasn't real because it didn't come with the label *Romance*. But in fact as they looked back what they had with this friend was the real love of their lives.

If we really want to find happiness, it's time we stopped giving friendship a second-place status compared to love.

Is the solution Jackie found the solution for you? Have you been running yourself ragged looking for love when what will really satisfy you is true friendship?

Option 2:

LOVE AS YOUR FOUNDATION.

Meredith's Story

"I wish it hadn't taken me so long to realize what I wanted. Because I'd had it all the time.

"Paul and I fell in love, we got married, and I wanted it to be great. But it wasn't. And that made me mean and miserable. All I did was complain to Paul about what he wasn't giving me. He wasn't warm. He wasn't passionate. He was too withdrawn. I wasn't important enough to him. I spent a lot of money dragging Paul to marriage counselors trying to make my marriage as excellent and special as I tried to make everything else in my life. 'Why can't you be wonderful?' was my message to Paul for years.

"So of course he felt hurt and he withdrew. The more I complained, the more he became like the man I was complaining about.

"Then the best thing that ever happened to my love life happened to me. I got elected mayor of our little town. Believe me it's no big deal being mayor here, but it is a full-time job and it keeps me busy. I know it kept me too busy to complain about all the things I wasn't getting from Paul. Instead of my asking him to really, really, really love me and be wonderful, I asked him to do things like take care of the kids and have some food ready when I got home from a late meeting. *That* was stuff he could do. And he did do it.

"For the first time I was happy with love in my life. I'd been making myself miserable looking for something I didn't really want. The real thing was that I wanted to have a life. I wanted to be a person with a life. It's just that I wanted that life to have as its foundation someone who loved me. That's what I wanted: just to know that Paul was there and that he loved me. It was so easy."

The place Meredith found for love that worked for her was a place where love was both authentic and yet mostly below the surface. She'd been so geared up to be swept away that when she wasn't feeling swept away she was feeling that nothing was happening.

But most of us are like Meredith in some respect. We make a big noise about not getting something that in fact we don't really want all that much. Who knows what Meredith would've done if Paul had turned into the superattentive lover. It might have just annoyed the hell out of her.

In any case Meredith lucked into getting what she really wanted. She never counted on how incredibly liberating and comfortable it would feel to have a life and know that deep down at the heart of that life was someone who loved her. And neither she nor Paul would have to do much about it. It was just there. That was the point.

Is the solution Meredith found the solution for you? Have you been running yourself ragged looking for love in your life to be

more than it is—because you think it should *be more than it is—
when what will really satisfy you is knowing that you have love
as a foundation?*

Option 3:

LOVE AS A NETWORK OF OUTLETS
FOR WHAT YOU HAVE TO GIVE.

June's Story

Jackie's and Meredith's stories were about finding places for love in their lives by redefining what they expected from the special person in their lives. For Jackie, love worked when she discovered how happy she was being best friends with her special guy. For Meredith, love worked when she discovered how satisfied she was just knowing her special guy was there. But both of these women held on to the idea that love meant having a special person, however you define "love."

For June, love had a special place in her life once she let go of the need to have a special person. You'll see what I mean in a minute.

"What is love anyway?" June said. "I can't speak for anyone else, but for a long time I'd thought that you have love in your life when you have someone who loves you. I'd cry about that on the phone with my girlfriends. 'I just want someone to love me.'

"And then I got what I thought I was looking for. This great guy really loved me. And I'd go around saying, 'He loves me, he loves me, he loves me.' Yeah, he had a lot to offer, but jeez hc was such a boring guy. I'll never ever forget lying in bed one night after we'd made love and I felt so empty and I kept saying to myself, 'He loves me,' but then it suddenly hit me. What do I feel? What do I get from his loving me? I'm feeling nothing. I'm saying this is love, but if you go by what I feel, this is nothing.

"The whole thing just felt really wrong to me. Anyway, the

first thing I did was something I never thought I'd do. I broke up with him. A great guy loved me, and I just kicked him out. It was more complicated than that. We had to go through a divorce. But that's what it amounted to: getting a dead tooth pulled.

"Then I said to myself, 'Great, now what do you have?' So of course I panicked. But I said, 'Okay, I'm just going to live my life.' I had my kids, and I loved them. I had my friends, and I loved them too. And there's my job—I run a group home for retarded women, and I have to tell you I really love those women, and to be honest, some of them aren't so lovable. And I don't blame them because they've got a lot to deal with. So I'm saying to myself where's the love, because I don't see a man who's in love with me.

"But then I realize *I'm* filled with love and *my life* is filled with love. I have so much love to give. And giving love gives me a wonderful life."

What was the place June found for love in her life? It was a whole network of relationships. All based on what June had to give. Who loved June? Not one person, but the love she gave others gave her a life. And it was her life that loved her back and made her feel good.

Is the solution June found the solution for you? Have you been running yourself ragged looking for someone to love you when what will really satisfy you is a whole network of outlets for the love you have to give?

Option 4:

BEING WILLING TO WAIT FOR PERFECTION.

Holly's Story

She didn't get married until she was forty-two. So many people repeated that fact about her so often that Holly got to the point where she was afraid they would engrave it on her tombstone.

Oooohhh, wow—a woman who didn't get married until she was forty-two.

Holly got to be sick of people asking her why, particularly her mother and two sisters. As if there had to be something incredibly wrong with a beautiful woman who simply *doesn't* get hooked up with anyone. Holly was tired of having to explain herself.

But she explained herself to me.

"For years all I said to people was that I was waiting for the right guy. I didn't want people to think I was Miss Picky. It was a lot easier to let people think oh poor Holly she's had such bad luck with men.

"But here's what really happened. I went to a Catholic school and I was a very good girl. But I was smart and I got into Barnard. The leap from St. Rosa's to Barnard was huge. I was a total slut there. I slept with everyone I could. You know how it is. You get involved with older guys. I mean I was sleeping with graduate students, professors. I bagged a trustee. I got to take a bite out of all the candy in the candy store. Rich guys, smart guys, cool guys. And I'd say that maybe half of these guys—maybe not quite half—talked about having some kind of permanent relationship with me.

"I'd say I was spoiled except I think most women go through a slut period. I mean if you're halfway attractive and you want to sleep around, you'll sleep around. And to be honest I was more than halfway attractive.

"So sue me—I was spoiled. But I just didn't want to settle. I mean some people make scientific discoveries or have these great religious insights. The big discovery of my life was that somewhere out there was the real thing and if I had to stay single until I was a dead old lady, I would because I didn't need a man for company. I didn't need a man for money. I didn't even need a man for orgasms. And I didn't need a man for validation. If I couldn't find a guy who was wonderful, who loved me madly, and who I loved madly, well, forget it.

"You have to understand that the whole time I was holding out for something special my women friends were getting involved with men and getting married and doing nothing but complain about their men. I was the happy one. I was free. I never had to ask myself whether I should settle or not. I never had to ask myself if a guy was good enough or not. I know I created an impossible standard. But I was happy, I was busy, I had a life. And I wasn't dragged down by any second-rate relationship.

"When I turned forty I said to myself, okay, you're still single. Fine. That's the way you played the game. That's how you thought things would turn out. That's how they did turn out. But you've had fun. You've had a rich life. And you like being alone so you can't say you gambled and lost. You gambled and got exactly what you thought you'd get. That's why hooking up with Sam was such a surprise. I'd been thinking, wow, you set your standards so high no one could meet them, but Sam did meet them.

"We're both business writers, financial journalists. He's got a column, I'm freelance. I make more money, but his work is steady. We're both interested in the same things. We're both incredibly lazy. We both find the world of business incredibly interesting up to a point. And then that's it, we're completely bored by it. And we've both spent twenty years talking about money and now we're ready for love I guess.

"You can't say why you're lucky, because then it's not luck. Luck is when you can't say why. All I know is that when I was ready to give up on finding true love in my life, I met someone exactly like me except for the fact that he had a penis, and we totally dug each other. I said I was going to hold out until I found something that was the way it was supposed to be and I did. Last night, for example, Sam and I got into bed and started talking about the best meals we'd ever had in Paris. We started arguing about which restaurant was better. At two o'clock in the morning we got out of bed, got dressed, packed, and got to the airport in time for the first flight to Paris. We just had to settle that food fight."

I think Holly made this clear but let me make it clear myself. Holly's solution wasn't to hang around until she got lucky.

That would be a complete misreading of what she did. Holly's solution was to refuse to settle for anything less than what she thought was the best for her even if it meant she'd never get lucky. The place Holly decided love should have in her life was the best or nothing. She was willing to live with nothing when it came to love because she had so much else going for her.

Obviously this isn't an option for most of us. It's like going on vacation. For most of us, when we want a vacation we want a vacation. Who would say I'm not going to go on vacation unless it's perfect? You've got to know yourself. But I think more women could benefit from Holly's option than actually do. It's a choice, and I think some of us should take it. And I think we should support women who choose this option.

Is the solution Holly found the solution for you? Have you been spending too much time complaining about the men in your life when in fact you should refuse to settle for anything less than something wonderful?

Option 5:

LOVE AS DAILY BALANCE.

Lily's Story

You've already met Lily. She talked about love as part of her daily health regimen. Lily's solution is what I call the checklist solution. It's totally about balance. Every day, love has got to be part of your routine like showering, eating, and exercising. It's not in the background. It's more than that. But it's not the foundation either. Lily's point of view is by far the most common one. I'm not saying that most of us live like Lily. I am saying that an awful lot of us think we should live like Lily.

Many of us feel that this solution to the problem of finding a place for love in our lives is so obvious that anything else is unthinkable. The key word for this solution is *balance*. People who subscribe to this solution believe that your husband doesn't have to be perfect. You don't have to have a perfect relationship. But to go through life without a significant other is like getting dressed up to go out and forgetting to put on makeup. It's part of your ensemble.

Lily's solution is an excellent one, like the others here. But I think there's something just a little misleading about it. Because it's such a commonly followed solution, and because it seems like *the* normal solution, a lot of women assume that it's easier and more satisfying than it really is. When you were a kid, did you ever try to walk a fence? I did. It was hard, wasn't it? You kept falling. Because balance is hard. That's my point about Lily's solution. It's hard to achieve balance day after day. And in your attempt to achieve it you could easily have the sense more often that you're losing your balance than that you've found it.

By all means, choose this solution if you've looked at all the options and are convinced that this one's right for you. But don't make yourself crazy by thinking it will be easy just because it feels normal.

There are other dangers too. Sometimes men who marry women like Lily are in for a surprise. The woman wanted to get married so badly, but once she's got him she's not as into him as he thought she'd be. But why would she be? This solution isn't based on the idea that love is everything. It's based on the idea that love is just a piece of the puzzle. Once you've had your daily dose of vitamin C, you don't have to be busy with vitamin C for the rest of the day.

I think that those of us who are like Lily are the salt of the earth. Lily is practical. She knows what works for her. What's healthy for her. And Lily's honest. But for Lily love is something she has to fit into her daily life to be healthy.

The key is to know yourself. If you've got to have a man in your life, you've got to have a man in your life. If that's what you need to feel empowered to go on and have a life, what's wrong with that?

Is the solution Lily found the solution for you? It is if you

need to experience being in a relationship as part of everyday life.
Every day you need a little bit of this and a little bit of that,
including a hit of being in your relationship.

Option 6:

LOVE AS YOUR TOP PRIORITY.

Janet's Story

"I was married for fifteen years before I realized the true place I wanted to give love in my life. Like a lot of women I'd wanted to have it all. So I thought it was okay when I had the husband, the kids, the job, my friends, my garden—you know how it is. The whole tapestry, all woven together. [Janet is talking about a vision of perfect balance like the one Lily wanted.] Then I got sick. Breast cancer. It was the usual thing. You get very scared. Everyone's worried. There's the chemotherapy. The radiation. In a way you're sicker from the treatment than from the disease. But you welcome it because you're fighting the disease. And the whole time all you can think about is how scared you are.

"I was lucky. I turned a corner. I got better. I don't want to talk about cure, because I think that's bad luck. But if you've been in remission for five years, as I have, you'd have to say that's a good sign. But you don't come through something like that without it changing you. You look at your world, your life differently. That's when I realized what love meant to me. Eddie and I would go for long walks. We'd read to each other. After all the time he'd spent taking care of me I wanted to spend some time taking care of him. It's almost as if we'd been drifting apart before I got sick and then somehow we came together again. Eddie, my relationship with Eddie, my love for Eddie became my priority.

"I'm saying love has become everything for me. It's not that Eddie's perfect or that our relationship is perfect. But just the way my house is my physical house, my love is my emotional house. It's where I live emotionally. I know that this is unbalanced. I know I'm putting all my eggs in one basket. I know it's sort of stupid to be a grown woman who's faced death and come away sounding like a high school girl who's all gooey for her boyfriend, but what can I say? My kids are great but they're going to go off and lead their own lives. Work is just stuff you're busy with. For me love is the only thing that's real. So it's the only thing that really matters to me.

"As long as Eddie and I can spend time together, enjoy each other, take care of each other, then I have everything I need."

I've discovered that more women are like Janet than you might think. You don't have to have faced death to be in her situation. Your relationship does not have to be all that wonderful and special. But for women who've found this solution, their love is their life. Everything else is a part-time job.

Interestingly, some incredibly successful women give love the same place in their lives that Janet gave it. So what if they're famous and successful? They'd say they're just lucky. But if for the sake of their relationship they had to pick up stakes and go live on a sheep farm in New Zealand, they'd do it in a minute.

Is the solution Janet found the solution for you? Have you been confused by all kinds of priorities when in fact the person you love is the only priority that makes any real difference for you? Everything else comes in second.

Option 7:

VARIETY IS THE SPICE OF LIFE.

Margo's Story

"I'll tell you right away what the bottom line is for me. Variety. Change. Something different from what I've just had. I fall in love and things are great but then I just get bored with the person. I'm not bored with love. I absolutely adore falling in love. But real human everyday guys just can't seem to live up to my expectations for the kind of three-ring circus I want love to be. They're normal people, I guess, and I guess they just want to relax into being themselves. I can understand that, but I want them to be someone different.

"What pisses me off is that it took me, like, fifteen years to figure this out. I remember back when I first came to Boston and got involved with James. At first things were great. But then I started getting annoyed with him, more and more. *Now* I know that I was just bored with him. But *then* I blamed it on there being something wrong with James. I'd just find these things to criticize about him. So I'd get on him for not wanting to try new things. Or for being closed. Or for not being a better lover. Or for . . . well, whatever. Then he'd be like, well, you liked the way I was a month ago. And he was right because I did like the way he was a month ago. I just got tired of him.

"But going through it, it was like this sad thing, oh, my relationship didn't work out. And then I'd go on to the next one and it would be another sad story of another failed relationship.

"It was this gay guy, a friend of mine, who kind of showed me the light. He said, hey, you're making this big drama show out of your love life when the fact is that you want new experiences. Your relationships aren't failing. They're successful but then you just get bored with them. That's what he said. And it was so true.

"I like myself a lot better now, and I feel a lot safer. I don't have to keep thinking that the rug's always going to get pulled out from under me, because I know that I'm going to be the one to fold up my rug and move on. I'm honest about it. Well, I'm not totally honest. You know if I get into a guy, I say, well, we'll try it and see what happens, no promises, no commitments. But I guess they're thinking that I'm thinking that maybe it could work out. But I'm thinking, no, I know it's not going to work out, but I'm going to enjoy it like crazy while it's still new and fresh.

"Can I keep this up? I have absolutely no idea. I'm thirty-six. Ask me in ten years. I just don't want to make myself miserable by creating this hope I'll find some guy I won't get bored with. I do want kids, and it's got to be sooner rather than later, but it feels funny having kids when you just know before they're born that you're going to end up divorcing their father. But I'm doing what's right for me now. This is who I am."

Is the solution Margo found the solution for you? Have you been chasing after that one excellent relationship and wondering why so many of your relationships fall apart when in fact the place love has in your life is a place marked by variety? It's not that variety is an accidental by-product. It's what you're looking for.

Option 8:

UNBALANCED YEARS ADD UP TO A BALANCED LIFE.

Bettina's Story

Sometimes our lives are divided into chapters. If you remember, Bettina's story was like this. She talked about four chapters in her life: artist, lover, mother, and then artist again. What can be nice about this is that when you're living through an experience, you're totally in it. When it's over, it's over, and you can move on to something new.

Most women, for example, experience their life having chapters when it comes to being a mother. There's a time when you weren't a mother. Then suddenly—oh so suddenly—you're completely absorbed by being a mother. Then after several months or years your kids move from the core to a place a little away from the core of your life. You'll always love them.

But you're a lot less busy with them. And what's wrong with that?

It can be the same kind of thing when it comes to love. Love wasn't a big deal in your life, then there's a period when it's everything, then it's not such a big deal again. A chapter. A stage. An experience. Like that trip down the Amazon you'll remember forever. It was incredibly intense. You're glad you did it. You'll always remember it. But you don't necessarily want to do it again. At least not for a while.

It's nice when this solution works for you, the way it worked for Bettina. All this solution requires is a slightly different concept of balance. Instead of your life being balanced because you have a little bit of love in it every day, with this solution it's balanced because there's a period when you have a whole lot of love. And then so what if there's a period without so much love. It's just a different concept of balance. It's balance over the course of your life, not over the course of your week.

Is the solution Bettina found the solution for you? Have you been trying to shoehorn yourself into some concept of balance that's too narrow for you? Have you been too worried about balance in the short run when all you need is balance in the long run? Your life can be balanced even if individual days or years are completely unbalanced.

Choosing an Option

The point of this chapter is custom-tailored liberation. There's more than one way to get it right when it comes to finding a place for love in your life. There's more than one way to *live* your commitment to the real thing when it comes to love.

As women who care about love, it's time we celebrated what brings us together as well as celebrating the ways we're different. What brings us together is the need we have for love in our lives, the respect we give it, the way we acknowledge love's fundamental value and importance. A life with no love at all is an empty life indeed. We all agree about that.

Let's also celebrate that we can choose different options. The point of stories like Bettina's and Janet's and Holly's and Jackie's and Margo's and Lily's and Meredith's and June's is that there are so many good ways to have love in your life.

Be grateful that you're a warm, giving, loving woman. Be happy that you know love matters. Be aware that you're ready, willing, and able to pay your dues when it comes to love. Accept all these things so that you can feel free to follow your own path.

It might be that you're a pioneer. Have you held out your whole life waiting for the love that feels just right? Have you focused your experience of love on one special period of your life? Have you spread your love over a variety of people? Have you felt more comfortable with love as friendship than love as romance? Have you said about love that you just want to know it's there? Have you tried to have just the right amount of love every day of your life? Have you decided that love is everything for you?

We're all pioneers as we explore these options. How can you know what's right for you until you've tried it? Just think of how powerful this idea is—finding the way to have love in your life that's right for you. For most women there's an instant surge of hope. No more blaming yourself for not living up to some abstract ideal. No more focusing all your energy on the need to find that one great person to love. No more trying to fit who you are and what works for you into a narrow straitjacket. The world is full of options when it comes to having a life full of love.

I honor you for being an explorer in the land of love. I urge you with all my heart to find what's right for you in this land.

ELEVEN

The Best in Love, the Best in You

Both of us, you and I, have been on a quest for a long time. We've been searching for something very basic, yet essential. An answer to a question.

Can you find love without losing yourself?

This book was designed to bring you good news. We no longer have to make a trade-off between finding love and finding ourselves. That ancient dilemma is no longer operative. Now we've learned a new truth. *Only* when the real you is fully present throughout every experience of love in your life will you have a chance at having real love itself. If it's not good for you, it's not good love.

The best in love is many things, but it always has something to do with bringing out the best in you.

Love without the real you isn't real love at all. It's a charade. It's a job. It's something where you wear a mask for the sake of allaying fears of loneliness. But of course, by wearing the mask you're only driven into the deepest kind of loneliness possible, the loneliness you find when you face a lifetime of false intimacy.

And this is good news. It means you can look forward to the sense of real intimacy if you move forward insisting that the real you be present in every experience of love.

We give love. That's something women have the capacity for. But should that drain you? Should it exhaust you? Should it make you less than you were when you started? *No!* Strong, smart women with a sense of who they are find that real love, when they give it, makes them better, richer, happier, more self-confident, and more fulfilled.

I grew up not knowing if love like this was possible for anyone. Now, finally, after a long and difficult journey, I know that love like this is possible for everyone. For you. You're holding all the answers in your hand, and in your heart.

INDEX